SWORD
OF
SCOTLAND

SWORD
OF
SCOTLAND

Jocks at War

by

Anthony Leask

Pen & Sword
MILITARY

First published in Great Britain in 2006 by
Pen & Sword Military
an imprint of
Pen & Sword Books Ltd
47 Church Street
Barnsley
South Yorkshire
S70 2AS

ISBN 1 844 15405 X

A CIP catalogue record for this book is
available from the British Library

Typeset in Sabon by
Phoenix Typesetting, Auldgirth, Dumfriesshire

Printed and bound in England by
Biddles Ltd, Kings Lynn

Pen & Sword Books Ltd incorporates the Imprints of Pen & Sword
Aviation, Pen & Sword Maritime, Pen & Sword Military, Wharncliffe
Local History, Pen & Sword Select, Pen & Sword Military Classics and
Leo Cooper.

For a complete list of Pen & Sword titles please contact
PEN & SWORD BOOKS LIMITED
47 Church Street, Barnsley, South Yorkshire, S70 2AS, England
E-mail: enquiries@pen-and-sword.co.uk
Website: www.pen-and-sword.co.uk

Contents

Preface

When my father, Lieutenant General Sir Henry Leask KCB, DSO, OBE, retired from the Army in 1972, he was asked by Philip Warner, then senior lecturer in military history at the Royal Military Academy Sandhurst, to write a military history of Scotland – the story of Jock, the fighting man. I do not know why Philip Warner selected my father, but his service in the Army was unusual in that he had served with all the infantry regiments of Scotland, some several times.

Commissioned into the Royal Scots Fusiliers (now The Royal Highland Fusiliers), he commanded 8th Battalion The Argyll and Sutherland Highlanders in the Second World War and 1st Battalion The London Scottish immediately after it. Later he commanded a brigade of Royal Scots and King's Own Scottish Borderers' battalions, and then 52nd (Lowland) Division with battalions of all the lowland regiments. His last appointment was as General Officer Commanding Scotland, Colonel Commandant of the Scottish Division of Infantry and Governor of Edinburgh Castle. So he had considerable knowledge of all the regiments and their histories.

When my father died in 2004, I found the manuscript in his papers. It is an account of Scottish arms from Roman times to the present day. The theme which runs through the book is the development of the Jock, the fighting man, from the barbarous Caledonian who faced the Romans to the sophisticated fighting men and women of today. It may seem there is little connection between the two. Yet the character of any modern soldier is, to a large extent, the result of his past and the traditions that he has inherited. The Jock is no exception. Passionate, romantic, sensitive, he can be all of these but underlying them is a steely determination and fierce loyalty which make defeat unthinkable.

Compressing 1,000 years into these pages inevitably means over-simplification and generalization. That said some details have been included on comparatively minor incidents. While this may be a little misleading, these stories nevertheless give a human insight into how different generations of fighting Jocks responded as individuals to the circumstances in which they found themselves.

Much of the information for the earlier part of this book has been obtained from research into the works of the ancient chroniclers such as Fordun and Barbour, and the later works of Chalmers, Innes, Hailes and Skeane. The Roman period, so well recorded by Tacitus, presents few problems. For the next 600 years it was necessary to draw on chroniclers of varying reliability whose accounts are often contradictory. They have been included because they are all we have to get a picture of the scale and type of fighting at that time.

My father was indebted to the authors of Scottish regimental and divisional histories, from which he drew a great deal of information, and to: Sir James Grant KCVO, WS, then Lord Lyon King of Arms; Professor J.D. Mackie CBE, MC, MA, LLD, then Emeritus Professor of Scottish History at the University of Glasgow; Professor G. Donaldson MA, PhD, DLitt, then Professor of Scottish History at the University of Edinburgh and to Philip Warner, himself an eminent military historian.

The book is, in the main, that written by my father. I have updated it and added more detail on the First and Second World Wars. Although both only covered six years in our nation's history, the commitment and sacrifice made during these wars merit more coverage than was given in the first unpublished edition. I could not have done this without much help from many people. They include Brigadier Duncan Cameron OBE, late The Black Watch; Major General John Cooper DSO, MBE, late The King's Own Scottish Borderers; Lieutenant General Sir Peter Graham KCB, CBE, late The Gordon Highlanders; Major General Jonathan Hall

CB, OBE, late The Royal Scots Dragoon Guards; Major General the Honourable Seymour Monro CBE, late Queen's Own Highlanders; Lieutenant Colonel Ian Shepherd, late The Royal Highland Fusiliers and Secretary to the Trustees of the Scottish National War Memorial; Major General Mark Strudwick CBE, late The Royal Scots; Major General David Thomson CB, CBE, MC, late The Argyll and Sutherland Highlanders; the Regimental Secretaries of all the Scottish regiments and their staffs; the Curators and staffs of the Scottish regimental museums, and the staff of Regimental Headquarters Scots Guards.

Professor Colin Kidd of the University of Glasgow; Professor Hew Strachan FRSE, FRHistS, Professor of the History of War at All Souls College Oxford; Professor Dennis Harding, Professor of Archeology at the University of Edinburgh and Dr Diana Henderson LLB, TD, FSA Scot, Director of the Scots at War Trust and Fellow of Queen's College, Cambridge provided invaluable assistance to me. Jack Alexander, Patrick Mileham and Robert Sigmond have kindly allowed me to draw on their specialist knowledge and books. Philip Biggs produced the maps. Finally, many ex-soldiers helped me with this book by sharing their experiences or lending pictures. I am indebted to them all. Any errors are mine.

This book would not have been published without the painstaking work of Sue Ellis MA. She has improved it in numerous ways.

This is not a history of the Scottish regiments so, on occasions, I have used the most well known names of individual regiments, even though they may not have been recognized at the time.

My father was immensely proud of his connection with all the Scottish regiments and the part they and their soldiers have played in shaping Scotland's history. This book is his work. Wherever he went, he made it clear at every opportunity that it is the soldiers – the Jocks – regular and territorial, who are the foundation of their respective regiments. It is they that wield the Sword of Scotland.

All the proceeds from the sale of the book will be donated to Erskine Hospital, the home for disabled ex-servicemen outside Glasgow. This is also their story.

Sword of State

The Sword of State, on display in the historic Crown Room of Edinburgh Castle, was presented to King James IV by Pope Julius II in 1507. It was accompanied by a scabbard and belt, and all three pieces are outstanding examples of Italian Renaissance craftsmanship. Their creator was Domenico da Sutri.

The Sword of State comprises one element of the Honours of Scotland, the Scottish royal regalia. The two other elements are the Sceptre, presented to King James IV by Pope Alexander VI in 1494, and the Crown of Scotland, made for King James V in 1540. They were first used together as coronation regalia at the enthronement of the infant Queen Mary in Stirling Castle in September 1543.

From the time they were taken from Edinburgh Castle in 1650 to be used at the coronation of King Charles II at Scone on New Year's Day 1651, they have had an eventful history. Between 1651 and 1660 the Honours were prevented from capture by Cromwell's army, at first in Dunnottar Castle on the Kincardineshire coast and, with Dunnottar besieged, smuggled out by the wife of the minister of nearby Kinneff Church, and buried under the church floor. After the 1707 Treaty of Union between Scotland and England, the Sword, Sceptre and Crown were locked away in the Crown Room at Edinburgh Castle and the doors walled up. Walter Scott, with the permission of the Prince Regent (the future King George IV), had the room unblocked and the chest forced open. All three Honours were rediscovered and immediately displayed to the public. They have remained on display ever since, except for a period during the Second World War when they were buried once again, this time in David's Tower.

The Sword of State, Sceptre and Crown of Scotland continue in use as sovereign regalia, presented to each new sovereign at a National Service of Thanksgiving held in the High Kirk of St Giles, in Edinburgh's Royal Mile.

(With acknowledgement to Chris Tabraham, Principal Inspector of Ancient Monuments at Historic Scotland)

Foreword

Rt Hon Michael Ancram QC MP
Marquis of Lothian

It must be rare in military bibliography to find a Lieutenant General undertaking the writing of a national military history. It must be even rarer to find a Major General completing that. It is surely unique that the two are father and son, Henry and Anthony Leask, both distinguished soldiers in their own right.

Their subject, the military history of Scotland, is a daunting one stretching back into the mists of Roman involvement in Scotland, travelling the roads of the dark and middle ages, the rises and falls of the periodic assertions of Scottish nationalism, and the leading role played by Scottish soldiers in both the building and the dismantling of empire. It is the story of a particular brand of soldier, but one which also reflects a particular brand of people and of national spirit. It is a moving story of courage and resilience and individual acts of derring-do. It is above all the story of a nation,

All nations are proud of their armies; but the Scots more than most. The 'Scottish Soldier' is part of Scottish culture and of the Scottish psyche. Indeed the history of Scotland itself was largely born out of and formed by its military prowess – whether on the winning or the losing side. From the Borders to the Highlands, from the Western glens to the North Eastern seaboard the tradition of sending young men to war, of singing songs celebrating their victories – and sometimes mourning their defeats – has been part of the rhythm of Scottish life.

What young Scot has not been raised with the exploits of that Scottish Soldier 'far from the green hills' ringing in his ears and embedded in his heart? 'Breathes there a man with soul so dead . . .' I was brought up in the Scottish Borders to stand in awe of a tartan Elysian field of heroes, maybe a few from the battlefield of the oval ball at Murrayfield, but the overwhelming majority from the annals of Scotland's regiments and Scotland's fighting men.

So what makes the Scottish Soldier such an icon? It is because the Scottish Soldier individually and collectively has always punched above his weight. This nation which is one third of the landmass but less than one tenth of the population of the United Kingdom has written its name in British history, partially through the skill of its entrepreneurs and businessmen, but much more through the courage, professionalism and commitment of its soldiers. In victory and defeat the Scottish regiments have always shone. Their pride in their history and tradition, their confidence in their fighting ability and their determination never to let themselves down have made them a fighting machine which is respected and feared throughout the world.

It is hardly surprising that their current merger into a super--regiment has been met with such dismay. It should not have happened. But now that misguidedly it has, there should be no doubt that the Scottish Soldier will rise to the occasion and that the remarkable history of the Scottish soldier will march proudly on.

Leask *pere et fils* have assembled a history which is not only a remarkable record of this military phenomenon but is also highly readable and a thumping good tale. It is told with commendable military dispassion but cannot hide the excitement of military ventures which tested the skills and courage of the Scottish Soldier to the full. It records the numerous acts and actions of exceptional valour which can be attributed to Scottish courage and dedication. At the same time they do not spare us the failures and the disappointments. They set out in measured terms the strategic challenges from the earliest times to the present day. They paint a full picture, one which adds effectively to the inevitably specialised and thus disjointed records which have gone before.

We are frequently told that the first duty of any sovereign government is the defence of the realm. That has always been extended to include the defence and advancement of our national interests overseas. In both cases there have been no better exponents than the Scottish Soldier. Rarely before have we been vouchsafed how this almost legendary figure evolved. This history leads us through the avenues of that evolution and gives us at the end, a portrait of which we can all be proud and in which we can all claim a share.

Sword of Scotland is an important history. It is also a great story – the story of the Jock. I saw him in action in Northern Ireland in bad times and in good. He was always scrupulously professional, enthusiastic and determined to carry out the duty to which he had been assigned. He was fierce and resolute against aggression while friendly and understanding in his dealings with frightened and sometimes traumatised communities. He was and is a soldier of our time, well suited to the new peacemaking and peacekeeping requirements that are increasingly part of modern soldiering. Yet his skills were learned in the skirmishes and battles of previous wars.

To the end the image of the Scottish soldier persists – the skirling of the pipes, the legendary courage and the shining loyalty, the fierceness tempered by irrepressible humour and innate kindness, that special mix that made him at once so feared and respected.

There are many myths about Scotland past and present. We are anything but a self-effacing nation and we are certainly not immune to a little self glorification. Indeed it has not been unknown for us on occasion to seek to rewrite our history – particularly in so far as the English are concerned!

Sword of Scotland however avoids all these Scottish weaknesses. It is fluent, factual and inspiring. It does what it sets out to do; it tells a story, and it tells it well. From the first page to the last it makes one feel good to be a Scot.

Scotland

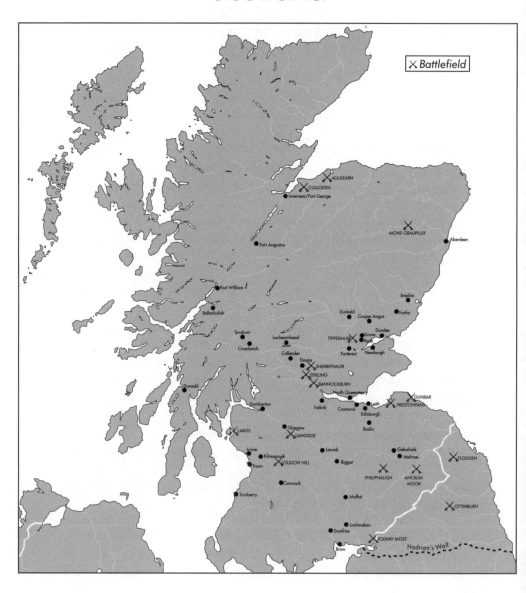

Chapter One

Early Caledonia

The history of any country must be, to a large extent, the history of its military endeavour, and most countries owe their birth, and indeed their survival, to force of arms. Scotland is no exception, and few countries have had a more violent and bloody history.

The military history of Scotland is the story of the Scottish people, and the sword has played a significant part in fashioning their character. One reason for this lies in the geography of the country.

Scotland is on the north-west frontier of Europe, and for many hundreds of years this was the periphery of the civilized world. Mountains and rivers divided its people in early times into separate groups who developed distinctive characteristics and intense hostility to each other. A fierce spirit of independence of family and clan was bred in the soul of its people from these early beginnings. From these roots grew the martial spirit which was to characterize the Scottish nation throughout much of its history.

During the first millennium BC, and before the Roman invasion, immigrant peoples swept into Scotland from the east, the south and the west. They came by land from England, by sea up the west coast from Ireland and south-west England, and across the North Sea from the heart of Europe. Scotland was, and remained all through its history, the high-water mark of these waves of invasion which carried with them not only new cultures, but also new methods of warfare. Not all immigration came as colonization in the wake of invasion. Some may have been the benign consequence of trade and the exchange of ideas, although this did not mean that indigenous people of the time were incapable of independent development. This was a gradual process whereby 'cumulative Celticity' was introduced into Scotland over many years.

There is little but legends and scattered earthworks on which to base Scotland's early history, before the birth of Christ, and the coming of the Romans. These primitive earthworks show a recognition of the need for defence, even if only at the community level, and they are to be found throughout the country.

The earliest fortifications found in Scotland are of the Iron Age, and probably date from about 500–200 BC. During this prehistoric period there appeared along the western coast a large number of small circular forts or 'duns'. These were probably built by the early invaders from Ireland or later by immigrant tribes fleeing from the advances of the Roman legions in southern Britain. The dun varied in size but essentially provided a stoutly-built dwelling surrounded by a wall, to provide shelter and protection for a family or small community. They were mostly sited on high ground or on small islets to give them every advantage of a long view and early warning.

In the far north, and in the islands of the west, a more advanced fortification was the 'broch', a potential forerunner of the castle. Its chief characteristics were its single entrance, thick walls honeycombed by galleries, and its high defensive tower. The long and narrow access, security measures such as bar holes and perhaps a guard cell on the stout wooden door, absence of windows and tapered circular design gave the broch particular strength. Archaeological opinion is divided but, in the context of what is known of Iron Age fighting techniques, they would surely have afforded a secure stronghold, with just a few defenders being able to hold off a much larger force for a considerable period. Occupants would have been vulnerable to long-term siege, but with conflict more often taking the form of hit-and-run raiding of livestock among rival neighbours, the broch was certainly safer than open farm settlement. Several hundred of these brochs have been identified, but the best example is to be seen at Mousa, on the east coast of the Sumburgh peninsula of Shetland.

A variation of the broch was the 'crannog' or island fort. These fortified homesteads were mainly constructed of wood and were often located in lochs or sheltered inlets – either built on stilts or using natural or reinforced islets – to provide additional security. Hill forts were another major type of defended settlement during and beyond the Iron Age and there is a classic example of one at Castle Law in Abernethy, Perthshire. Such forts were likely to have had a timber-frame closely following the line of the hill, which was then faced with stone. This made it effective against attack from both battering ram and fire. The similarity of the structures in Scotland to a later version described by Caesar after the capture of Avaricum suggests external influence in their design, if not direct involvement in their construction.

Two hill forts – considerably larger than any of their contemporaries or successors – present an intriguing puzzle. One is Eildon Hill near Melrose, Roxburghshire, where a great hill overlooks the approaches to this ancient Border town. Dominating the valley of the Tweed, and protected on two sides by the loop of that river, its selection as a defensive position shows canny tactical appreciation. Complete with stone ramparts and ditches to give depth to the defences, it would be a stubborn position to take in the twentieth century. The other large hill fort is Traprain Law in East Lothian. Two miles out of Haddington on the A1 high road to Dunbar, it commands the flat country all around and, like Eildon Hill, seems to have been a very large defended settlement.

Both Eildon Hill and Trapain Law were clearly very important sites, although neither shows much evidence of pre-Roman occupation. Previously thought of as major defensive strongholds on the eve of the Roman conquest, more recent research suggests that their dating and use as major community centres may have been more complex than previously appreciated. Without a sizeable force, the defence of a 40-acre enclosure would have been difficult. Archaeological thinking now leans towards their possible use for major tribal events where security would have been of paramount importance, such as the inauguration of kings. Whatever their use, they remain striking examples of early Scottish fortification.

These various defended locations of dun, broch, crannog and hill fort all existed more or less simultaneously, each created in response to the local geography, availability of materials and level of turbulence. It is likely that many were partly dismantled, re-occupied, adapted and rebuilt, although the extent to which they continued to change was related to the impact (or lack thereof) of the arrival of the Romans.

What of the weapons which these earliest warriors of Scotland used? From the relics found in duns and brochs the main armament appears to have been the sword, spear and shield. Types of weapons carried varied according to the status of the individual. Chiefs had shields and swords, often finely chased. There is also evidence of chain mail at that time. The ordinary fighting man usually carried a long spear and a much plainer shield. Made of iron, many of these weapons show in their design the traces of an early culture of craftsmanship brought to Scotland by the Celts. From caches found of thousands of slingstones, the sling may also have been in use, wielded perhaps by those with a specialist skill.

From out of the mist of the early past emerges that first fighting vehicle, the war chariot. Introduced into Scotland by immigrant tribes from the south during the period 300–200 BC, it became the main offensive arm of tribal forces in the Lowlands and on the plains of north-east Scotland, before the advent of the Romans. We will see with what effect they were used against the legions of Rome.

Scotland was to the Romans what the north-west frontier of India was to the British Empire in the nineteenth century. It was both a challenge and a commitment. That wild and barbarous country inhabited by a poor but proud people could not be ignored. A frontier with these barbarians had to be established. The question was, where? As always, opinions were divided. The 'doves' were for pulling back to a line out of contact with the fiercest tribes of Caledonia, who inhabited the northern part of Scotland. The 'hawks' were for subduing the whole country.

The earliest written history comes from the Romans and we owe this largely to the historian Tacitus who, as son-in-law of the Roman General Agricola, was in an excellent position to record the events of the first century AD.

It was Agricola who led the first Roman army into Scotland in the year AD 81 along the axis Carlisle-Moffat-Lanark, and he was a 'hawk'. During the next three years he conquered the whole of the Lowlands as far north as the line between the Forth and the Clyde, and constructed a line of forts to seal off the north of Scotland at this narrow neck of land. In the process he encountered great resistance from the tribes in Galloway. Forced to mount a special operation in AD 82 to subdue them, he is said to have sailed with a force from Kirkbride Loch in Cumberland, and landed at Brow at the Lochar-mouth on the Solway.

In AD 83 Agricola decided to extend his rule to the north of the Forth-Clyde line, as he dreaded a general rebellion amongst the northern tribes, who had hitherto been disunited but who might join together to face the common foe. The Roman army was supported in all its operations by the fleet and Agricola, guided by his naval advisers, decided to cross the Forth at Inchgarvie near the present Forth Bridge and land at North Queensferry in Fife.

Agricola now found himself for the first time engaged with the real Caledonians, whose spirit was still unshaken by defeat. They immediately sprang to arms, and without waiting to be attacked, started offensive operations against the nearest Roman outposts – these were the forts between the Forth and Clyde along the line Falkirk-Kilsyth-Kirkintilloch-Clydebank.

It so happened therefore that while Agricola was advancing eastwards up the Fife coast towards Kirkcaldy, closely supported by his fleet and marines, he found himself attacked in the rear. This daring assault considerably alarmed the Romans, as the garrisons of these forts had been reduced to strengthen the main force in Fife. Such was the alarm amongst Agricola's staff that he was actually advised by them to retreat behind the Forth, rather than risk defeat by the savage tribes. But Agricola was made of sterner stuff, and rejecting his staff's advice, he determined to continue his campaign northwards to subdue the Caledonians with a new plan of operations.

The Roman army suffered from two disadvantages. It was considerably inferior in numbers, and it was fighting in an unknown land. To counter these disadvantages Agricola reorganized his army into three columns. The columns were mutually supporting but able to operate on a larger front than hitherto, and so avoid the dangers of encirclement by a numerically superior enemy. One of these columns, consisting of the Ninth Legion which had suffered considerable losses in previous engagements, reached the area of Lochore, two miles south of Loch Leven, when it was heavily attacked in its encampment in the middle of the night. The Ninth Legion was saved only by the timely arrival of Agricola with reinforcements, and the Romans were able to drive back the Caledonians to their hills and woods. The encampment can be seen to this day.

Agricola's plan of campaign appears to have been typical of many other commanders of sophisticated forces who have had to face an irregular enemy in difficult country. Because of their dependence on supply transport and heavy equipment, the Romans tended to stick to the easier tracks, and these usually ran along the low ground. The Caledonians shunned tracks, and were happy to keep to the high ground from which they could conduct their guerrilla warfare with advantage. This meant that the Roman army, like many another before and after, commanded only the ground it stood upon.

The Romans continued their advance northward from the Dunfermline-Loch Leven area, through the Ochil Hills, with their main axis probably along the line Glen Devon-Glen Eagles, down into the lower ground of the valleys of the Allan Water and River Earn. This gave Agricola lateral communication, essential to his forces, along the line Perth-Auchterarder-Doune-Callander, and from this line he pushed forward to establish forts to block the exits from the mountains to the north at Callander, Braco, Comrie, and Inchtuthil, near Coupar Angus. Inchtuthil was a major administrative base capable of housing over 5,000 men.

So long as the Caledonians stuck to their guerrilla tactics, using the mountains and forests as their allies, the Romans were unable to defeat them. Agricola may well have despaired of victory at this stage in the campaign, when he viewed the mountain barrier of the Grampians ahead.

But it was now that the Caledonians made the fatal mistake of offering battle to the Romans on the invaders' terms. Why they did this is not clear, but it may well be that they were emboldened by their greatly increased strength as a result of the confederacy of tribes. This brought together for the first time many who had hitherto fought the enemy only in their own tribal areas.

The site of the Battle of Mons Graupius (the Grampians) is not certain, but there is a strong possibility that it was at Ardoch, near Braco, that Agricola came upon the Caledonian host drawn up under command of their greatest chief Calgacus. Some historians believe the battle to have been fought near the mouth of the Spey, and others place it in Aberdeenshire or Angus. It seems unlikely that it could have been very far north in view of the time covered by Agricola's operations. He started his advance across the Forth at the beginning of the summer of AD 83, and the battle is supposed to have taken place at the end of that summer. As his usual method of advancing was to secure firmly the ground he had captured before proceeding further, it is most likely that he was still in the area of Strathearn and Strathmore when he was challenged by the Caledonians in great strength.

The armies which faced each other in the first recorded battle fought in Scotland had little in common.

The Caledonian host, according to Tacitus, numbered 30,000, but this is probably an exaggeration. Their main strength was in their infantry, whose swiftness of foot gave them a great advantage in making sudden and savage assaults. Tactics were simple – a swift charge accompanied by much noise and the call of the carnyx (battle trumpet). Timing and use of ground would have been all-important. Like their Highland descendants, they were in the habit of throwing off the greater part of their clothing before closing with their adversaries in hand-to-hand conflict. They were armed with spears and long swords. The sword, which was the early edition of the Highland claymore, had no point and was meant only for cutting. Their defensive equipment consisted only of a small targe.

The Caledonian cavalry, mounted on small Highland horses, described by the Romans as swift, spirited and hardy, were armed like the infantry, and indeed often fought dismounted. Cavalry and infantry were frequently mixed; foot soldiers may have held on to horses' manes or the legs of the horsemen, like their descendants, the Scots Greys and Gordon Highlanders, are said to have done at Waterloo centuries later.

7

The Caledonians were very expert in the use of their armoured fighting vehicle – the war chariot. The similarity of this vehicle's use, nearly 2,000 years ago, with the modern armoured personnel carrier is striking.

The chariots provided mobility and fire power. They may have been armed with scythes and hooks, attached to the wheels and axles, for cutting and tearing the enemy ranks as they charged through them, although there is no archaeological evidence to support this. Each chariot contained a charioteer, with one or two additional warriors. The Caledonians appeared to manage these vehicles with considerable dexterity, and by their bold use they were occasionally able to break into the Roman line. At the start of an engagement the chariots would circle the enemy at high speed while the warriors on board threw their javelins into the enemy formation. When they had broken into the line, the warriors leaped from the chariots and fought on foot, while the drivers retired a short distance to await developments. It is generally believed that they were more often used as a means of rapid manoeuvre of foot soldiers than as a fighting vehicle.

The tactics of the Caledonians were simple. The mass of the infantry was placed in the centre and the horse and chariots on the wings. An interesting custom not paralleled in modern battles was the use of families. These were massed in the rear to serve as both a protection and an encouragement. We are told that the shrill cries which they were in the habit of raising, acted as an incentive to their fathers, husbands and sons, to fight to the last in defence of all that was dearest to them.

How different were the Romans? Their army consisted of 8,000 foot, 3,000 horse and some 11,000 auxiliaries, mostly recruited from Gaul and the south of Britain. They had only about 4,000 genuine Roman legionaries. But every possible advantage was on the side of the invaders in a pitched battle like this one. They were highly disciplined veteran troops, completely equipped with both offensive weapons and defensive armour which was the best of its day. Moreover, they were led by an experienced and able general.

The issue of such a battle could not have been long in doubt, in spite of the desperate bravery of the Caledonians, who fought for their homes and freedom.

It was before this battle that Calgacus made an appeal to his men which has lived down the ages, and has perhaps been echoed many times by other defenders of their native land.

They make a desert, and they call it peace. March then to battle, and think of your ancestors – and think of your children.

But this appeal was to no avail, and the might of Rome was more than plain valour could overcome. The battle was very bloody.

The Roman army was deployed with its horses on the flanks and the auxiliaries in the centre. The legionaries were drawn up in the rear in general reserve. It was against the centre that the Caledonians threw themselves, but they were repulsed by the superior skill and weapons of the Romans. The Caledonians then attempted to take the enemy in the flank, but this move was defeated by Agricola in person, at the head of his legionaries.

Ten thousand Caledonians fell, while we are told the Roman losses were only some 400 men. Such was the victory of military might over the brave but unsophisticated tribes of Scotland.

Shortly after this battle Agricola was recalled to Rome, and with him went the 'forward' policy. From then on the Romans were on the defensive, and for the next 100 years the tide of imperial power was to recede south, leaving the Caledonians in possession of their native soil.

This process of withdrawal inevitably produced a Maginot Line strategy, and about AD 121 the Emperor Hadrian began the construction of a mighty stone wall from Newcastle to Carlisle to hold back the increasingly bold tribes pressing down from the north. This great work, which took some eight years to complete, formed the rear line of a deep defensive system. Forward of the Hadrian Wall, as a form of outpost line to the main position, another defensive line called the Antonine Wall was constructed about AD 142. This ran roughly along the old line of the Agricolan forts between the Forth and Clyde, and indeed made much use of the original positions. It was, however, a very much more developed affair, with forts at regular intervals along its length, connected by a military road. There are signs today that

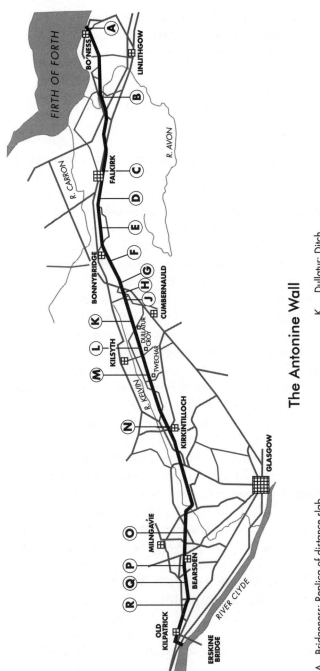

The Antonine Wall

A Bridgeness: Replica of distance slab
B Polmonthill: Ditch (Grangemouth)
C Callendar Park: Ditch (Falkirk)
D Watling Lodge: Ditch
E Rough Castle: Fort, rampart, ditch, Military Way and beacon platform
F Seabegs Wood: Rampart, ditch and Military Way
G Castelcary: Fort
H Garnhall and Tollpark: Ditch
J Tollpark and Arniebog: Ditch (Cumbernauld)

K Dullatur: Ditch
L Croy Hill: Ditch, 2 beacon platforms, site of fort
M Bar Hill: Fort, rampart and ditch
N Kirkintilloch: Site of fort (Kirkintilloch)
O New Kilpatrick cemetery: Rampart base and ditch (Bearsden)
P Thorn Road, Bearsden: Rampart base and ditch (Bearsden)
Q Hutcheson Hill: (Glasgow)
R Duntocher: Rampart base and site of fort (Dunbartonshire)

this line was protected by a ditch covered by ramparts in many places. Nor were the sea flanks neglected, as naval forces were stationed at the ports of Cramond on the Forth, and at Troon in Ayrshire.

These static defensive positions were held by Roman auxiliaries, and the Antonine Wall was probably garrisoned by a force roughly the equivalent of twelve modern battalions in manpower, perhaps less than 10,000 men in total. As time went on and these soldiers saw the power of Rome waning, they could have had little heart for their task of keeping back the barbarians. They found this increasingly difficult, and again and again the Caledonians broke through the forward position of the Antonine Wall.

Rome's final attempt to hold the Caledonians in check came in the year AD 208. In that year the Roman Emperor Severus sallied forth from the Antonine Wall and advanced through Fife up to the Moray Firth, supported on his sea flank by naval forces based at Cramond. This expedition achieved little, as the Caledonians never again gave their enemy the chance they had at Mons Graupius. Their tactics now were always to harry the enemy by day and by night, to ambush, to cut his lines of communication and, above all, to use the wild and forbidding country to their advantage. They must have become masters in the art of guerilla warfare.

The Romans gradually withdrew from what was to them a dark and inhospitable land of mountain and forest; first from the forward position of the Antonine Wall and finally from the main position of the Hadrian Wall.

Chapter Two

The Dawn of Scottish History

430–1034

With the departure of the Romans, Scotland entered a dark and obscure period of its history, without benefit from reliable contemporary records for nearly 600 years. It was during this period that the tribes of ancient Caledonia, enriched by the influx of tribes from outside, were forged first into four separate kingdoms and then into one Scottish kingdom and nation.

These two steps of amalgamation took place against a setting of inter-tribal conflict that was fierce, merciless and bloody. It was the 'Dark Age' of warfare, as in much else. We know little of the arms or tactics employed by the forces of this time, but there is no evidence to suppose there was any major advance in either of these fields until the Norman influx towards the end of the period. While it may have been a time of military stagnation, it was not one of inactivity.

By the fifth century the tribes of Scotland had been grouped into four kingdoms. In the north the Picts, the original 'painted men' of Roman chroniclers, were the most powerful of the peoples of Caledonia. At the time of the Roman exodus they held sway, under their great chieftain 'Drust of the Hundred Battles', over the area of the present counties of Kinross, Fife, Perth, Angus, Kincardine, Aberdeen, Moray, Inverness, Ross, Sutherland, Caithness and the northern part of Argyll. The original capital of this kingdom was Inverness. It was later moved to Scone in Perthshire.

The Scots, who ultimately gave their name to the whole

country, were a warlike Celtic people originating in the north of Ireland. They moved northwards into Argyll and the Hebrides, establishing their capital at Dunadd, near Crinan.

The Britons, the most sophisticated of the four peoples, inhabited the kingdom of Strathclyde which stretched from the Clyde to the Solway, covering the present western counties of the Lowlands. Their capital was at the ancient fortress of Dumbarton.

The fourth kingdom was that of Angles which spread from the Forth southwards down into Northumbria, and included the Lothians and eastern Border counties. This was the furthermost point of invasion reached by the Teutonic tribes who had crossed the North Sea and moved up the east side of Britain.

Little is known of the history of the Pictish kingdom in the north until its long conflict with the Angles of the south-east. The Angles pressed northwards to extend their dominion north of the Forth during the fifth and sixth centuries, and the capital of Scotland probably takes its name from the Anglo-Saxon King Edwin of this period. In opposition to the advice of his counsellors, King Egfrid, a successor of Edwin, crossed the Forth and the Tay and penetrated through the defiles of the Pictish kingdom, plundering and destroying the country as he advanced, much as the Romans had done 500 years before. But on 20 May 685 his advance was halted by the Picts under King Brude at Dunnichen near Forfar (also known as Nechtansmere), and, after being completely routed there, the Saxons withdrew behind the Forth. It is probable that scenes from this battle are depicted on the carved stone at Aberlemno. Some believe they show Pictish horsemen and foot soldiers, armed with swords, shields and spears, defeating their Angle enemies.

The Picts then turned their attention to the Scots and, under command of their great warrior King Ungus, they invaded Argyll. The pendulum of war swung back and forth for years, with the war bands of each side carrying the sword into the heart of the enemy territory. Typical of such expeditions was one carried out by Ungus in 736, in revenge for the abduction of his niece by Dungal, the son of the Scots King. Ungus led his forces from Forteviot in Strathearn, through the mountain passes to Lorne in Argyll, following the line of the present A85 and A82 roads by

13

way of Crieff, Comrie, Lochearnhead, Crianlarich and Tyndrum. The unfortunate Lorne was laid waste with fire and sword. After destroying the Scots fortress at Duror, four miles south of Ballachulish on the present A828, and taking Dungal prisoner, he withdrew along the same route to his capital at Forteviot.

In a fury the Scots, under King Muredach, collected their forces together and gave chase, overtaking the Picts at Comrie. There a fierce battle took place, in which the Scots were defeated with great slaughter, and Muredach himself perished.

The tide of success turned against the Picts in 761 when the Scots under Aodhfin took the offensive in force, using the same route through the passes of Glenorchy and Breadalbane, into the heart of the Pictish territories. A simple study of the map shows why this route was trod and re-trod in most major operations between Picts and Scots. Remembering that Dunbartonshire was then part of the kingdom of Strathclyde, it is the only route which makes maximum use of the main passes through otherwise inaccessible mountains.

The Scots offensive ended at Forteviot, where a doubtful battle was fought with the Picts under their King Ciniod. The Scots situation appeared at one time to be extremely serious, as the Picts had seized the main defiles in the mountains behind them, thus threatening their line of withdrawal. However, by great skill Aodhfin succeeded in leading his army round the enemy positions, using the rugged paths through the mountains to the north of the main axis, and safely back to Lorne. The Picts did not dare to follow.

From then until 842 the Scots remained in the ascendancy, winning the final round in the last battle fought at Forteviot, where the Pictish King was slain fighting in defence of his capital and kingdom. The Scots King, Kenneth MacAlpin, who won this redoubtable victory, had already laid claim to the Pictish throne through his family ties. He now united the two crowns in his own person, establishing a kingdom of all Scotland north of the Forth-Clyde line, and moved his capital from Dunadd to Forteviot. He and his immediate successors styled themselves Kings of the Scots and Picts, and under his rule the two peoples began to become one.

In the south of Scotland the two kingdoms of Strathclyde and the Angles were also constantly at war during this period. The Angles, having found it unrewarding to advance north against the Picts, turned their attention against the Britons.

As early as 603, the Angles had defeated a Scots army which had come south to help the Britons at the Battle of Degsaston (Dawston in Roxburghshire). Thereafter they increasingly thrust westwards up Liddesdale to the Solway and northwards up the valleys of Nithsdale and Annandale, into the very heart of Strathclyde. They reached the Briton capital of Dumbarton, which they sacked, in 756. It is likely that the present-day A74 and A76 roads from Carlisle to Glasgow follow closely the lines of advance of these invaders of Strathclyde.

The Britons were the most Romanized of the four peoples and, in imitation of their former protectors, they had tried to defend their country's eastern Border by the erection of a defensive wall which would have done credit to the Romans. Indeed it may have been started by them. The wall stretched from Galashiels in the north to Peel Fell, at the eastern extremity of Liddesdale in the south. It consisted of a broad and deep fosse and double rampart, and was defended by forts built at intervals along the line, on the summits of the neighbouring heights. Some remains of this interesting defensive work, which is known as the Catrail, may be found south of Hawick. The best examples are to be found running due east from Robert Linn Bridge, ten miles south of the town on the B6399 road. This great defensive line was turned by the Angle thrust, first to the Solway, and then north through Dumfriesshire.

The kingdom of Strathclyde never recovered from this attack by the Angle invaders, and its plight was made worse by periodic assaults of Danish seaborne war bands that sailed up the Clyde. The most disastrous of these assaults was in 870 when Dumbarton itself fell to the Danish invaders after a long siege. The city was sacked and its inhabitants put to the sword.

The final chapter in the history of the unfortunate Britons was written in 973, when they were roundly defeated by the Picts and Scots in a battle at Abercorn, near Grangemouth. The Britons exhibited the utmost courage in fighting this defensive battle

15

against Kenneth, King of the Picts and Scots, but the military power of the Britons had been too weakened by the successive attacks of powerful neighbours, and they were unable to offer any real resistance. The kingdom of Strathclyde ceased to exist and was annexed by the victorious Picts and Scots.

By now, all Scotland was being subjected to repeated attacks by fierce marauding bands from across the North Sea. The fury of the Norsemen lashed like a scourge around the coast of Scotland with unabated ferocity for well nigh 200 years. Starting in the eighth century with minor incursions by parties of Viking pirates, the attacks grew until the Norsemen came in such strength they were able to capture, hold and settle in large areas around the coast. They conquered Orkney and Shetland, the Hebrides, Caithness and Sutherland, in addition to establishing settlements wherever they could gain a foothold.

Two things resulted from this savage sea invasion. First, the blood of the adventurous sea kings was mixed with that of the native Caledonians, to produce Scots with an affinity to the sea. Second, the pressure of invasion from outside was undoubtedly a major factor in the unification of Scotland.

It is said that the northern pirates sailed up the Tay in 893 and were defeated at Collin on the banks of that river near Scone. They again sailed up the Tay in 904 and penetrated to the Scottish capital Forteviot, where they were defeated once more. In 907 they returned to plunder Dunkeld, but failed in an attempt to take Forteviot and were driven from the country. King Constantine of the Picts and Scots, with the help of the Angles, repulsed another Viking assault in 918 at Tinmore (probably Tynemouth in East Lothian).

An important engagement was fought at Findochty in Banffshire in 961. Known as the Battle of the Bauds it resulted in yet another defeat for the Norsemen, and a considerable number of barrows on the adjacent moor marked the site of their burial ground until recent years.

The Norsemen never seemed to be dismayed by their repeated defeats, and this may well be because the raiding parties were from separate parts of their vast sea empire. In any event they continued their expeditions, and spread their attacks to different parts of the coast. They must have become very expert in commando tactics.

In 990 a notable battle was fought against a Viking expeditionary force at Luncarty, near Perth. The battlefield lies four miles north of the city, to the east of the A9 road. The battle was long and fiercely contested. At first the two wings of the Scottish army were compelled to give way but they rallied behind the centre, which was commanded by the King, Kenneth III, in person. Reforming on the high ground in the centre, the Scots managed first to beat off the Norse attack, and then to drive their enemies back to their ships in the Tay with great slaughter. Monumental barrows, filled with the relics and arms of the slain, have been found on the site of this battle, known as Denmarkfield.

At the beginning of the eleventh century the Vikings, who had by then conquered and settled in Shetland and Orkney, made their appearance in great strength on the coast of Moray. They seized and fortified the promontory called the Burghhead, where they found a large harbour area for their ships. Here they developed a forward base from which to launch expeditions along the coast. Their main base was Orkney, the centre of a Viking sea empire which by then included all the offshore islands of Scotland, as well as Caithness and Sutherland on the mainland. The Viking Earls of Orkney became so powerful that they were, in reality, kings of their sea dominions, owing allegiance to neither Norway nor Scotland.

The martial prowess of such Norse leaders as Sigurd the Mighty and Thorfin the Mighty are legendary, but their authority ultimately depended on sea power. In turn the exercise of this sea power depended on how much could be carried in their small ships and the changeable weather conditions always prevailing in the northern seas. This meant that operations were usually much more in the form of raids to collect tribute and plunder, rather than protracted campaigns against the main enemy forces. The Vikings were nearly always roundly defeated when they gave battle against such forces on dry land.

In 1010 Sigurd the Stout, Viking Earl of Orkney, continued to raid along the shores of the Moray Firth, even after he had formed an alliance with King Malcolm by marrying his daughter. Friend

17

and foe alike suffered at the hands of these ferocious marauders. But once again the sea hawks were defeated on land near Mortlach, Dufftown, after a protracted battle resulting in great slaughter. It is said that Malcolm II had made a vow on the field of battle that he would endow a religious house if his arms were blessed with victory. He kept his word, and such a house was established near the scene of the battle. Although legend, there seems little doubt that the original church here was founded about this time, and Mortlach became the seat of an early Scottish bishopric. The skulls of Viking warriors who fell in the battle are said to have been built into the walls of the church, and the scene of this bloody conflict was marked by a number of sepulchral mounds, containing human bones, broken armour, and other relics of the slain.

In spite of severe reverse, the Norsemen immediately returned to the attack, this time on the coast of Angus. A large army under Camus, a renowned Viking chief, landed near Panbride and advanced inland. They got as far as Aberlemno, when they were halted by a Scottish force under Malcolm. Again they were driven back to their ships. A tall, monumental stone is supposed to mark the spot where Camus was slain in this battle.

The last attempt by the Vikings to expand their dominion into the north-east of Scotland came in 1014, when a large force made a landing on the coast of Buchan. The spot can be found about a mile west of Slaines Castle near Cruden Bay. This time they were thrown back by the local commander, or mormaer, and this part of the mainland was never threatened again.

Although the Norsemen, who had been the scourge and terror of every country in Western Europe, had been baffled in their attempts to establish themselves on this side of Scotland, they continued to maintain their rule over the Western Isles, Orkney and Shetland, and parts of Caithness and Sutherland for another 200 years. This was probably because the broken country and coastline of the far north and the west favoured their 'commando' tactics, and hampered the defence. In any event, wherever they settled they left their mark by the infusion of their fiery blood into the local populace.

By now the King of the Scots ruled over most of Scotland,

except that part still under the sway of the Norsemen, and the south-east and Lothians area. This region had long been disputed territory between the Angles and the Scots, and the final blow to unite all Scotland was struck at the Battle of Carham. The Northumbrian kingdom at that time stretched up the north-east coast of England to the Firth of Forth. Uchted, Earl of Northumberland, had been laying claim to this part of Scotland for many years and had made frequent forays into it. In 1018 Malcolm II decided to put a stop to it. He led an army south into the Northumbrian-held Lothians, and encountered Uchted's army at the village of Carham, near Wark, on the southern banks of the Tweed.

Although the issue seems to have been in some doubt until the end of the day, final victory rested with the Scots, and as a result of this battle the Lothians and south-east Scotland came under the rule of the Scottish king.

In 1034, it was Duncan, known to us as the saintly and venerated figure of Shakespeare's 1606 tragedy, *Macbeth*, who became King of all Scotland, always excepting that part of the far north still under Norse domination. It was a kingdom united by the sword, but a nation whose people retained the distinctive characters of their different forebears. Mountain and flood continued to separate clan from clan, and province from province, so that the Pict, Scot, Briton and Angle kept their separate individuality. To this day the Islander, the Highlander and the Lowlander show this difference. The Islander, invariably a seafarer, became fiercely independent. The Highlander, often unable to subsist within the mountain regions, became a natural aggressor and a master of the attack, but always with one eye on survival. The Lowlander, without the advantages of mountains, has been forced throughout history to defend his land and property. This has made him as determined and skilled in this role as the Highlander is in his. The use of the horse is but one example. It was mainly in the Lowlands that the horse was used for fighting purposes and where cavalry developed.

One other powerful agent united the Scots at this period of their history. The Christian faith had been spreading through the wild heathen tribes of ancient Caledonia since the fifth century, and by the time Scotland was united by the sword, it was also united by the cross. It is interesting to note that its church historically went its own way – even under Rome it tried to retain a greater degree of autonomy.

For the next 500 years, the military history of a united Scotland is largely the story of its wars with the English.

Chapter Three

The Kingdom of Scots

1034–1286

With the union of Scotland into one kingdom came developments in the military system. The ancient Caledonians, except at the Battle of Mons Graupius under Calgacus, had fought as single tribes. Later the military forces of the four separate kingdoms of the Picts, Scots, Britons and Angles were little more than a collection of war bands raised for a particular operation. From this stage the armed forces, although still retaining their tribal nature for recruiting, developed into regional forces commanded by provincial governors. This development continued throughout the period leading up to the unification of the country under one crown.

From the middle of the eleventh century there began to emerge two different systems of military service in Scotland. In the south, east, and north-east, probably through the Norman influence, a feudal system developed with barons being responsible for raising and providing forces from their lands. In the north and west, including the greater part of the Highlands and Islands, the old way of life continued in matters military, as in all else. The chief of a clan was the father of a clan family, and if he decided to go to war, his clan family also went. Serving one's clan chief was a personal matter, a family matter, and – as clans could be widely spread – it did not necessarily connect to a land tie or where the man lived.

As time passed these two systems blended together, often through the intermarriage of chiefs and nobles, and all were in any case drawn together in the service of the king. The King as head of the state called upon the loyal support of Highland chief and

Lowland baron alike. They, in swearing allegiance to the monarch, were pledging the support of their own followers, many of whom were now meshed into the complex structures of clan loyalty.

The composition of military forces in the Lowlands was also undergoing a considerable change through Norman influence. The offensive arm was now the heavily armed and armoured cavalry mounted on sturdy horses. The nobility and knights were invariably included in this arm, the balance being made up of high quality men-at-arms. The cavalry weapons were the heavy lance, the long sword, and the double-edged battle axe. The sword was also double-edged and often two-handed, requiring a strong man to swing it whether on horseback or dismounted.

Another weapon which gained popularity about this time was the mace, a club with either a knob on the end adorned with spikes or a spiked ball attached by a chain. The mace was much favoured by the clergy who were not allowed to carry weapons with blades.

The personal armour of rider and horse was heavy and cumbersome in the extreme. Although it provided protection it also considerably reduced mobility. If dismounted, the horseman was at a great disadvantage when confronted by a lightly-armed adversary.

The infantry in the Lowlands was armed with long spears to repel mounted attack, and short swords for personal defence. The bow had now become a major weapon, and archers were also armed with the short sword.

Forces raised in the Highlands were very different. Usually only men of high rank would be mounted, and they would seldom wear any except the lightest armour. The rank and file fought on foot, and were armed with the claymore, the dirk, and the targe. But what they lacked in arms and armour they more than made up for in ferocity and speed of manoeuvre. And this remained true for much of early history.

Some of the best examples of the weapons of this period, used in both Highlands and Lowlands, can be seen in the Great Hall at Edinburgh Castle.

About this time, again through the Norman influence, there appeared the great castles which still exist in Scotland, particularly in the south and east. These were usually developed from existing fortresses, but the Normans brought many new ideas to the building of strongholds. Sited tactically on ground difficult for an enemy to cross unobserved, and often protected by a moat, these castles were now built to hold larger garrisons, including families. They also provided a centre for government and trade.

Apart from the ceaseless raids which raged across the Border, and a number of minor operations against the English, the first great battle involving Scottish forces during this period took place on 22 August 1138. It was probably also the earliest fully recorded battle fought by a considerable Scottish army outside Scotland.

David I, in domestic matters a most progressive monarch, was keen on English adventures with a view to expanding his territory. In 1135 he became involved in the civil war which rent the southern kingdom. He seems to have played a complex political game, siding first with one side and then the other. The military operations, however, which emanated from this devious foreign policy were fairly easy to follow.

Following a period of anarchy after the death of Henry I of England, his nephew Stephen had been acclaimed King in preference to Henry's daughter Matilda, who had contracted an unpopular marriage. In support of Matilda's claim, David led an army into England and took possession of the whole country north of Durham. In this he was supported by many of the northern English barons. When Stephen advanced north to Durham, the Scottish army withdrew first to Newcastle, and later back across the Border. The war then entered a period of stalemate, while prolonged negotiations went on in an effort to reach a settlement.

These negotiations were finally broken off in 1137 and David, at the head of a large Scottish army, again entered Northumberland and ravaged the countryside, destroying everything in its path. At the beginning of 1138 Stephen took the field once more to defend his realm, and David fell back to Roxburgh, where he took up a defensive position and awaited the approach of the English. They were, however, reluctant to follow the Scots into their own country and in March David re-entered Northumberland at the head of a formidable force now united under the Scottish crown. It was on Cutton Moor, near Northallerton in Yorkshire, that the Scottish host came up against the English, on 22 August 1138.

The battle which ensued was called the Battle of the Standard because of the remarkable standard used by the English as their rallying point. This consisted of the mast of a ship mounted on a four-wheeled cart, with a large crucifix at the top. A silver box containing a consecrated host was borne on the centre of the cross. For them this was indeed a holy war in defence of Christ's Church against the barbarians.

The 'barbarian' Scots, whose ensign was a lance with a sprig of heather wreathed around it, advanced to the attack in several divisions. The vanguard, commanded by King David's son Prince Henry, consisted of the men of Lothian and Teviotdale, of Border troopers from Liddesdale, and of the fierce men of Galloway. Next came a division of Highlanders and the men of the Isles, armed only with claymores and small targes. Behind them marched the King with a strong body of Anglo-Saxon and Norman knights, men-at-arms, and archers mostly from the Lowlands. The rear was brought up by a division consisting of men from Moray, north-east Scotland and Aberdeenshire.

It seems likely that the English army numbered about 10,000 while the Scots were stronger with about 16,000. However, on the whole the Scottish soldiers were not as well equipped or armed as the men-at-arms who made up the majority of the English army.

The Scots hoped to take the English by surprise, using a thick fog to cover their approach march. They were only partially successful, getting at least to the battlefield before the alarm was raised in the English ranks. A most embarrassing argument then broke out in the Scottish army over the positions of honour on the battlefield and who, among the very different sections, was to take precedence. The King had decided to put the most sophisticated part of his army, the men-at-arms and archers, in the centre of the front. This was the place of highest honour. Unfortunately the men of Galloway had already claimed this post, maintaining that by ancient custom the privilege of commencing the battle belonged to them. In the end the King had to give way to the men of Galloway, and as a consequence the whole Scottish army was required to regroup. This could not have been easy under the watching eyes of the English host.

This incident, not important in itself, serves to emphasize the very strong tribal and regional spirit which governed the activities of the Scots in all they did. Although united in one kingdom, their loyalties were still very narrow, and each clan or regional group regarded itself as infinitely superior to all others. This deep conviction in the superiority of family, clan and, later, regiment, has been an abiding characteristic of the Scottish soldier. It became his great strength. But in the Battle of the Standard it did not do him much good.

The Gallovidians opened the battle by charging the English centre, held by spearmen and archers. This single-minded attack might have succeeded, had they not been facing an army that had deployed its forces in interdependent elements. English men-at-arms had dismounted as a screen in front of their archers, thus enabling the bowmen to continue shooting right through the Scottish charge. As a result, and in spite of the ferocity of their assault, the Gallovidians were unable to break the English formation. Perhaps frustrated by this lack of progress, Prince Henry then charged at the head of the Scottish knights and men-at-arms. A dashing cavalry leader, he overdid it. Having routed the enemy immediately before him, he proceeded to chase them off the battlefield, and the Scots' attention was thus dangerously diverted.

At this critical moment, an English soldier raised on his lance what he supposed was the head of the King of the Scots. Thinking their King to be dead, the rest of the Scottish army panicked and was thrown into complete confusion. By the time Prince Henry returned from his impetuous pursuit of the enemy centre, he found the battle lost.

Nearly half of David's army was destroyed in this encounter and he was forced to withdraw to Carlisle with the remnants. The English, however, had also suffered considerably from this bloody battle and were in no condition to follow up their advantage. Shortly afterwards the Scots took the offensive again, and although there was no other major engagement in this campaign, they were able to obtain very favourable terms when peace was concluded between the two countries on 9 April 1139.

These were still early days in the life of the Scottish kingdom, and its acceptance by some outlying parts of the country was either nominal or non-existent. Whenever weakness was shown at the centre, trouble started in the more remote parts of the kingdom, as well as outside it. So it happened when David died in 1153, and was succeeded by a boy of eleven, Malcolm IV, known as the Maiden.

Rebellion broke out in Moray, and Somerled, Chief of Argyll, sailed up the Clyde in 1164 with 160 galleys to destroy Glasgow. Also encouraged by the weakness of the Scottish kingdom, the Norwegians landed a force which sacked Aberdeen. Galloway, always a troublesome province despite its participation in the Battle of the Standard, rose in revolt against the central government of Scotland. Military action during this period was therefore largely a series of royal expeditions to bring rebels under control, or hurried assemblies of forces to repel the sporadic assaults of marauders on the coasts.

In 1165, however, King William the Lion concluded a formal treaty of alliance with France. Known as the Auld Alliance, this treaty created a bond of friendship between the two countries which lived for many years after its usefulness had ceased.

Encouraged by this French support, William launched a campaign against England which ended in disaster at Alnwick, in Northumberland, in 1174. The battle itself is of little military significance, but it is noteworthy as heralding a period of 100 years of peace between the two countries.

The last battle against the Norsemen took place in 1263. It arose from the efforts of the Scottish kings to bring the Hebrides under control of the Crown of Scotland. In an attempt to retain Norse control over the Western Isles, King Hakon sailed from Norway on 7 July 1263 with a powerful force. Having reached Shetland in two days, he continued on to Orkney where he remained for several weeks, exacting levy from the inhabitants both of the islands and of the nearby mainland of Caithness.

Hakon then sailed south down the west coast of Scotland, being joined on the way by various Hebridean chiefs, until his force had grown to more than 100 ships, all well provided with men and arms. Dividing this mighty force, he sent fifty ships to plunder Kintyre and five ships to attack the Isle of Bute, while he himself remained with the rest of his fleet at Gigha, a small island between Kintyre and Islay. The squadron which sailed against Bute compelled the Scottish garrison of the castle of Rothesay to surrender and a large part of it was put to the sword.

Having recalled his forces from these various expeditions, Hakon then sailed around the Mull of Kintyre, up the Forth of Clyde, and anchored in Kilbrannan Sound, between the Kintyre peninsula and the Isle of Arran.

Panic had seized the Scots and attempts were made to buy off the Norsemen by offering to give up the whole of the Hebrides to Norway. Luckily for Scotland, Hakon would not listen to terms, and shortly afterwards he dispatched a fleet of sixty ships up the Clyde into Loch Long. This detachment plundered and laid waste to both sides of the Loch, and then dragged their boats across the isthmus from Arrochar to Tarbet into Loch Lomond, a distance of two miles. This was a considerable feat by any standards, as the boats had to be manhandled on rollers made from felled trees. Once in Loch Lomond, the Norsemen carried fire and sword along its shores, and on to the islands in the Loch.

But the delays caused by abortive negotiations and minor expeditions had given King Alexander time to assemble his army. Moreover, the delays had carried operations into October, and the elements now began to act against the Norsemen. A violent storm destroyed ten of the Norse ships in Loch Long, and soon after, on 1 October, the rest of Hakon's fleet in the Clyde encountered a tempest of such tremendous force that several ships were cast ashore. The surviving vessels, many badly disabled, made for Largs on the Ayrshire coast, and next day Hakon landed the remnants of his forces.

By this time the Scottish army under King Alexander had moved up into position on the high ground which commands the town and port of Largs. It consisted of a large body of well-equipped infantry armed with spears and bows, and 1,500 cavalry well mounted and armoured. It greatly outnumbered the Norse army.

The Norsemen were drawn up in three divisions, one of which occupied the eminence now called Castle Hill, south-east of the modern town of Largs, and the other two were stationed on the beach due west of Castle Bay, with the double role of protecting their ships, and also giving depth to the position. This necessity to protect the ships and the natural desire to hold forward on the high ground split the Norse forces. Against such a superior Scots force defeat must have been inevitable.

As the battle was about to start, Hakon was persuaded by his chiefs to return in his barge to his fleet off the island of Cumbrae, and then return with every available man to reinforce the battle front. But he never got back, as another storm blew up and made landing impossible.

The Scots approached the Norse position down the general axis of the present A760 Paisley-Largs road, enveloped the Norsemen on Castle Hill and put them to flight. The fleeing Norsemen fell back on to the Norse positions on the beaches and threw this part of their force into complete disorder. The rout soon became general. Many of the Norsemen leapt into their boats and tried to get back to their ships standing off the shore, but many boats became overloaded and were swamped.

The rest of the Norsemen retreated along the shore, closely pursued by the victorious Scots, making a stand whenever the ground gave them a chance to do so. The battle was furious and bloody, the carnage great. The Steward of Scotland was slain. The King himself was wounded in the face by an arrow. Hakon, nephew of the Norse king, and a large number of Norse leaders perished in the fight. Nor would any Norseman have survived this bitter conflict, but for the timely arrival of reinforcements from the fleet, who eventually managed to make a landing through the surf over the storm-torn beaches south of Largs.

The remnants of the Norse invasion force re-embarked in their boats and managed to get back to their ships, only to continue the fight against the elements. The storm continued to rage with unabated fury and Hakon's once magnificent fleet was shattered and broken upon the Scottish shore. The last Norse invasion of Scotland was over.

Chapter Four

The Rise of Wallace

1286–1298

On the death of King Alexander III in 1286, Scotland was plunged into a struggle for survival. The wars of independence against England lasted for nearly 100 years and were fought with a ferocity unsurpassed before or since.

The circumstances which caused these two countries to fly at each other's throats were themselves tragic. Alexander's first wife, two sons and one daughter had all died before him and, when Alexander himself was killed in a riding accident, the only direct heir to his throne was his three year-old granddaughter, Margaret the Maid of Norway. Edward I of England, always scheming to annex Scotland under the English crown, now stepped on to the scene with a plan for his son to marry the infant Margaret, and she was sent from Norway in 1290 for this purpose.

But death struck again at the succession; the little Queen Margaret died at Orkney on her journey to her throne and marriage. With her death, Alexander III's line was extinguished and Scotland was now exposed to all the evils of a disputed succession, and the dangers of foreign intervention.

Civil war loomed, with no less than thirteen competitors for the Crown. Two were serious claimants – Balliol and Bruce, grandfather of King Robert I and known as Bruce the Competitor. Edward of England, however, had not given up his plans for enlargement and he threw his support behind Balliol, who was crowned King in 1292. Such backing came at a high price, and

29

after four years of humiliating submission, Balliol renounced his allegiance to Edward and took up arms against him.

Edward promptly invaded Scotland, a country sadly divided within and quite unable to resist attack from without. After sacking Berwick he advanced to Dunbar, where he utterly defeated Balliol, imprisoning him for a time in the Tower of London before exiling him to France.

The story of the Battle of Dunbar does little credit to Scottish arms and the blame must be laid at the feet of the Scottish leaders. Dunbar was the key to the Lothians, and Edward had ordered the Earl of Surrey to take it. Surrey had a considerable force and he invested the fortress. While he was thus occupied, a relieving Scottish army of far greater strength arrived on the scene and occupied the high ground to the west of Dunbar. Rather than stay in this strong position, the Scots abandoned it when it seemed to them the English were in difficulty crossing a steep-sided burn. It was this headlong rush down the hill that led to the English repulsing the Scots attack with great slaughter and taking many prisoners.

The Dunbar operation concluded, Edward moved on through the country, putting all who resisted to the sword. The English army captured Edinburgh, Stirling, Perth and Elgin. After this victorious campaign, King Edward finally returned to Berwick where, on 28 August 1296, he received the submission of the Scottish nobility and clergy, who were compelled to recognize him as King.

Scotland was now at the mercy of her conqueror, a victim of her own disunity and the selfish conduct of her leaders. The spirit of the nation was sunk in despair.

At this critical moment there arose a new leader and champion of freedom. Sir William Wallace of Lanarkshire was certainly not alone in his hatred of the foreign yoke, but it was he who first awoke the Scottish nation to a new consciousness of its strength and gave it the leadership it so needed at this critical time.

With Wallace at its head, the resistance movement spread rapidly throughout Scotland, and soon took the form of guerrilla warfare. Wallace started in his home county of Lanark where he quickly succeeded in gathering around him a body of men whom he imbued with his own fierce and determined spirit. As his fame spread he attracted to his banner more and more men and operations spread further afield. One of the first to join him was Sir William Douglas, who brought with him a large body of retainers.

At first these rebellious activities were dismissed by the English as those of robbers and brigands. As they developed, Edward began to take alarm and he took action to ensure the security of his newly-acquired dominions. Orders were issued to Surrey, Edward's viceroy in Scotland, to crush the insurrection. Accordingly a large army under Henry Percy and Robert de Clifford moved across the Border into Scotland. They advanced up Annandale on the line of the present A74 to Lochmaben, where they suffered a surprise night attack by the Scots. It was only by the light of their own burning tents that the English army could see just how small a Scottish force had attacked them.

After this inconclusive engagement the English army pressed on to Irvine, moving along the line of the present A76 road through Cumnock and Kilmarnock. At Irvine a considerable Scottish force was deployed to give battle to the enemy. Although weak in cavalry, it was strong enough numerically to have given a good account of itself. But dissension amongst the barons destroyed it, and it disintegrated before any action could be fought. Once more stubborn pride and selfish family and clan interests were their undoing.

Wallace retired in disgust to the north, accompanied only by his own retainers. But such was his appeal to ordinary Scotsmen that his army of irregulars grew rapidly and he soon found himself once more in a position to take the offensive. He energetically set about the capture of all the English strongholds in the north-east. The castle of Dunnottar was surprised; Forfar, Brechin and Montrose were also taken. Aberdeen fell after the English garrison had set the city on fire and abandoned it. Wallace was besieging Dundee when he heard that a large English army under the command of the Earl of Surrey was advancing on Stirling. Leaving the citizens of Dundee to continue the siege of the English garrison in that city, Wallace moved his forces rapidly south to hold the crossing of the Forth at Stirling.

Stirling was of immense strategic importance. Its wooden

31

bridge, a little way upstream from the present bridge, was the lowest crossing of the Forth and therefore the gateway to the northern counties. It was extremely narrow, allowing only two horsemen to ride abreast.

Wallace got to Stirling before the English and took up a commanding position in the area of the Abbey Craig ridge, now crowned by the Wallace Monument.

The English army advanced to the bridge from the south. It included a large number of heavy cavalry under Sir Marmaduke Twenge, a brave and experienced soldier. The English commander-in-chief, Surrey, was also an experienced soldier, and he realized that to attack the strong Scots' position by a frontal assault through the defile of the narrow bridge, with a difficult deployment on the north side, was to court disaster. Unhappily for him, he was persuaded against his better judgment by his impatient followers to do just this. He ordered an immediate attack.

On 11 September 1297 the Battle of Stirling Bridge began with the advance of the English across the bridge, led by Sir Marmaduke Twenge and Hugh de Cressingham, the English Treasurer of Scotland. Once across the bridge with his leading troops Twenge made a fatal mistake. Instead of consolidating his footing on the north bank of the river to secure a bridgehead for the remainder of the English to cross, he pushed on along a narrow causeway through the marshy ground to Causewayhead at the foot of Abbey Craig. This had the effect of canalizing the English advance and preventing the deployment of their cavalry, making them very vulnerable to attack on the flanks, as well as from the heights of Abbey Craig.

When about half the English army had crossed the bridge without opposition, part of the Scots army made a rapid detour round the right flank of the English on the north bank, and got between the English and the bridge. When he saw the retreat of the enemy cut off, Wallace ordered a general assault on all the English on the north bank. The English horse, unable to deploy, found themselves attacked on all sides and many hundreds were killed or drowned attempting to ford the river. The infantry fared no better; attacked before they had time to form up and unable to deploy their archers effectively, they were thrown into utter confusion.

At this moment Surrey attempted to save the day by ordering reinforcements over the bridge. This only added to the confusion and slaughter, as the new arrivals were unable to deploy in the confined space once they got over, hemmed in as they were by the Scottish spearmen.

Finally, a part of the Scottish force managed to cross the river by a ford west of the bridge and attacked the so far uncommitted part of Surrey's army in the rear. The English army disintegrated under this new blow, and it fled. No quarter was given and the slaughter was appalling. Although figures are often exaggerated, it is said that 20,000 men fell in the battle and subsequent pursuit.

One notable survivor of this bloody contest was Sir Marmaduke Twenge, who cut his way out from the very centre of the Scots and escaped.

The great victory at Stirling Bridge was due to the brilliant generalship of Wallace, using the ground to best effect against a superior enemy, so that the river obstacle, and the commanding ground which covered it, placed the English at a major disadvantage. As his aim was to prevent the English capturing the bridge, he could have been expected to take up a defensive position south of the bridge to protect it. A lesser general might have done so, thereby consigning an inferior Scottish force to a pitched battle in the open. Wallace's men would have been hammered against the very obstacle which had given them victory.

After the English defeat at Stirling, most of the strongholds they had occupied were surrendered and Wallace proceeded to carry out a number of large-scale reprisal raids over the Border to collect plunder. At home he became master of Scotland and did much to restore order in the country. Amongst his reforms in the military sphere were the organization of military districts throughout the country, and the introduction of muster-rolls of all between the age of sixteen and sixty who were capable of bearing arms. This is one of the earliest examples of conscription for national military service, itself a system perfectly supported within a feudal society.

Records suggest he introduced an organized chain of command to control his forces. The largest unit was 1,000 strong, divided into ten companies each of 100 soldiers. There is some evidence for further sub-division, with five platoons within each company, each again divided into sections and subsections.

Apart from these necessary reforms to instil some sort of discipline into his otherwise highly irregular forces, Wallace had neither time nor means to strengthen them before he had to face another major conflict with the English.

About the middle of 1298 an English force under the Earl of Pembroke landed in the north of Fife, and began to lay waste to the countryside. It is not clear what the purpose of this expedition was, but their depredations were cut short when Wallace attacked them on 12 June in the forest of Earnside near Lindores Abbey in Newburgh. Assisted by local people, he defeated them with the loss of 1,500 men.

The attention of the English monarch, Edward, had been elsewhere, engaged as he was in conflict with the French. Realizing that he had lost control of Scotland, he started to make preparations to regain it. Hurrying north, Edward joined his general, the Earl of Surrey, at Roxburgh and placed himself at the head of the most powerful army that had ever entered Scotland. It was further reinforced shortly after by the arrival of troops pulled out of France from Gascony.

Edward advanced with his huge army from Roxburgh across the Lammermuir Hills, through Lauder and along the present A68 to Kirkliston, six miles west of Edinburgh. Everywhere the English went they found the country deserted and stripped of supplies. Wallace collected his forces just out of reach of far superior enemy numbers but continued to harass them on all sides, depriving them of any means of living off the country. He also deprived them of intelligence, as Edward was never able to make contact with the main Scots force. The movements of the English King, however, were closely watched by the Scottish light horse.

As a result of this 'scorched earth' policy the English began to suffer acute privation. The scarcity of provisions became so bad that Edward decided it was impossible to remain in the field any longer, and he ordered a retreat to Edinburgh. It looked as if Wallace's shrewd strategy was to be crowned with success.

But treachery was at work, and just as his army was starting its retreat, Edward got information from collaborators that the Scots were encamped close by in the forest of Falkirk. He also heard that it was Wallace's intention to surprise the English by a night attack, and to thereafter harass them in their retreat. Edward immediately changed his plans and issued orders to press on towards Falkirk.

Having advanced along the line of the present M9, the English army camped late on the 21 July 1298 on the heath immediately to the east of the town of Linlithgow. It was a hungry and disgruntled army which lay down to sleep that night. Men and horses had been on short rations for many days and morale was low. Indeed the Welsh troops, who numbered about one-third of the English army, had earlier mutinied because of their conditions. Insubordination had only been quelled after English cavalry had ridden in upon the mutineers and put eight of them to death.

Matters were not improved in the English army when King Edward suffered an accident during the night. Like his men, Edward lay on the bare ground with his shield as a pillow and his war-horse tethered beside him. In the middle of the night the horse kicked the king, breaking two of his ribs, and in the confusion the whole camp awoke. It stayed awake when Edward mounted his horse and gave orders to continue the march.

As the sun rose behind them, the English army passed through Linlithgow and came upon the Scots outside Falkirk. The Scots were outnumbered three to one, and out-classed in arms and equipment.

Now Wallace made his fatal mistake – a mistake made so often before and since by guerrilla commanders. He decided to give battle to the English on the open ground on which they stood. Why he did this it is difficult to say. He may have reckoned that retreat was too hazardous in such close contact with the enemy. Perhaps he thought the morass which lay in front of the Scottish position was more of an obstacle than it proved to be. In any event, his decision was calamitous.

The Scots infantry was drawn up in four main divisions called 'schiltrons'. These infantry squares bristled like porcupines, the spears thrust forward all round by three ranks closely packed together. The front rank knelt, the second rank stooped, pointing their weapons between the heads of the front rank, while the third rank stood erect with their weapons pointed between the heads of men in front. The archers, commanded by Sir John Stewart, were in the spaces between the schiltrons, while the cavalry was positioned in the rear.

The English attacked in three lines. The first line, under command of the Earl Marshal, advanced straight towards the Scots but, when it reached the soft ground of the morass, it swung round to the left and so came upon the Scots obliquely from the flank. The second line, under command of the Bishop of Durham, noting the obstacle ahead, swung round to the right and so attacked the Scots on the opposite flank. Seeing their infantry being attacked on all sides by vastly superior forces, the Scots cavalry broke and fled. This left the Scottish infantry to fight it out alone; and bravely they did. Again and again the enemy cavalry charged the squares, and still they held.

At last Edward withdrew his horsemen and ordered forward his archers and slingers. The Scots were now subject to the concentrated fire of the English bowmen whose longbows were much superior to the Scottish short bow. The Scottish squares wavered and finally broke. The English cavalry then swept forward to overwhelm them while they were in disorder, and the day was lost. Thousands of Scots lay dead on the field.

With the remnants of his army Wallace fell back into the shelter of Torwood, six miles from Stirling on the present M9 Falkirk-Stirling road. He then retreated to Stirling before the advancing enemy, and true to his policy of leaving nothing for them, reduced the town to ashes. His army defeated and dispersed, Wallace became a fugitive until his capture and execution by the English in 1305. So passed this great Scottish soldier and champion of freedom.

The conquest of Scotland was, however, a bitter prize for the English, since the country was in ruins as a result. Indeed, Edward found it impossible to maintain his army in Scotland and withdrew practically all his troops from the country. Perhaps Wallace's 'scorched earth' policy gained him the ultimate victory after all.

Chapter Five

The Struggle for Freedom

1298–1307

For the next eight years the English kept returning to Scotland in force to try and strengthen their hold and maintain their claim of sovereignty. The country had no leader and no proper head of government. Any organization to administer and defend it rested in the hands of a few barons.

In the summer of 1300 Edward marched into Scotland again at the head of a considerable army, using the westerly route through Carlisle. According to Walter of Exeter, a Franciscan monk who accompanied this expedition, it must have been a splendid affair. Eighty-seven of the greatest barons of England were in this host, which also included knights of Brittany and Lorraine. This formidable army marched into Annandale, captured the fortress of Robert Bruce at Lochmaben, and then besieged the castle of Caerlaverock on the Solway Firth, about nine miles from Dumfries. Caerlaverock was a very strong fortress indeed, having only three sides and surrounded by a very deep moat. With a garrison of only sixty it held out for a long time against an English force numbering about 3,000, equipped with siege engines.

But Caerlaverock eventually fell and the English army dispersed over the south of Scotland, plundering and laying waste to the country as it went. The Scots wisely reverted to the harassing and skirmishing tactics of guerrilla warfare. Edward controlled the operations of his troops from Dumfries until the summer of 1301 when, after a visit to England, he established his headquarters at Linlithgow, probably on the site of the present palace. As a centre of communications to every part of Scotland, this was a far better location for Edward's headquarters, and he spent the winter there.

Little action seems to have taken place until the end of 1302, when a short truce expired and the campaign was resumed. During this lull much of the English army must have withdrawn home, as the resumption of military operations saw the advance of Sir John de Segrave from Berwick to Edinburgh, at the head of a force which some historians put at 20,000 men. On arrival in the Edinburgh area the English army initially based itself at Roslin in Midlothian, but split into three divisions in order to live off the country. This gave the Scots a chance to seize the initiative after the reverse at Falkirk four years before.

A hastily assembled Scottish force of only 8,000 men under John Comyn and Sir Simon Fraser marched through the night from Biggar, in Lanarkshire, to Roslin, where it surprised and destroyed the first division of the enemy in a dawn attack on their encampment. Segrave himself was captured. No sooner had this engagement ended than the second division of English appeared, but were promptly dealt with in the same way. The English army paymaster, Ralph the Cofferer, was taken prisoner. The third English division under the command of Robert Neville hurried to the support of the other two divisions but it arrived too late and suffered a similar fate.

Dealing with the enemy piecemeal was certainly effective for the Scots, though this was more through luck than good generalship. Nevertheless, the Scottish commanders must have shown high qualities of leadership to persuade their men to fight three battles in quick succession after a night march. In any event, the victory at Roslin temporarily boosted Scottish morale and cleared the country of the enemy's main forces.

In 1303 and 1304, however, Edward returned to Scotland with another large army to punish the Scots for their continued rebellion and for his losses at Roslin. His progress through the country, capturing once again Edinburgh, Linlithgow, Perth, Dundee and Aberdeen, took him as far north as Kinloss in Moray. He is said to have used prefabricated pontoons to cross the Forth. Retracing his steps he reduced the castle of Kildrummy in Aberdeenshire, and reached Dundee on 20 October 1303. Then he marched on Stirling and finally took up winter quarters at Dunfermline.

Throughout all this one-sided campaign the Scots did little but harass his columns, cut off stragglers and deny supplies. Resistance was piecemeal and there was certainly no national coordination. Few castles showed much resistance, their owners being afraid of the consequences. A notable exception was the defiance shown by the castle of Brechin in Angus. Commanded by a courageous knight and soldier, Sir Thomas Maule, it refused to surrender to the invader for twenty days, only capitulating when Sir Thomas was killed in the siege.

At Stirling, also, the garrison of the castle, 140 strong under Sir William Oliphant, put up a brave resistance. The English army numbered 7,000 and used their siege equipment to bombard the castle. For three months the siege continued but in the end the garrison succumbed to starvation.

It was at this new low ebb in the tide of Scotland's military strength that there emerged another champion of its freedom. Always a contender for the throne, Robert the Bruce – the competitor's grandson – had played an uncertain part in the affairs of the country.

On 27 March 1306 Bruce had himself crowned King of Scots at Scone and the gauntlet of defiance was once more thrown down at the feet of the English. When the news reached the English King he rapidly dispatched an army under the Earl of Pembroke to try once more to subdue the Scots. On 26 June Pembroke heavily defeated the small Scots army at the Battle of Methven. The site of this battle is on the northern outskirts of the village of Methven, eight miles west of Perth, on the present A85 road.

The remnants of the Scottish army scattered, and Bruce himself, with about 500 men, retired into the fastness of the Highlands. The party had to keep on the move to avoid capture, and suffered a miserable existence living off the country. With the approach of winter Bruce had decided that he must try to get back to his own family area in Carrick, and moved his small force along the banks of Loch Tay, through Glen Dochart to Crianlarich, following the line of the present A827 and A85 roads. The route they followed

39

was the same as that trod 500 years earlier by Pict and Scot forbears; as the only way through the mountains, it was ideal for ambush. As Bruce's band moved up the narrow defile of Strath Fillan near Tyndrum they were ambushed by a greatly superior force of Macdougalls, committed through their family to the enemy. Although a small encounter it was a very bloody one, with great losses on both sides. The long pole-axes wielded by the Highlanders decimated Bruce's horsemen and, while there are tales of Bruce's tremendous feats of bravery and prowess with his battle-axe, he himself was lucky to escape. The site of this battle is south of the Free Church Manse of Dalry (Dali Righ) or the 'King's Field'.

After this skirmish, Bruce wandered over the Highlands and Islands, a fugitive with dwindling support and apparently little prospect of ever taking the field again. Yet throughout the bleak winter of 1306, he remained determined to continue the struggle to free Scotland, and it is to this perseverance, as much as to his generalship, that he owed the final victory.

With the spring of 1307 he took the field again. He arrived in Arran with a small body of followers under Sir James Douglas, later known as the Black Douglas. From Arran he planned to cross to the mainland to raise troops in his ancestral lands of Carrick in Ayrshire, and for this seaborne operation he had been able to raise about 300 islanders with a number of galleys. A small advance party was sent ahead to locate the English forces in the area, and to report on the mood of the vassals he hoped to recruit. If conditions were favourable, the advance party was to signal the go-ahead by lighting a signal fire on the coast near Turnberry. On the appointed day, a beacon was spotted and Bruce set sail with his force as darkness fell, using the light to steer their course. Unfortunately the fire had either been lit by mistake or by the enemy. On land, Bruce found that not only was there a very strong English force under Lord Percy in the area, but his own vassals were not disposed to join him. Bruce would have had every reason at this point to turn back. Instead, in the face of such bad news, he resolved to press on.

Lord Percy had foolishly split his forces between Turnberry

Castle and the village of Turnberry and this gave Bruce the chance of dealing with at least part of the enemy. In the dead of night he fell on the English troops billeted in Turnberry village and put all to the sword. Hearing the uproar in the village but not knowing the strength of the attackers, Percy dared not sally forth from the castle.

From Turnberry, Bruce withdrew into the mountains of Carrick, where he awaited reinforcements being raised by his brothers Thomas and Alexander in Ireland. But these reinforcements never reached him. They were intercepted on landing at Loch Ryan in Galloway by the enemy under a powerful chief, Duncan McDowall, and were completely destroyed.

The forces in all these operations were small but for Bruce they were critical. With only 300 men in the hills of Carrick, Bruce had needed the reinforcements from Ireland, who had numbered 700. Their loss was a disaster and it meant that he had to stay in those hills.

However the gloom was partly relieved with a daring operation by the Black Douglas on his former home, Douglas Castle on the Douglas Water in Lanarkshire. On 19 March 1307, leaving only the cook and the porter behind, the entire English garrison marched to the Church of St Bride for the Palm Sunday service. Black Douglas, with a handful of followers, mingled with the procession and, at a given signal, fell on and destroyed the unfortunate English. On taking possession of the castle, Douglas heaped everything they could not remove in the courtyard, flung the bodies of the dead on to the pile and set fire to the whole place to prevent its further use by the enemy. The Church of St Bride stands to this day.

Meanwhile Bruce and his small band of followers continued to wage guerrilla warfare from their hideouts in the mountains of Carrick with considerable success. An English force sent to drive them out of the mountains was itself ambushed at Glen Trool and forced to withdraw with heavy losses. As their successes grew, so more and more Scotsmen flocked to Bruce's standard. With greater numbers at his command, he descended to the plains and drove the English garrisons out of most of the fortresses in

Ayrshire. The districts of Kyle, Cunningham, and Carrick were completely cleared of the enemy. During these operations in 1307 Sir James Douglas ambushed an English force of 1,000 men under Sir Philip Mowbray on the march from Bothwell to Kyle and completely routed them. The remnants of this English force fell back to Bothwell, while their commander took refuge in the castle of Inverkip.

Pembroke now determined to halt this wave of Scottish success in south-west Scotland and, early in May 1307, he moved into Ayrshire with a force of 3,000, most of whom were heavy cavalry. Bruce, with a comparatively small force, was at this time at Galston, north-east of Ayr, and on hearing of the English advance he moved along the axis of the present A71 road to take up a battle position astride this road south-east of Loudon Hill. The position he chose showed his remarkable ability as a general.

Realizing that his meagre force of about 600 spearmen could not beat off such a vastly superior enemy without cunning use of the ground, he selected a part of the road which passed between two marshes. To narrow the front still further, he dug a triple line of deep trenches on each flank. The combined effect of this was to force the enemy to attack on such a narrow front that their numbers could not be fully deployed. Finally he covered his rear by positioning his baggage and camp followers on Loudon Hill itself.

On 10 May the Battle of Loudon Hill started with the advance of the English along the road from the east. They swept forward to the attack in two divisions astride the road. The front line, with levelled lances, charged the Scottish spearmen who were formed into a solid block completely barring their passage. The Scots stood firm and, with no room for manoeuvre, the English horse were thrown into confusion. Many were unhorsed; others fell back upon the second wave which itself became disorganized. Panic ensued and in a short time the whole enemy force had been put to flight.

By launching his army on a frontal attack of this sort, Pembroke showed little tactical ability and no imagination. He was presumably relying blindly on his superior strength. Bruce, on the other hand, had used the ground to defeat the enemy army.

The Scots victory at Loudon Hill had two effects. First, great numbers of Scots now rallied to the standard of Robert the Bruce. Throughout Scotland he was acclaimed as the deliverer of his country and patriotic fervour once more swept the land. Secondly, King Edward I resolved to crush the Scots once and for all.

Chapter Six

The Triumph of the Bruce

1307 – 1330

Now was the scene set for the climax of this long and savage struggle between the English and Scots. So much blood had been spilt by both sides, with nothing to show for it but a devastated land. Much more was yet to be spilt.

Edward I, the 'Hammer of the Scots', set out on his last campaign a sick man. He never made it and died on 6 July 1307, aged sixty-eight, at Burgh upon Sands on the Solway, within sight of the country he had tried so hard to enslave. He died a bitter man, his hatred for Scotland declared even in his death wish that his bones be carried at the head of his army and remain unburied until the Scots had been subdued. His death at this time must have been a tremendous relief to the Scots, as the son who took over command of the campaign was not of the same calibre as his father.

Within months, Edward II abandoned the campaign, withdrawing the greater part of his forces and leaving only a few fortresses fully garrisoned. Bruce took full advantage by turning his attention to the rest of the kingdom and, during the winter of 1307, he carried out operations in the north-east to assert and establish his authority. On 25 December he roundly defeated the Earl of Buchan at Old Meldrum in Aberdeenshire, just outside Barra Castle near the town. He then crushed all further resistance by his old enemy the Comyns in Buchan, with a severity and brutality long to be remembered in the area. The castles of Aberdeen and Forfar were captured, their garrisons put to the sword and the fortifications demolished. Whenever possible, Bruce reduced captured fortresses in this way to deny their future use to the enemy. He also neatly avoided the need to garrison them. The strength of his army was still such that he certainly could not afford to leave static guards and this attacking strategy kept his forces focused and mobile.

Bruce then marched against the MacDougalls of Lorne to settle his old score with them. During his advance into Lorne the enemy attempted to ambush his force as it negotiated the Pass of Brander between Dalmally and Bonawe, on the line of the present A85 road. In 1309 this pass was but a narrow track between the mass of Ben Cruachan towering on the north and a precipitous slope to the water on the south side. Warned of the enemy's intention, Bruce sent Douglas and his men ahead to encircle and trap them. He himself advanced in to the ambush with some of his troops. The enemy were put to flight with great slaughter, and Bruce moved on to capture the MacDougall stronghold at Dunstaffnage, north of Oban.

Throughout 1309 and 1310 Bruce continued to consolidate his position, extending his rule over most of northern Scotland and a good deal of the south. As the tide of success swept on, so more men joined his cause, and the Scots army grew strong enough to carry the war into England itself, plundering and laying waste to the counties of Northumberland and Durham. Meanwhile the remaining English-held castles in Scotland fell one by one into the hands of the Scots.

Not all victories were attributable to sheer force of numbers. The immensely strong fortress of Linlithgow fell not by brawn but by brain. A local partisan farmer called Binny, who normally supplied the castle with forage, managed to conceal eight armed men in a delivery of hay entering the castle. When the hay cart reached the exact mid-way point of the gateway, the armed men leapt out and overpowered the guard. With the cart in the way, the drawbridge could not be raised, nor could the gate be shut or portcullis lowered. Access achieved, the main body of the attackers rushed in and seized the rest of the castle.

Roxburgh Castle, commanded by De Fiennes, a Burgundian knight, was strong in both defence and garrison. In spite of this it fell to the Douglas. He had chosen his date very carefully. Tuesday, 7 March 1312 was the eve of the Lenten fast and the garrison's usual discipline had lapsed. While its attention was on wine and merriment, Douglas and a small party of picked men scaled the walls with rope-ladders and captured the outer defences. The garrison were then driven back into the keep where they made a determined stand for twenty-four hours before being forced to surrender.

Even the fortress of Edinburgh Castle fell to the Scots after a daring assault carried out on a dark night on 14 March 1312, by Thomas Randolph, Earl of Moray. The castle had been besieged for six weeks but its immense strength had defied all attempts at capture. These days Princes Street Gardens, the railway lines and the church yard at the bottom of Lothian Road are at the foot of its northern flank. In 1312, Randolph had no access to this approach, protected as it was by a loch which stretched along the whole valley. This prevented any large force deploying close to the castle on that side. The west and south flanks were equally well protected by the precipitous slope of the castle rock itself. This left the eastern side as the only possible approach for a besieging force to attack in the conventional manner. Difficulties were further compounded by a causeway leading to the drawbridge so narrow that attackers had perforce to thin and hence become easy prey for defenders.

It was probably this which lulled the garrison into a false sense of security, and so caused the fall of the fortress. The bold attackers scaled the great rock in the most unlikely place, took the garrison by surprise, and although outnumbered, forced it to surrender.

The loss of all these strongholds was too much for the English to bear. The last of the fortresses still in their hands was Stirling, and when it came under siege King Edward assembled an army to relieve the castle and retain at least one significant foothold in Scotland. He had not much time in which to do it as the English garrison had agreed to surrender if not relieved by Midsummer Day. This arrangement made between Edward Bruce, King Robert's brother, and the Governor of Stirling Castle, Sir Thomas Mowbray, was an embarrassment to both sides. The English King could hardly ignore the challenger to his arms. The Scottish King could not allow the English to relieve Stirling without losing most of the ground won at such cost over the past six years. Like those who came before him, Bruce would be at a disadvantage if forced to abandon his guerrilla tactics and fight a pitched battle against an enemy force superior in both experience and numbers.

The English army assembled in Northumberland in June 1314 was probably the most powerful force yet to fight against the Scots. Chroniclers of the day put its strength at 100,000 men. In reality, it was probably about 3,000 heavily-armed cavalry and 20,000 infantry, but the quality of its men and equipment was superb.

Having completed their assembly, the English army started its advance on 17 June, moving up Lauderdale to Edinburgh along the line of the present A68 road. As they advanced north, supplies were carried by sea to Leith. On 22 June they reached Falkirk, with two days in hand to accomplish the relief of Stirling by Midsummer Day. Horse and foot had marched 100 miles in six days.

Bruce had collected his forces in Torwood half-way between Falkirk and Stirling. The location was redolent of bad memories, as this was where the unfortunate Wallace had found himself and the remnants of his army after their defeat at the battle of Falkirk in 1298. During the evening of 22 June the Scottish scouts made contact with the might of the English army, streaming through Falkirk. Subsequent reports to Bruce were so depressing that he ordered them to be kept secret. And well he might, for the Scottish army was outnumbered four to one and miserably equipped by comparison. Against the English host Bruce could muster only some 5,000 infantry, most of whom were spearmen armed with twelve foot spears, a few archers and 500 light horse.

But one advantage Bruce did have. His men were fighting for hearth and home on their native soil. By now he had inspired all ranks of his little army with that precious battle-winning spirit – the will to fight for a cause, both personal and national, which all recognized and for which they were prepared to die. To reinforce this he drew up his men and reminded them of all that they had suffered, what they had won and what they stood to lose. He encouraged any man, not prepared to fight to the death for him and for freedom, to leave the army.

Bruce's leadership in inspiring his men with the will to fight was equalled by his generalship. Realizing the weakness of his forces and acute deficiency in cavalry, he deployed his meagre army in such a way as to use the ground to maximum advantage against the heavily-armoured enemy. To this end he selected a piece of ground near the village of Bannockburn on which to offer battle to the English.

The field of Bannockburn lies south of Stirling near the village of Bannockburn, on the present A80 road. Bruce organized his forces in four main divisions on the high ground in this area facing south-east. His front extended from the Bannock burn on the right to the small village of St Ninians on the left. The right was protected by the steep sides of the Bannock burn itself. He reinforced this position by having rows of pits dug wherever the ground permitted. These were filled with sharp stakes and then camouflaged with bracken and branches. Preparations were completed by scattering caltrops or iron spikes between the pits and along any ground suitable for cavalry approach.

These dispositions made maximum use of the high ground and natural obstacles, as well as providing depth to his defence. From them Bruce would be able to fight in any and every direction the enemy attacked. In the event this is exactly what he had to do. During the afternoon of Saturday, 23 June the English army reached the Bannock burn after a forced march of ten miles from Falkirk. It was a hot day and the heavily armoured cavalry must have felt the heat as much as the marching infantry. Both were at the end of a long week of forced marches and they were tired and hungry.

The English armoured knights who formed the vanguard of the enemy under command of the Earls of Hereford and Gloucester were the first to close on to the natural obstacle of the Bannock burn. They must have presented a magnificent but terrifying picture to the Scots formed up on the other side. The remainder of the English army was still strung out to the south behind them along the line of the Roman road running from Torwood through West Plean.

To the surprise of the Scots the English cavalry went straight into an attack across the burn, without waiting for the main body to close up and deploy for battle. King Edward and his cavalry commanders reckoned that, with their superiority in numbers and armour, they could tackle the Scots without delay.

So unexpected was the English attack that Bruce himself was nearly killed. While carrying out a reconnaissance of the front he was suddenly charged by one of the English knights, de Bohun, who was heavily armoured and mounted on a powerful war horse. Before the eyes of his whole army, and despite being comparatively lightly armoured and mounted on a sturdy pony, the Scottish King rode forward to meet the charge. As his adversary thundered up to him, Bruce side-stepped the heavy charger, rose in his stirrups and, with a single blow of his battle-axe, split his enemy's head open. To the watching Scottish army this was indeed an omen of victory.

The Battle of Bannockburn had begun. The cavalry of the English vanguard, as yet unsupported by their trailing infantry, struggled to get across the Bannock burn and through the belt of caltrops and anti-cavalry pits without success. After a time they fell back in disorder and their commander, the Earl of Gloucester, was unhorsed.

A second body of English cavalry about 600 strong, under the command of Lord Clifford, now tried to move round the Scottish left between the low marshy ground known as the Carse and the high ground occupied by the Scottish army. Foreseeing this very move, Bruce had left a strip of firm ground in this area into which to entice the enemy. Some might argue he had no alternative, with hardly enough troops to hold the high ground let alone the low ground stretching to the Carse. Nevertheless, he was a good enough general to realize the tactical potential of this piece of ground and, when the time came, to use it to his advantage.

Clifford's orders were to get his force into a position between Stirling and the Scottish army and so cut off its retreat. This operation failed completely. As soon as Clifford's force got into the 'killing area', Randolph's division of the Scottish army descended from its position near St Ninians and threatened the English flank. As so often happens in this situation, whether in ancient or modern warfare, Clifford's force swung round to face the new threat. In spite of its orders to press on to the Scots rear, it wheeled left and engaged Randolph's division.

Randolph's men immediately halted and formed schiltrons, presenting an impregnable wall of spears around each formation. Undeterred, the English horsemen hurled themselves at the hedgehogs of spears but nothing could break the Scottish infantry. Lord Clifford himself died in the charge, and great was the slaughter of men and horses in his force.

The fighting on the first day of the Battle of Bannockburn was over. So far only the advance guard of the English army had been deployed, but its two unsuccessful attacks from the south and south-east had badly shaken the morale of the whole army. By the same token Scottish spirits were high as a result of the day's operations.

As nightfall approached Bruce now had a difficult decision to make. He realized that, in spite of his considerable successes that day, he was still greatly outnumbered, and he could have had no illusions about the dangers he would run in closing with the main body of the English army next day.

His decision to stay and fight it out may have been influenced by the redeployment of the English that evening. Having failed to take the Scottish positions with attacks from the south and south-east, King Edward decided to strike the next day from the east. To this end, and also to get at a better water supply for his horses, he moved the main body of his army round to the east of the Scottish position across the Bannock burn to camp for the night in the flat marshy land of the Carse. This would bring him closer to Stirling so that he could relieve it next day. It did not seem to occur to him that Bruce with his inferior numbers would leave his strong position and attack him. He could not have made a bigger mistake and Bruce realized it.

To have deployed an infantry force in boggy low ground dominated by the enemy would have been bad enough; to place a heavily armoured cavalry force in such a position was disastrous. After passing a damp and uncomfortable night in marshy surroundings the English were soon to realize how disastrous it was.

As Sunday, 24 June dawned, and the pale light of daybreak

spread across the battlefield, the two armies prepared for battle. The Scots knelt in prayer, and to receive the blessing of the Church, and mass was celebrated at the head of each schiltron. In the English camp the knights and men-at-arms put on their armour and saw to their chargers. The scene was almost peaceful but for the blare of trumpets calling the English troops to fall in on their battle stations.

But the trumpet calls came too late. It was at this moment, before the English had time to assemble in any sort of battle deployment that Bruce struck. The Scots had said their prayers in battle formation and they started to advance down the hill towards the unprepared English in three solid phalanxes of infantry, ringed by forests of glittering spears. Down the hill marched the schiltrons like a steadily moving wall of steel.

Bruce's plan was simple. First, he wanted to get the advantage of surprise by attacking the enemy before they were ready. Second, by rolling his infantry down upon the English, he could press them back against the extremely boggy ground of the Carse.

Chaos reigned in the English ranks. The cavalry tried desperately to charge the advancing Scottish infantry but they were so cramped and restricted in their movements that they were unable to make any impression on those steely squares. The English archers were redundant. Having camped behind their cavalry, their weapons were masked by the solid mass of their own horsemen.

The English army, unlike the Scots whose main arm was infantry spearmen, depended on its armour and its archers. Both were now literally bogged down. However, at this stage some archers began to move round the left flank of their cavalry to get a clear shot at the Scots. In so doing, they placed themselves in a most dangerous position as they were in the open and without their normal protection of pikemen.

Bruce realized how vulnerable his packed infantry formations would be to the accurate and intense shooting of the English archers. He also realized that he now had a chance to destroy one of the English army's main arms with a single blow. He promptly ordered his small cavalry force under Sir Robert Keith to charge the bowmen from the flank. The English archers were annihilated.

51

Steadily the Scottish infantry pressed on down the hill, forcing the luckless enemy cavalry further and further back towards to the marsh behind them. The ring of steel round the English was closing rapidly as Bruce brought his right flank round the south and cut off escape in that direction. The battle raged with great fury.

At this moment Bruce decided to throw in his reserve – the Islanders under Angus Og, Macdonald of the Isles. These had in fact only just reached the battlefield, after a forced march from the far west, but they launched themselves against the northern flank of the English, driving them into the narrow gorge of the Bannock burn where the course of the burn forms a large loop.

The whole Scottish front now surged forward on to the thoroughly disorganized English with renewed energy, the officers cheering their men on with cries of 'On them! On them! They fail! They fail!' Even the camp followers joined in. From their area on Gillies Hill, so called from that very day, emerged 2,000 servants and camp followers, reinforced by local farmers, and all determined to join in the fight. Whether or not they did so out of enthusiasm for the cause or a desire for plunder, their arrival on the battlefield with makeshift banners made out of blankets and horse rugs was decisive. At the sight of what they thought to be further reserves, the English broke and tried to flee. But fleeing was not easy. Whichever way they turned they found either the spears of the Scots or the marsh and the waters of the Forth to its north. The Bannock burn and the marsh of the Carse became choked with struggling horses and men. Many who got across the marsh drowned while attempting to swim the Forth. Most of the shattered survivors of the English army fought their way out to the north, towards Stirling. These included King Edward surrounded by a band of knights determined to save their king.

Edward reached Stirling Castle only to be told by the Governor, Sir Philip de Mowbray, the castle must surrender to the Scots next day in accordance with the terms of the truce. The King was therefore forced to flee south. Accompanied by some 500 men, and pursued by Douglas, he finally reached Dunbar where he took a boat for Berwick and safety.

Among the many thousands slain or taken prisoner were 700

knights and many of England's greatest nobles. The Scots captured 500 men of high rank and a great number of lesser degree, all of who were treated with generosity and clemency because they represented a valuable asset.

So ended the Battle of Bannockburn, the greatest victory in Scottish history and the worst disaster to English arms since the Norman conquest. Although it did not immediately end the war, it finally extinguished English hopes of conquering and annexing Scotland. For the next fifteen years, until Bruce's death in 1329, the Scots carried the war into the north of England where they were able to operate at will.

The significance of this battle in the history of the Scottish nation is difficult to exaggerate. It raised Scotland from the condition of a conquered and subordinate province to that of a free and independent country. It began the process of welding the Scots into a proud nation with a strong heritage of military prowess.

Robert the Bruce's selection of ground and the dispositions of his meagre forces on that ground were the keys to his success. It should be remembered that initial dispositions in medieval battle – and indeed up to the time of modern field communications – were usually vital. Once deployed it was difficult and slow to change position. But his conduct of the battle once joined must surely place him amongst the great commanders of history. Above all he was a leader, able to not only instil into his soldiers a sense of mission and a love of cause, but also a preparedness to die for them.

Chapter Seven

Fruits of Victory Lost

1330 – 1371

With the death of Robert the Bruce in 1329 Scotland's military strength declined rapidly. Bruce's generals Douglas and Randolph died soon after their leader and the throne was occupied by David II, a boy of five. The country's weakness inevitably encouraged trouble from those dispossessed and disinherited by the wars of independence.

A large force of the disinherited under Edward Balliol sailed up the east coast from England, landed at Kinghorn, and overran Fife in August 1332. At Dupplin Moor near Perth they completely routed a numerically superior Scottish force under the Regent Earl of Mar, a weak man and an incompetent general. The Scottish army had been camped on the northern bank of the River Earn. The English, having discovered a ford over the river, were able to cross the Earn undetected and surprise the Scots by a skilful night attack. Mar had not only neglected to post sentries, but had permitted his troops to relax with more than the usual amount of help from the local brew. With such disregard of the normal military requirements of security and sobriety, the unfortunate Scots suffered enormous losses, including their leader Mar. However, the English success was only temporary and the pro-English Balliol was driven from Scotland within the year.

In the spring of 1333, Edward III of England, who had come to the throne in 1327 at the age of fourteen, marched north in an attempt to take Berwick, a city which had been resisting his forces for some time.

Edward first tried to storm into the town, filling in the defence ditches and planting scaling ladders against the walls. Although the attacks were repulsed with great loss, the siege became so complete that the garrison agreed to surrender if not relieved by a certain date and it gave hostages in support of this pledge. Before that date was reached, the Regent Douglas, at the head of a considerable Scottish army, advanced to the relief of Berwick along the south side of the River Tweed. He actually succeeded in getting into the besieged city a small force under Sir William Keith but otherwise his efforts had to be confined to creating a diversion to ease the pressure on the garrison.

When the date for surrender of the city arrived, Edward demanded its capitulation in accordance with the agreement, but Sir William Keith, who had now become the governor, refused to comply on the grounds that he and his party had reinforced the garrison. The pact was therefore dead. Edward replied by hanging Thomas Seton, one of the hostages and son of the former governor of Berwick, in full sight of the city walls.

Under pressure from the panic-struck citizens of Berwick, Keith reached a new agreement with Edward. Unless the Scots reinforced the garrison by 200 men or defeated the English in a pitched battle by 19 July, Berwick had to be surrendered. The Scottish Regent found himself making the critical decision to risk all on a pitched battle. Crossing the Tweed on 18 July 1333, he encamped at Dunse Park, a few miles north of Berwick.

The English army was drawn up before him in a strong position on the top of high ground called Halidon Hill. Organized into four divisions with large numbers of archers in support, their front was covered by a swamp stretching along the low ground between the two armies. The Scottish army was also divided into four divisions, three forward and one in reserve under the Earl of Ross. The Battle of Halidon Hill was fought on 20 July on a site just off the A6105 road about three miles north-east of Berwick.

As the boggy ground prevented the use of cavalry, the Scottish mounted troops dismounted and continued in a headlong charge towards the English waiting on their hill. Unfortunately the conditions proved almost as difficult an obstacle for heavily armoured men on foot as for those on horseback, and the Scottish charge was soon slowed down and broken up. They then came under accurate and sustained volleys from the English archers. Hundreds fell, but the Scots eventually extricated themselves from the soft ground of the marsh and resumed their charge up the hill. The impetus however had been lost and those who reached the top of Halidon Hill were driven down again. The reserve under Ross was unable to affect the outcome and, by the end of the day, the defeat of the Scots was complete. Berwick fell, and the young King David II was sent to France for safety.

It is difficult to find any excuse for the way in which the Regent Douglas conducted this engagement. Robert Bruce had always warned his commanders against falling into the trap of taking on the English in a pitched battle, because of their superiority in heavy cavalry and the 'fire power' of their archers. At Halidon Hill the English had the additional advantage of a major obstacle – to infantry as well as to cavalry – across their front. A frontal assault in these circumstances was doomed to failure.

In King David's absence, the conflict between England and a rudderless Scotland dragged on under a series of regents. About the end of July 1336 a large body of Flemish troops under command of the Count of Namur landed at Berwick to reinforce the English campaign in Scotland. The intelligence on which their subsequent movements were based was woefully inadequate. Believing the south of Scotland to be firmly in English hands, the Flemings pressed straight on to Edinburgh. The city was not garrisoned, its Castle defences having been reduced in earlier fighting. But Edinburgh was not as vulnerable as it appeared, and Flemish forces were suddenly attacked by the Scots under the Earls of Moray and March, and Sir Alexander Ramsay.

A fierce battle ensued on the Borough Muir, the area between the Meadows and Blackford Hill. The Flemings, clad in complete armour, had at first the advantage, but when Scottish reinforcements came down suddenly from the Pentland Hills under Douglas of Liddesdale, they had to beat a hasty retreat. The Flemings were forced into the narrow thoroughfares of the city. At the spot where Victoria Street enters the Grassmarket, the battle-axe of one Scottish knight, David de Annand, is reputed to have struck one of the mailed Flemings so hard he killed horse and man in a single blow, shattering a huge flagstone in the pavement in the process. The Flemish could not withstand such ferocity and they were driven street by street up on to the high ground on which the Castle esplanade now stands, where their misbegotten foray on behalf of the English was ended.

In 1336 the English themselves sallied forth. Their army actually penetrated as far north as Lochindorb in Moray, although their progress was by no means unimpeded. The castle of Leven, situated on an island in the middle of the beautiful loch of that name, was held by the Scots under Alan de Vipont. Another Scotsman, Sir John de Strivelin, was campaigning in the interests of Balliol, and he proceeded to invest the castle with a large force of English troops. Strivelin built a temporary fort in the churchyard of Kinross, where a narrow neck of land juts out into the loch. From this base the English attempted to capture the castle by boat attack, but without success. Then one dark night the Scottish garrison in Loch Leven Castle turned the table on their besiegers by carrying out a boat attack on their base in the temporary fort, and inflicting so many casualties that the siege had to be lifted.

Another stirring episode in this period was the defence of Dunbar by the Countess of March. A daughter of Randolph, Earl of Moray, she had inherited her father's indomitable courage. She was called Black Agnes because of her somewhat dark complexion.

The Earl of Salisbury, commander of the English besiegers, used every device to take the castle of Dunbar. Great engines of war were brought up to throw massive stones against the walls, but they made no impression and merely gave Black Agnes an opportunity to show her disdain for the enemy by ordering the walls to be dusted down after each salvo. This contempt for danger inspired her followers. Salisbury also used the machine called a 'sow', which had been used very effectively at the siege of Berwick. The sow was a very large armoured box on wheels enclosing twenty or thirty soldiers, and was pushed with its load to the base of the wall to be scaled. Black Agnes was ready to deal with the sow as with most other things, and the moment the sow reached the foot of the walls it was crushed by an immense rock hurled from the parapets.

When Salisbury found he could not take Dunbar by assault he sat down to starve it into submission. But he failed in this too. Sir Alexander Ramsay of Dalhousie sailed on a dark night right into the castle, through a gate on to the sea, with a load of provisions he had collected on the Bass Rock just up the coast.

After five months Salisbury raised the siege and withdrew – defied and defeated by a heroic woman.

By 1339 the tide was turning once more against the English, and in that year Robert Stewart, now Regent, captured Perth. During the next two years, the enemy was swept out of most of Scotland, culminating in the re-capture of the great castle of Edinburgh on 17 April 1341. The castle which had been rebuilt by the English was captured by a trick. Under cover of a supply column delivering rations to the English garrison, a small party of Scots seized the gate and drawbridge and held it while a larger force rushed in to overwhelm the garrison. Encouraged by these successes, King David II returned to Scotland from France and assumed the government of the country. Sadly he was not the man for the job. Scotland needed peace – it got more war, and David lacked the years of campaigning experience of his illustrious father.

On 17 October 1346, having very unwisely invaded England, the twenty year old King was utterly defeated by the English at the Battle of Neville's Cross, near Bishop Auckland in Durham. The engagement started when a very large English army advancing to encounter the Scots came upon the Douglas of Liddesdale out on a foraging mission for the main Scottish army. As he only had a squadron with him he tried to avoid the English but he was pursued, attacked, and routed. The remnants of his force escaped to give the alarm.

The Scottish army was then quickly formed up in three divisions. King David led the centre, the right was commanded by the Earl of Moray, and the left by Robert The High Steward.

The ground on which the Scots found themselves committed to battle was tactically poor. They had no advantage of height or a commanding view over the surrounding country. Moreover, their position was intersected by ditches and obstacles which made it difficult for the divisions to support each other.

58

A chance to do something to correct this unfavourable tactical situation presented itself as soon as the English army drew near, but the chance was not taken. The first English to approach the Scots position was a large body of their key troops – the archers. Sir John Graham, an experienced soldier, realized how vital it was to stop the archers getting into a position to shoot, and he asked the King for permission to charge them before they could form up. Forgetting the lessons of Bannockburn, David refused. Nothing deterred, Sir John tried to attack the archers with his own small band of retainers, but they were too few to make an impression and were beaten off.

The English began their attack with an assault on the Scottish right wing. Preceded by a hail of arrows from their archers, the men-at-arms charged into the gaps forced on the Scottish defence by the formation of the ground. Moray fell dead and the division was overrun. The King's flank was thus uncovered and the English pressed on to the centre. A furious battle raged around David. His generalship may have been poor, but he was a brave and courageous soldier. Wounded by two arrows, he fought on at the head of his nobles, encouraging his men to the last, until he was overcome by the enemy and taken prisoner. The centre fell. The left wing of the Scottish army retreated from the battlefield and the day was lost.

Robert Stewart now once more became Regent and faced the task of rallying the Scots in their defeat. He did not do badly. Berwick was recaptured in 1355, and in that same year a Scottish force under the Earl of Douglas defeated an English force at Nisbet Muir near Norham. Norham with its castle is on the Border, on the present B6470 road, and at the time of the battle it was in English hands.

The action arose from a Border raid by Northumbrians to plunder the estate of the Earl of March in Scotland. As a reprisal a cunning plan was conceived to destroy the English garrison at Norham. Sir William Ramsay was sent into Northumberland with 400 men to lay waste to the countryside, while Douglas, with a much larger force formed an ambush at Nisbet Muir well inside Scotland on the road from Norham to Duns. After Ramsay had plundered Norham village and the surrounding country, he proceeded to drive his booty into Scotland in full view of the exasperated English garrison in Norham Castle.

The English took the bait and, sallying forth under their Governor Sir Thomas Grey, they set off in pursuit. Ramsay, however, fled before them in accordance with his orders, and lured them right into the ambush at Nisbet Muir. Few of the English escaped.

But despite these minor successes the fortunes of Scotland were at a low ebb. The country was economically exhausted, militarily weak, and leaderless. King David II was returned to Scotland on payment of a huge ransom which the country could ill afford. So much achieved by Robert the Bruce in the field of national unity and military organization had been frittered away. The sword of Scotland had become severely blunted.

Chapter Eight

The Stuarts

1371 – 1587

With the weakening rule of the monarch came an increase in the power of the barons and chiefs in the provinces. They built bigger and better castles and from these strongholds became increasingly defiant towards their king.

During the wars of independence many of the fine castles built in the thirteenth century had been destroyed to prevent them falling into the hands of the English. In the fourteenth and fifteenth centuries, some of the more important castles such as Bothwell, Dirleton, Caerlaverock, and Kildrummy, were rebuilt and made even stronger.

In the Highlands and Islands, the most powerful call to arms still came from clan. All over the rest of Scotland, however, the form of military service was changing. The barons began increasingly to exact a different kind of tribute from their tenants, in the form of money or goods. With the wealth thus collected, they were able to hire mercenaries to garrison their castles and fight their battles. They were in fact forming small regular armies and, being composed of professional soldiers, they were more effective. Such armies, though, could be unreliable. Men serving solely for the pay, having no loyalty to leader or cause, could change sides for better terms of service, and they often chose the most awkward moment in the campaign to seek improvements.

The weapons and tactics had changed little, any innovation originating in England or France. The exception was guerrilla tactics, in which the Scots at times excelled, and it was a pity they did not stick more often to this form of warfare. After Bruce, whose ability as a general in both guerrilla warfare and set-piece battle made him the outstanding commander of medieval Scottish history, there were few commanders of note.

Much of the fighting of this period took the form of raids carried out by one baron or chief upon the territory of his neighbour. The object was usually booty, and the action took the form of a 'hit and run' operation. The Borders were particularly subject to raids of this sort since the barons on both sides of the Border did not have to even look for an excuse because a state of semi-permanent warfare existed between the two countries along its length.

When the first Stuart king, Robert II, ascended the throne, barons and chiefs in every part of the country challenged the authority of the crown. In the Highlands and Islands the chiefs grew more and more powerful and independent, with great clans like the Macdonalds and Macleans practically running separate kingdoms. In the Lowlands the great barons like Douglas, with their military power increased by private wars against the English, paid scant regard to the authority of the king. Indeed much of the fighting at this time was carried on, not between Scotland and England, but between Douglas on one side of the Border, and Percy of Northumberland on the other. Perhaps it is from this period of history that the Borders developed their separate character, and started to produce soldiers with an identity quite distinct from the Highlander or the Lowlander.

The families of Armstrong, Elliot, Johnstone, Maxwell, Scott, Kerr, and Hume all figure largely in the stories of the endless Border affrays of this time. A tradition of fighting and raiding, known as reiving, became established. Caused in part by the general poverty along the Border it was mainly carried out in the autumn and winter. Rustling, burning of homesteads, and murder were all part of daily life in this area of lawlessness. Inevitably it produced its own architecture, culture and people. These people had to fight just to survive.

One of these Border battles was fought in 1388 at Otterburn, a village in Redesdale, about thirty miles from Newcastle, and has been made famous in history by the song 'Chevy Chase'.

The Earl of Douglas had led a daring raid into England, reaching as far as the gates of Durham. At Newcastle, following an encounter with his hated enemy, Sir Henry Percy (renowned by the name of Hotspur) he began to withdraw back into Scotland along the route of the present A696 and A68. On 5 August he reached Otterburn and camped for the night, choosing a location with marsh on one side and woods on the other. Douglas positioned his supply wagons between these two natural obstacles, under the charge of his camp followers and, thus protected, the Scots relaxed for the night.

Hotspur had pressed on after them and, having learned their position, attacked at sunset with great fury. His first barrier, though, was not unprepared Borderers, but a wall of wagons, all manned by armed camp followers who were disinclined to abandon their charge, and it was this that gave Douglas the time to assemble the rest of his force for battle. He led them round the wood protecting his flank and fell on the unsuspecting English rear. After a bitter struggle Hotspur was taken prisoner and the Scots were victorious. Such victory came at a price and Douglas himself died on the field of battle.

Internecine squabbles raged elsewhere. In 1396 a fight took place on the North Inch of Perth that might have come straight from the pages of Homer. To settle a dispute between Clan Chattan and Clan Cameron, thirty men from each clan stepped forward to fight a fierce and bloody contest in the presence of the King. At the end of the day, only twelve men stood, with just one survivor from Clan Cameron remaining.

Another example of the ferocity of inter-clan and inter-family warfare occurred in Aberdeenshire. Donald Macdonald, Lord of the Isles, had extended the rule of his clan over much of the western islands. In 1411 he marched a strong force, said to number 10,000 and included his own clan and the Macleans under Red Hector Maclean of the Battles, right across Scotland to Aberdeen to support his claim to the Earldom of Ross. If he succeeded in this, he would become the ruler of northern Scotland. To oppose him, a force of about 1,000 nobles and burghers assembled under the Earl of Mar. Although outnumbered ten to one, Mar's force was much better armed. The battle known as

Red Harlaw took place at Harlaw, a village just off the present A96 road from Inverurie to Huntly, and was fought throughout the day with great ferocity. Although militarily indecisive because both sides thought they had lost, it resulted in the withdrawal westwards of the Macdonalds and Macleans, leaving Hector Maclean dead on the battlefield. A great red granite monument marks the site of the battle, probably the most bloody ever fought in north-east Scotland.

When James I assumed the government of the country in 1424 he was determined to curb the power of the barons and chiefs. His opportunity came in 1428 when Alexander of the Isles, with about 10,000 Islanders and Highlanders, sacked Inverness. The King carried out a punitive expedition against him which ended in victory for the Crown. James had to take the field against the clans again in 1431, and, after defeating the rebels under Donald Balloch of Islay, he managed to restore his rule in the Highlands. He also took steps to quell the rebellious nobles of the Lowlands, and one by one their power was reduced. James died in 1437 having not fully achieved his objective. Black Douglas, most powerful of all the barons, was not finally broken until 1455, at the Battle of Arkinholm, near Langholm in Dumfriesshire.

About this time cannon appeared on the military scene. James II was an enthusiast about this new artillery, some of which he obtained from the Low Countries through his marriage to Mary of Gelders in 1449. The immense cannon in Edinburgh Castle, nicknamed 'Mons Meg', probably came from Flanders at this time. Flemish influence may also have been behind the installation of the first gun platform in a Scottish stronghold, at Ravenscraig, a castle owned by James's wife. The place of artillery was assured in 1456, when James II ordered some of his barons to provide guns with trained gunners, as part of the forces they were obliged to provide to serve the Crown when required. For James, the fascination with guns was to prove fatal and he was killed when one of his own cannon burst at the siege of Roxburgh in 1460.

James III ascended the throne as a boy of nine, and Scotland was ruled again by a regency for the next nine years. When he did take over control of the government, he proved to be a weak King and this encouraged the nobles to make trouble yet again.

The English also took advantage of Scotland's weakness, and in 1482 an English army captured Berwick. A group of disgruntled nobles under the Earl of Angus, chief of the Red Douglases, and Lord Home, and with the support of the Earl of Argyll, rose in rebellion and proclaimed James's young son king. The northern barons and burghers could not allow this challenge to the balance of power and they put a considerable force in the field in support of James. Unfortunately, he could not lead them. On 11 June 1488 he met the rebels at the Battle of Sauchieburn, near Stirling. James lost control of his horse, which bolted away from the battlefield and threw him. When the enemy caught up at Beaten Mill, they murdered the King while he lay defenceless.

This period saw large numbers of Scotsmen begin to serve as mercenaries in France, and to a lesser degree in some other countries. As Scotland imported culture with the Auld Alliance it exported soldiers to France. As early as 1419 a Scottish force of 6,000 men under the Earl of Buchan had landed at La Rochelle, and took part in many engagements in the service of the French king. Another force of 10,000 Scots under the fourth Earl of Douglas followed in 1424. They must have been good, as it was from this body of Scotsmen that Charles VII picked the Garde Écossaise, his personal bodyguard. Twenty years later, when he formed a regular army, this Scottish guard became its senior unit and for many years adventurous young men from Scotland, often younger sons from the great families, came to refill its ranks. Many of them at this time came from the Lowlands. Some Highlanders did come south to join but it was not until much later that significant numbers of Highlanders took service abroad, in many cases because they had to.

Many Scotsmen rose to high rank in the service of France. Buchan became Constable of France, Commander-in-Chief of the French army. Douglas was made Duke of Touraine.

But France was not the only country to see Scottish soldiers. In 1502 a force of 2,000 was dispatched to Denmark. Scotland may have been a poor country in many other ways, but she produced excellent fighting men. They were motivated to serve abroad by their limited prospects at home, a sense of adventure and money.

There is no doubt that the idea of raising and maintaining

regular forces of the Crown, which started in Scotland in the fifteenth century, came largely from France as a result of the military connection built up by the Auld Alliance. The idea of having a regular force, however small, on which to build on mobilization, had many advantages. It meant the King did not have to rely so much on his barons to produce forces, whose allegiance in any case was first to their lords. In a country where the power of the barons had grown apace, and where many of them were employing regular mercenaries, some form of paid force which gave the monarch more power as well as independence was very attractive. Moreover the advent of artillery meant that training of gun crews became important, and the only efficient way of making best use of these new engines of war was with a regular cadre. It is interesting to reflect that the earliest formed bodies of regular troops in any country, apart from the personal bodyguards of the monarch, were usually the artillery.

There was only one major disadvantage to the maintenance of a regular force – it had to be paid. It is presumably for this reason that such forces were slow in appearing, and when they did they were small.

It was James IV (1488–1513) who restored the power of the King and did much to establish the monarchy in Scotland on a far firmer footing than it had been before. Under him centralization of authority gradually took place. But it was not without a struggle – particularly in the Highlands.

James IV had a military mind, constantly bent on organizing and training, and under him the art of warfare took a leap forward. Like his father and grandfather James was interested in guns, and he had the force and ability to put this interest into practice. Under him the art of gunnery developed. The number of cannon was increased, and some were even cast in Edinburgh Castle under his direction.

Perhaps most remarkable of all his schemes were the measures he took to ensure every man in the country possessed a weapon, and was trained in its use. The 'wapynschawingis', the equivalent of the modern rifle meeting, was introduced in each district. Men considered to be of military age were required to report from time to time with their weapon and fire six shots. Fines were levied on any who failed to attend. The term 'wapynschawe' (weapon show) still survives in some Scottish regiments to describe a rifle meeting.

Not content with activities on land, it was James IV who gave Scotland her first regular navy. He started in 1493 by giving instruction to all coastal cities and towns to provide a ship of at least twenty tons, complete with crew. Then he built three men-of-war, the *Margaret*, the *James*, and the *Michael*. The *Michael*, which was launched in 1511 at Newhaven in Midlothian, was the largest ship launched in Scotland up to that time and a powerful ship by any standards of the day. It is said to have a crew of over 1,000 seamen and gunners. The records show that James's fleet at one time reached a strength of twenty-six ships of various sizes, considerably more than the English Navy had at that time.

With that same determination and ability which he displayed in organizing his forces, James set about the business of pacifying the Highlands and Islands. It was not easy. In this vast area north of the Highland Line, little had changed for centuries. The ancient patriarchal system of the clan continued to be the way of life and the basis of organization for war. Its great strength was its simplicity. The chief was the father and the clansmen his children, and every member, from great chief to shepherd, regarded themselves as equals.

This clan system bred a sense of pride in name and family, and a loyalty to it. Such an overriding core value gave the Highlanders and Islanders an immense strength as fighting men and it was a martial spirit that would be harnessed into later Scottish regiments.

When James IV started to tackle the turbulent Highlands, determined to bring some sort of order amongst the warring clans, he set about it in a fashion quite unlike his predecessors. He actually went to see the Highlanders and Islanders in their glens and islands, and he went to them in peace. What is more, he spoke to them in Gaelic – something no previous King had ever done.

It must have seemed to the clans that here was a man after their own heart, and at first he registered great success. Unfortunately, the pace of their response was too slow for his liking and, losing patience, he switched to a less diplomatic feudal approach, eventually detailing two powerful clans, the Gordons and the Campbells, to take on the task of maintaining order. The Gordons were responsible for the northern isles and Highlands and the Campbells for the west and south-west. This rather poorly conceived intervention escalated the existing problems, turning every other clan against the Gordons and Campbells and increasing inter-clan feuding. In an effort to strengthen and support his policy of pacification of the Highlands, James established garrisons which controlled communications at such places as Inverlochy and Urquhart in Invernesshire, and Tarbet in Argyll.

After years of effort this policy had some success, and an uneasy peace reigned beyond the Highland Line. In the Borders James was more successful, putting down the 'reivers' (robbers and plunderers) with a firm hand. The military power of the King was now greater than that of the Border baron. It was as well that James IV had established some order and peace within his kingdom because the threat of war with England once more clouded the horizon. Henry VIII had ascended the English throne and was bent on war with France. The Auld Alliance was invoked and in the summer of 1513 Scotland was at war with England. It proved to be one of the greatest disasters in its history.

On 24 July James mobilized his forces, calling up the levies from the barons and burghs in the Lowlands, and the clans from the Highlands. The army he thus raised was a mixture of feudal and tribal, since many Highlanders responded to his call to arms. The fact that they did so was surely a tribute to his work in pacifying the Highlands. Thanks to his grandfather's foresight, his army also had cannon, complete with trained gun crews.

Much effort had been put into the individual training of the levies, as a result of James's policy. This and the natural skills of the Highlanders would have produced a high overall standard of weapon training in the Scottish army. But that was not to be enough.

On 22 August James crossed the Border at the head of his army and, after capturing several Border strongholds including that at Norham, he camped at Flodden Edge near Branston in Northumberland. On 7 September a large English army under the Earl of Surrey arrived on the scene. By moving a large part of his army round the flank of the Scots, Surrey was able to cut off their line of retreat, and also attack them from the rear. In the battle which followed, the Scots suffered their greatest defeat, with enormous losses. King James was slain, together with some 12,000 of his troops, including nine earls, fourteen barons, and many Highland chiefs. From castle to cottage, Scotland was turned into a land of tears, remembered to this day in the lament for the fallen: 'The Flowers of the Forest are a' wede away'.

What went wrong? There is no doubt the Scots fought bravely and to the bitter end. King James himself led his army in the battle, and there was no lack of leadership. Perhaps the answer lies in the fact that the English were better organized and better equipped. They also fought well, particularly in view of their very long march to the battlefield. But above all, and despite the transformation that James had effected on his nation's military organization, the English were better prepared. Surrey had planned his operation carefully, and in plenty of time. Some evidence suggests that he had even dispatched his guns to the north of England some time before the campaign started. The Scottish army had been collected together at the last minute by a king who had not wanted this war but who ended up paying for it with his life.

He was succeeded by his baby son, James V, and a regency once again ruled Scotland until 1528. When James V did take over the reins of government he proved to be a passionate and forceful man. Very soon he had subdued the Douglases and put down trouble in the Borders. In the Highlands and Islands, as usual restive when central government was weak, he acted with firmness, but there his policy was only partially successful. His attempt to win the favour of the Macdonalds at the expense of the Campbells was not a success, and – as one would expect – he finished up by making both of them his enemies.

It was not, however, until the last years of his reign, in 1542, while the country was still recovering from Flodden, that the Scottish forces fought any serious action. In August Henry VIII of England sent a force across the Border which was soundly beaten at Hadden Rig near Berwick. He promptly sent a second force which sacked the Border towns of Kelso and Roxburgh.

James V unwisely retaliated by marching into Cumberland at the head of 18,000 men. On 24 November he encountered a smaller force of English under command of Sir Thomas Wharton at Solway Moss. The site of the battle is halfway between Gretna Green and Longtown just off the present A6071 road. James's army lacked fighting spirit and it was badly commanded by his favourite, Oliver Sinclair. The result was another debacle for Scottish arms.

Within two weeks James V died and once more Scotland was under a regency during the minority of the new monarch, the baby Mary Queen of Scots. Scotland was also plunged into the Reformation, and became the centre of a struggle between England and Protestantism on the one hand, and France and Roman Catholicism on the other.

The first military act of this great drama took place in 1544 and 1545, when Henry VIII ordered an invasion of Scotland which laid waste to a great deal of the Lowlands. The Scots were de-moralized and quarrelled amongst themselves. As a result their resistance was feeble. But the situation was about to change, albeit temporarily. With no shortage of volunteers, Angus collected together a force of about 1,200 on the Border. He then defeated an English army of 5,000 men under Sir Ralph Evers on 17 February 1545 at Ancrum Moor. The site of this engagement is two miles north-west of the village of Ancrum in Roxburghshire.

Angus deployed his force on a reverse slope. Evers thought this movement signalled a Scots' retreat and his force charged over the crest directly into the sun. They were met by a wall of pikes. 800 were killed including Evers.

This minor success, however, did not halt the English invasion, and on 10 September 1547 an English army of 10,000 men under Somerset utterly defeated a much larger Scottish force at Pinkie, near Musselburgh, Midlothian. The Scots were initially drawn up behind the River Esk, but abandoned their position to cross the river and won an early success. The English foot, however, and some Italian musketeers with them, did deadly work and the Scots were soon routed. Some 6,000 of them are said to have been killed.

After this calamity the Scots had to suffer the establishment of

English garrisons at Haddington, the island of Inchkeith in the Forth, and Broughty Castle near Dundee. They remained in the grip of occupation until 1550 when the English, defeated in France, were required to withdraw from the Lowlands under the terms of the Treaty of Boulogne.

Scotland was now divided by religion as well as politics, and strange partnerships resulted. The Protestant faction in league with Protestant England had become very unpopular as a result of the English invasion. Their only strongpoint eventually was St Andrews Castle, and here in 1547 the Protestants gathered, only to be captured when the castle fell to a visiting French fleet. Bad luck indeed! The prisoners were shipped to France where many, including John Knox, finished up in the galleys.

The next decade saw the country's divisions reach the climax of a religious civil war and the birth of the Reformed Church. In this struggle, which did so much to shape the character of the country, there were few military engagements of note. There was one event, however, that was to have far-reaching consequences and it occurred at Leith in 1560.

A large French force sent to Scotland to support Marie de Guise, the Queen Mother, in her fight against the English-supported Protestants, was driven back to their base at Leith. Here they were besieged by an Anglo-Scottish army for six months. The Queen Mother took refuge in Edinburgh Castle where she died on 10 June. The French then surrendered, and were evacuated under the terms of the Treaty of Edinburgh.

Although militarily this event was of no great importance, its political significance was enormous. The death of the Queen Mother was itself a step towards peace. The Treaty of Edinburgh, which not only recognized Elizabeth as Queen of England, but also removed all foreign troops, English and French, from Scottish soil, had far-reaching results. The Auld Alliance was dead and the triumph of the Protestant faith in Scotland seemed certain.

When Mary, Queen of Scots, returned from France to assume the government of her country, in August 1561, she was eighteen, a widow and a Catholic. She faced a near impossible task.

Her short and troubled reign was brought to an end in the summer of 1567 when, betrayed and abandoned, she was forced to abdicate. Her son James was crowned at Stirling on 29 July, and yet another regency was set up under Moray.

A bid to restore Mary to the throne was made in 1568 when she escaped from captivity in the Castle of Leven in Loch Leven. At Hamilton she rallied her supporters, but on 13 May she was defeated at an engagement at Langside near Glasgow. She left Scotland never to return.

Mary's son ascended the throne as James VI when only one year old. For the next fifteen turbulent years Scotland was ruled by a succession of Regents while the country continued to be torn by religious strife. In 1583 James took over the government and tried desperately to bring the warring factions to a compromise. Brought up in the Protestant faith, he stayed a Protestant, but he had the sense to realize that sooner or later all denominations were going to have to live together.

The dawn of the seventeenth century saw the internal troubles of the country continuing, but against a new background. In 1603 James VI ascended the throne of England to become James I and the King of a new country – Great Britain.

Chapter Nine

The Union of the Crowns

The union of the Crowns changed little in Scotland. During the rest of James's reign the two countries of the union continued to lead a separate existence with their own parliament, law and church. The King of Scotland ruled from London instead of Edinburgh.

In religious matters James moved slowly but surely against the non-conforming Presbyterians, establishing the episcopacy so gradually that opposition did not unite against him. He seemed therefore to have won against the Kirk, but the deep religious convictions of many Scots opposed to a hierarchical church had merely gone underground. They were to come to the surface with a vengeance in the next reign.

In the suppression of disorder and rebellion in Scotland, James acted with a heavy hand from his throne in London. On his orders a permanent peacekeeping force under Sir William Cranston stamped out trouble in the Borders, while the Highland clans were gradually brought to heel and came to recognize the sovereignty of the King as they had never done before. A minor incident in 1602 had built up into a major feud between the MacGregors and Colquhouns. James had been convinced that the Colquhouns were the innocent party. When the MacGregors attacked and killed eighty Colquhouns in Glen Fruin the following year, the King was furious and they were dealt with in a ruthless manner. The Privy Council proscribed the name MacGregor and forbad anyone who had borne the name from carrying arms. The Campbells were charged with enforcing the law.

The Macdonalds of Islay were likewise dealt with by the Campbells acting as the King's policemen with the utmost severity. In the Western Highlands and Islands, and indeed across the central Lowlands, the power of the Campbells grew apace.

In the north of Scotland James's other 'policeman', the Earl of Caithness, also forcefully maintained the King's peace. When the Earl of Orkney was arrested in 1609 for oppressing his people in Orkney and Shetland, his son led an uprising against the Crown. The rebellion was crushed, the lands of the Earl of Orkney confiscated, and the Earl and his son executed.

But James's policy worked, and there was peace and order of a kind, at any rate during the remainder of his reign. When he died on 27 March 1625 Scotland had been transformed and begun to adopt the contemporary civilization of Western Europe.

Elsewhere in Europe, there had been an immense leap forward in weapons and equipment. The cannon, musket and pistol were now in common use, along with the pike and sword. Firearms had, of course, been in existence long before but their use had been limited largely to siege work. By the beginning of the seventeenth century they were beginning to show their tactical use in the battles of manoeuvre on the continent. Unfortunately military thought in Scotland, as in England, had not advanced at the same pace. In spite of the development of weapons there had been no change in tactics or organization for the last 100 years. There had been no major engagement fought in Scotland within living memory and military thought was often limited to lining up, firing at the enemy and then charging.

Hitherto the country had relied upon a hard core of professional soldiers – mercenary or locally enlisted – in the pay of king, noble or chief, reinforced by large numbers of levies mobilized for an occasion. These levies had been required to bring their own weapons when mustered; but firearms were beyond the means of the ordinary citizen, whose weapon had to be provided. Moreover the use of firearms required proper training, and levies were unlikely to have the time or opportunity to get this.

The armed forces therefore entered the seventeenth century very much as they had entered the sixteenth. Firearms had arrived on the scene but there was neither the organization nor the training to use them effectively. The next fifty years were to see this change, through the strong influence of returning Scottish veterans of the Dutch and Swedish armies on organizations, tactics and training.

Charles I, on ascending the throne of Great Britain in 1625, soon found himself in great trouble in both his kingdoms. In Scotland his handling of the Kirk resulted in civil war in 1639, when the Covenanters rose in open rebellion. Their cause received tremendous support throughout the Lowlands, but the Highlands and the north-east remained aloof. There the episcopacy was still strongly entrenched.

Charles gathered an army of 20,000 at Berwick intent on bringing the rebels to order. This merely increased the enthusiasm of the Covenanters who promptly raised more regiments. When the opposing sides met at Duns in Berwickshire in June 1639 a settlement was reached without a fight. It was as well for the King that a battle was avoided, since the Covenanters were in better shape in every way. The King's army contained practically no professional soldiers and was little better than a rabble. The Covenanters had the advantage of a large number of Scottish soldiers who had returned to Scotland from service in the Protestant armies in Europe. One of these, Alexander Leslie, was a commander of ability. He had started as a soldier of fortune in the Netherlands, later entering the Swedish service, in which he rose to be a general. He served under Gustavus Adolphus throughout his victorious campaigns and, when his master died, he succeeded him in command of the best army in Europe and was made a field marshal in 1636. It is little wonder that he was at once selected to command the Covenanters on his return to Scotland.

The 1639 settlement was short-lived, and in the summer of 1640 the forces of the Covenant under Leslie crossed the Tweed and advanced to the Tyne. At Newburn they forced a crossing and without much more difficulty entered Newcastle. Charles submitted, and the Covenanters withdrew back over the Border, having extracted a large sum of money by way of payment for their keep while on the campaign.

The incidents of 1639 and 1640 were known as 'The Bishops

War', though they would hardly merit the name. Operations, such as they were, were very one-sided and although the Covenanters' army was Scottish, it was not the army of Scotland. Large parts of the country, particularly the Highlands and Islands, were not represented because their sympathies were certainly not with the Covenant. And yet in a strange way the spirit of the Covenanters did much to form the character of the Scottish soldier, then and today, whether he is a Highlander or Lowlander. It imposed a stern discipline and moral conviction upon the native martial qualities which already existed.

In England things went from bad to worse, and in 1641 Charles came back to Scotland to try and win support in his northern kingdom against his enemies in the English Parliament. Alexander Leslie was made Earl of Leven and Argyll made a Marquess. Charles also agreed to some reforms in both Kirk and State. However all was overtaken by the outbreak of the Civil War in England the next year.

It was during this period that Charles I in 1642 raised the Scots Guards as a 'Guard of His Own Person', with the Marquess of Argyll as Colonel. The regiment thus became the oldest of all Guards regiments in the British Army.

At first the Royalists in England achieved a measure of success. The King's army at this stage was up against opponents no better trained or equipped than itself. In desperation, the English Parliament looked for ways in which they could gain advantage. They asked for help from the Covenanters, and they got it. In 1644 a Covenanter force of 25,000 men under the Earl of Leven marched south to join the English Parliamentary forces in Yorkshire. At the battle of Marston Moor on 2 July 1644 the Scottish Covenanters played an important part with both horse and foot. The Scottish Covenanter horse under David Leslie who, like his namesake Alexander, was a veteran of the Swedish army, was grouped with Cromwell's new Ironsides. It must have learned much from its close contact with the English cavalry, who were to become the best professional soldiers in Europe after the Swedish pattern.

But now at last the Royalist Highlands were rising in the King's cause, under the leadership of one of the most romantic figures in

Scottish history. James Graham, 5th Earl of Montrose, was a born leader of great courage and personal charm. He had been a Covenanter but then transferred his allegiance to the royalist cause; their successes in the next year were due to the genius of this one man.

In the summer of 1644, having been made a Marquess and Lieutenant General of the King's Army in Scotland, Montrose collected a force of Highlanders which was later joined by Scottish expatriates from Ireland and Royalists from the Lowlands. His whole force barely numbered 2,000 men, and he had no guns and little cavalry. Yet with this motley collection he won a series of victories over forces three times the size of his own.

In August he advanced from Blair to take Perth. On 1 September at Tippermuir, three miles from the city, he was confronted by a Covenanter army under Lord Elcho consisting of 1,000 horse, 7,000 foot and nine guns. He boldly attacked this considerable enemy force, his Highlanders inflicting enormous casualties, and put it to flight. Twelve days after his triumphant entry into Perth, this dynamic leader had arrived at Aberdeen, which he sacked.

He then carried out probably the most remarkable operation of his career. Finding lukewarm support in the north-east, he marched his army in mid-winter from east to west across the mountains to fall upon the Campbells, who were the main supporters of the Covenant in the Highlands.

Joined by the Macdonalds and Macleans he attacked Argyll's castle at Inverary and destroyed it. He then marched through the snow-covered mountains of Lorne, through Glen Coe and Lochaber, to Inverlochy, just outside the modern Fort William. Here on 2 February he inflicted another astonishing defeat on the Campbells.

Then with remarkable speed, considering most of his army was on foot, he crossed the Highlands again and captured Dundee in March. Moving north, he routed a Covenanter force under General Hurry at Auldearn in Nairnshire on 9 May. With a force of only 1,500 infantry and 200 horse he defeated an enemy whose strength was more than twice his own. His success was due to his well thought out tactics, but luck also played a part. Hurry tried to lure Montrose into a trap but this was compromised when his troops fired their muskets to clear damp powder. Montrose, now alerted, deployed a small force with the royal standard on a low hill hoping to deceive Hurry that this was his main position. The bulk of his forces he concealed behind a ridge to a flank. This deception succeeded and although part of Montrose's force acted prematurely this did not affect the outcome. Two thousand of Hurry's men were killed.

Montrose then retraced his steps to Aberdeen, and in July he defeated another Covenanter force under Baillie outside the city at Alford. This and all his other victories had been achieved with a very small number of men. He now started to build up his strength with new recruits, and by the next month his army mustered some 5,000 men. With this force he moved rapidly south-west to Kilsyth, a town about thirteen miles north-east of Glasgow, to prevent the junction of the enemy force under Baillie (which had followed him despite its defeat at Alford) with another one under the Earl of Lanark coming from the west. Without waiting for Lanark to arrive, the Covenanters decided to attack and began a flank march across the front of the Royalist army to get formed up. Montrose took advantage of this rash manoeuvre and ordered his men to charge. The Highlanders dashed upon the Covenanters with a suddenness and fury which broke the enemy formation, and soon the flashing claymores of the clans were cutting them down in hundreds.

This was Montrose's last victory, and after it he entered Glasgow in the King's name. Scotland was at his feet. In one year he had won victory after victory, and always against far superior numbers. But he had not yet come up against the crack troops of the Covenant who had been serving with David Leslie in Cromwell's army. The total defeat of the Royalists at Naseby in June 1645 allowed these Scottish Covenanter troops to be suddenly released and to return home to Scotland. This was to bring Montrose's succession of triumphs to an abrupt end.

After his resounding victory at Kilsyth, Montrose had planned to march south to restore the Royalist fortunes in England after Naseby. But this course of action came to nothing. Covenanters were not the only ones who wanted to go home and, by the time

Montrose reached the Border, many of his Highlanders had left, reluctant to fight further afield. There was a thick early morning mist on 13 September. On a piece of flat land at Philiphaugh three miles west of Selkirk, Montrose's sadly depleted force of about 900 suddenly came face to face with David Leslie and 4,000 veteran troops, all well-trained and well-armed. The smaller force was routed.

Montrose escaped from the battlefield with a handful of his men and tried to rally the Highlands again, but without success. Finally, on King Charles's orders, and as part of a deal with the Covenanters which eventually failed, he disbanded his forces at Blairgowrie and went into exile in Norway. He was to return to Scotland, in circumstances that none could ever have foreseen.

With the King of Scotland and England now a prisoner of the English Parliament, the balance of power fluctuated rapidly. In England the struggle had been between the King and Parliament. In Scotland it was between the King and Covenant and many Covenanters, in spite of supporting the English Parliamentarians, remained staunchly Royalist. In their view, the quarrel with the King was on religious grounds, not political, and in 1648, the Scots decided to send an army into England to support their demand for the liberation of their King. This operation was disastrous. In July the Duke of Hamilton crossed the Border and marched as far as Preston. There his army – badly organized and badly led – met a smaller force of some of the best troops in Europe and commanded by Cromwell in person. The defeat was total. Hamilton was captured and later beheaded in London, an act considered by many to be disgraceful, as he was a Scottish officer doing his duty to his King.

That King followed Hamilton to the block on 30 January 1649. Scotland was so shocked by the news of the King's execution that for a time the country was almost united in spite of religious differences. The King's son was immediately proclaimed King Charles II in Edinburgh, and Montrose returned from exile in April 1650 to raise the King's standard. In Orkney he collected some followers and then landed at Thurso in Caithness. But the expedition was doomed to failure from the start. Few men rallied to his standard and his small force was dispersed at Carbisdale, near Bonar Bridge, on 27 April. Much as they resented the English execution of their King, the more intransigent of Covenanters could not tolerate Montrose's return and he was captured and hanged in Edinburgh. So this great Scottish soldier died, a victim of the strange ebb and flow of politics in seventeenth-century Scotland. Although he died dishonoured, he has a special place in the hearts of his countrymen as a man of fearless courage and unswerving loyalty. Eleven years after his death, his remains were buried in St Giles Cathedral.

Charles II arrived in Scotland from exile on 23 June 1650, having accepted the Covenant. One of the first things he did was to re-form the Scots Guards. On 22 July, the very day the regiment was presented with new colours at Falkland Palace, Cromwell invaded Scotland.

With an army of 16,000 experienced troops, Cromwell crossed the Border and advanced up the east coast, supported by his fleet. His first objective was the capture of the port of Leith to secure his maintenance by sea. Finding the port too strongly defended, he marched round the south side of Edinburgh to seize Queensferry as an alternative supply base.

Meanwhile the invasion of Scotland had rallied the Scots, and an army under the Earl of Leven deployed to meet the invader, the field command being entrusted to David Leslie. As Cromwell circled Edinburgh, the Scottish army 'shadowed' his movements, barring his advance to Queensferry by occupying a strong position at Corstorphine, five miles west of Edinburgh.

The two armies confronted each other at Gogar Bank. Leslie's troops were drawn up in the area now occupied by the World Headquarters of the Royal Bank of Scotland, along the line of the present A8 road. Cromwell's army, having crossed the Gogar Burn, was formed up along the ridge on which stands the present Gogar Bank House, residence until recently of the General Officer Commanding Scotland. A railway line now traverses the low ground that separated the two forces. As so often before, it was the condition of the land that determined the outcome of the encounter. The 'Skirmish at Gogar' did not develop into a battle because opponents were drawn up on either side of a bog. Cromwell found that his heavy cavalry could not get across the obstacle, and without them he was not prepared to use his infantry. After an exchange of shots, Cromwell broke off contact and retraced his steps to Dunbar, camping at the foot of the Pentland Hills on the way. His need to re-supply from his ships was now serious.

Leslie followed Cromwell to Dunbar and took up a strong position on the high ground south of the town, where it completely dominates the road south to England. The English were encamped on the low ground near the town. With 22,000 men against 16,000 the Scots had the advantage of numbers although they were less well trained and lacking in experience. The Scots also had the tactical advantage and the position of the English was perilous. But now Leslie made a fatal mistake and Cromwell was quick to take advantage.

For some reason, Leslie abandoned the high ground and moved down to the low ground along the line of the Brox Burn. Before daybreak on 3 September Cromwell had managed to get some of his horse and foot across the Brox Burn near the sea. The Scots were not quick enough to react, and before long this penetration developed into a major attack. The Scottish right was broken. Cromwell's troops swung south, pinning the remainder of the Scottish army between the high ground they had abandoned and the burn. The Scots, thrown into disorder, broke and fled. Cromwell had outmanoeuvred Leslie and routed his army. But some regiments stood their ground and fought to the end. Three thousand Scots were killed and 10,000 taken prisoner. Many of these were to die in captivity. The site of this battle is marked by a stone some two miles south-east of Dunbar, just off the present A1 road.

Cromwell now occupied Edinburgh and proceeded to crush any opposition in the Lowlands. But the Scots would not accept defeat, and on 1 January 1651, almost as an act of defiance, Charles II was crowned King at Scone, and Leslie raised a new army.

In June Cromwell advanced to take Perth, but found Leslie in a strong position blocking the way at the approaches to Stirling. He decided therefore to switch his line of advance across the Firth of Forth and threw a strong force under General Lambert across the

81

river at North Queensferry. On 20 July, at Inverkeithing, Lambert came up against a Scottish Royalist force which had been hurriedly dispatched to stop his advance northwards. The fight which followed was ferocious.

The English heavily outnumbered the Scots and their ranks contained many veterans of the English Civil War. They were well disciplined and superbly trained. The Scottish Royalists were neither well disciplined nor trained. Their ranks included many raw recruits who had never seen action. But what they lacked in military experience, they certainly made up for in staying power.

Early in this engagement the Scottish cavalry were completely routed, leaving the Highland infantry, composed mostly of Macleans, to take the full weight of the enemy attack. They bore it to an exceptional degree. Eight hundred Macleans under Hector Maclean of Duart stood to fight; all but forty fell with him in an extreme example of loyalty to chief and clan.

The opposition smashed, Cromwell pressed on to Perth, leaving the bulk of the Royalist army with the King at Stirling. It must have seemed to Charles that the way to the south was uncovered and he went on the offensive, taking with him an army numbering 16,000 to invade England. Cromwell gave chase, linking up with his main army on the way, and on 3 September 1651 the two armies met at Worcester. The English numbering some 28,000 men, won a decisive victory, and Scotland lost yet another army at the hands of the English. Charles II managed to escape after the battle, and took refuge once again on the continent. Throughout this campaign he had been accompanied by his personal body-guard, the Scots Guards, who now made their way back to Scotland as best they could with the remnants of the Scottish army.

Not all of Cromwell's troops had headed to Worcester. General Monk had been left behind in Scotland to finish off the work, and he was doing it very thoroughly. With no serious opposition left, he sacked Dundee and took Stirling. By the beginning of 1652 Dunnottar Castle, in Kincardineshire, was the only castle that still flew the royal flag in Scotland. After an eight-month siege, it fell on 24 May.

For the next eight years Scotland, and the Lowlands in

particular, suffered military occupation, emerging only from this state at the Restoration. Charles II returned to his throne in 1660 amidst great rejoicing. One of his first acts was to order the withdrawal of all English troops from Scotland and the raising of a new Scottish army. Amongst the new units were two independent troops of dragoons, who later became The Royal Scots Greys and are now The Royal Scots Dragoon Guards, and the Earl of Mar's Regiment, who became The Royal Scots Fusiliers and are now The Royal Highland Fusiliers. The Scots Guards were reformed under the Colonelcy of the Earl of Linlithgow. It included men who had served in the original regiment and so maintained the direct link with Charles I's bodyguard.

Charles also brought back The Royal Scots from France. This regiment, the senior of all the British infantry of the Line, had been formed in Scotland in 1633 by Sir John Hepburn to fight for the French. During this time it had undoubtedly been joined by other Scotsmen already in the service of the King of France, and it followed the Garde Écossaise in the long tradition of that service.

Not all elements in Scotland took kindly to the new regime and it was not long before old religious differences once more divided the country. As a protest against the return to episcopacy a body of Covenanters took to the field and repulsed a Government force of three troops of horse, under John Graham of Claverhouse, at the battle of Drumclog in Lanarkshire in 1679. This was followed immediately by another engagement at Bothwell Brig when the Duke of Monmouth, sent to deal with the rebellion, heavily defeated the Covenanters with great loss. Despite this setback, the hard core of Covenanters was determined to continue its resistance. Under the leadership of a minister, Donald Cargill, and Richard Cameron, it took to the hills where, hunted and starving, it maintained its religion in defiance of the Government. Even the death of Cameron in another action with Government troops at Airds Moss in Ayrshire in July 1680 failed to crush this movement.

When Charles II died in 1685 he was succeeded by his brother James (VII of Scotland and II of England). Scotland was afforded a period of reasonable peace during his reign. But, by 1688, James realized that by favouring Catholics he had lost the support of Parliament to the protestant Mary. He fled to France. William and

Mary were proclaimed King and Queen, and trouble broke out immediately.

Throughout the Highlands many refused to accept the new monarch and remained loyal to the Stuart James II. John Graham of Claverhouse, Viscount Dundee, now raised the Jacobite standard to which the loyal clans rallied, and the Government dispatched General Hugh MacKay with a body of troops to put them down. Amongst MacKay's troops was a newly formed regiment. They had been raised only four months before in Edinburgh by their Colonel, the Earl of Leven, who recruited 800 men in two hours. This regiment is now The King's Own Scottish Borderers.

On 27 July 1689 the Highlanders attacked MacKay's troops with great fury at the top of the pass at Killiecrankie, in Perthshire. But Dundee himself was killed and without his leadership the Jacobite army ceased to be effective. He was succeeded in command by Colonel Cannon. Under him the Highlanders moved on to Dunkeld where they attacked The Cameronians, another new regiment formed from the survivors of the Covenanter followers of Richard Cameron. The Cameronians had taken up a defensive position in the local churchyard, and defended it so well that the Jacobite attack failed. Cannon was a poor leader and not respected by his men. It is said that he spent much of his time drinking with Lord Dunfermline. Without proper leadership, the Highlanders dwindled away, most of them returning to their homes. The last act of rebellion took place at Cromdale in Morayshire the next year. On 1 May the Battle of the Haughs of Cromdale was fought on the slopes two miles east of the village, between the dragoons, mounted infantry, of Sir Thomas Livingston and a force of Highlanders under General Buchan. The dragoons surprised the Highlanders and killed over 300.

The Government now embarked on a programme to break the will of the Highland clans not loyal to William. All were ordered to swear allegiance to the King no later than 1 January 1692. The exiled King James gave permission for them to do so and all but two chiefs took the oath. Macdonald of Glencoe was singled out for punishment, and on the night of 13 February thirty-eight of the clan were massacred at Glencoe by a Campbell party acting on Government orders. Although hardly a military operation, this dastardly act needs mention as its consequences were to reverberate for the next fifty years.

Meanwhile, Scottish regiments in the service of King William, as King of England as well as Scotland, found themselves serving abroad. All Scottish regiments in existence at that time took part in the campaign in Flanders, 1689–1697, and fought with distinction in the major battles of Walcourt, Steenkirk, Landen and Namur. The Royal Scots had already taken part in actions at Maestricht, 1673, and in Morocco and Tangier, 1680–83.

The seventeenth century came to a close and two years later Queen Anne ascended the thrones of Scotland and England, which became united into one nation in 1707. With this came the integration of the Scottish forces into the British Army in which Scots were to play a major part in the years ahead.

Chapter Ten

Union with England

Standing armies had already been formed under the Stuarts in both Scotland and England. The union of the two countries established the British Army and control of all units rested in the hands of the government in London. The seniority of most Scottish units depended on the date they first crossed the Border and they had a major part to play in the subsequent story of the British army.

Britain entered the campaigns of the eighteenth century with regiments of regular soldiers. Each regiment was the total responsibility of its Colonel who received a commission from the King to raise, train and command it. He also clothed and fed it out of stoppages of pay, or out of his own pocket. The Colonel of the Regiment <u>was</u> the regiment, and he gave his name to it, for example, Leven's Regiment and Argyll's Regiment. To the officers and men who served in it, the regiment meant everything.

This was the birth of the regimental system and although there have been changes and reforms the system exists to this day. It generated a strong sense of identity, unit cohesion and a pride that was to sustain the British soldier, Jock included, through all the campaigns and battles that lay ahead.

The weapons and equipment of the Scottish soldier had undergone enormous changes during the seventeenth century and new weapons were taken into use in Charles II's reign. The pike was rendered redundant when it became possible to fix a bayonet on to a musket. At the same time, firearms had become so effective that heavy armour was impractical and it too was discarded in favour of speed and mobility. The Royal Scots Greys, (then titled The Royal Regiment of Scots Dragoons, subsequently The Royal North British Dragoons and 2nd Dragoons, and now The Royal Scots Dragoon Guards) Scotland's only cavalry regiment, was now armed with swords, carbines and pistols.

There was also a revolution in tactics as a result of the development of fire power and the introduction of the bayonet. The infantry was now able to use its more effective firearms and artillery support to manoeuvre and close with an enemy, then use the bayonet to complete the operation.

The first operations involving Scottish troops were those in Germany and the Low Countries between 1702 and 1713. The Royal Scots Greys, Royal Scots, Royal Scots Fusiliers, and Cameronians all took part in Marlborough's tremendous victories at Blenheim, Ramillies, Oudenarde, and Malplaquet with great distinction.

No sooner were these major battles with the French brought to a victorious conclusion, and peace established by the Treaty of Utrecht, than trouble broke out again in Scotland. In 1715 the Jacobites rose under the Earl of Mar and proclaimed James VIII and III as King at Braemar. Support for the Jacobite cause in the Lowlands was small and the Highlands were divided, some clans coming out for King James, but just as many supporting the Government. The loyalties of English and Scots, Lowlanders and Highlanders crossed and re-crossed in this mesh of allegiance and belief.

The rebellion nevertheless grew apace and 12,000 clansmen joined Mar's army very quickly. The Government troops in the Lowlands, under the command of the Duke of Argyll, numbered only 4,000, the bulk of whom were stationed at Stirling. Mar occupied Perth without much difficulty, and there was little to stop him marching on Edinburgh and taking that as well.

But Mar was no general. Boldness and quick action might have given the rising a small chance of success. Mar's timid approach ensured its complete failure.

Instead of pressing on after occupying Perth, Mar wasted time by waiting for news of an English Jacobite rising. By doing so he lost the only opportunity he had of taking action against Argyll before he could be reinforced by regiments moving up from the south. In their frustration, some Jacobite clans took independent action. The Macdonalds and Macleans tried to take the Campbell stronghold of Inveraray, while the MacGregors attempted Dumbarton Castle. Both actions failed.

When Mar finally heard that the English Jacobites were rising, he sent 2,000 men under Mackintosh of Borlum to join them. Mackintosh, a leader of some initiative, tried to take Edinburgh on the way south but was prevented from doing so by the wily Argyll who, by now, had had enough time to move his troops to protect the capital.

At last Mar, hearing that Argyll was soon to be reinforced by regiments coming north from England, decided to move his main force south, and on 13 November the two armies met at Sheriffmuir, near Dunblane. The battle which followed was inconclusive. The Macdonalds and Macleans of the Jacobite right defeated the enemy's left. The Jacobite centre and left, however, were broken by Argyll's cavalry. The two armies then broke off contact and returned whence they came. The site of the battle can be found one mile due east of Queen Victoria School at Dunblane.

Although the battle of Sheriffmuir was a draw on the field, it spelt disaster for the Jacobite army, which now began to disintegrate, with disheartened clansmen disappearing off to their homes. Mar abandoned Perth and retreated north, and the landing of Prince James Edward did nothing to save the cause. Early in 1716 the rebellion collapsed, and James Edward and Mar sailed for France. The 'Fifteen' was over.

To make sure that nothing like this could happen again, the Government now took strong measures to curb the independence of the clans. The first thing was to disarm them. This was highly unpopular with clans of all persuasion. Nor was it particularly successful.

At the same time six independent Highland Companies were raised to police the Highlands. To make maximum use of local knowledge, each company was responsible for the district in which it was raised. This made them very effective although unpopular with the local population. These companies were later, in 1739, combined to form The Black Watch, a name the new regiment took from its dark tartan. Very soon after its formation at Aberfeldy in Perthshire the new regiment found itself fighting in Flanders against the French, alongside all the other five Scottish regiments which had fought with distinction at the earlier battle of Dettingen (1743). At Fontenoy, on 11 May 1745, The Black Watch received its baptism of fire. Prior to the main attack the Highlanders attacked and captured a forward redoubt, killing a considerable number of the French entrenched there. When the main attack took place they were placed in the front line. The French made three attacks to try and hold the British advance but all were repulsed. These attacks lasted several hours and all the time the British were advancing with the Highlanders in the van. But then the French made a further desperate attack, the British were pushed back and forced to retreat. During the retreat The Black Watch held together and covered the rear, beating off further attacks by infantry and cavalry. In this battle The Royal Scots lost 286 men and The Royal Scots Fusiliers over 300. The Black Watch's 123 casualties were surprisingly low. One reason for this was the regiment's tactics. The regiment advanced rapidly. When they saw that the French were about to fire they lay down. While the French were reloading they stood up, fired, charged, and then withdrew. This process was then repeated. Such tactics were in complete contrast to the usual ponderous attrition by volley fire.

Back in Scotland a new Commander-in-Chief had been pressing on with the pacification of the Highlands. General Wade was a great believer in the importance of communications to military operations, and he constructed 250 miles of military roads in the Highlands, to enable troops to be moved more rapidly. Many bridges in the Highlands stand to this day as monuments to this efficient and far-sighted general. In particular his military road system joined the important garrisons at Fort George (in Inverness – the present Fort George, at Ardersier, was built between 1748 and 1769), Fort Augustus, and Fort William, thus creating a line which cut the Highlands in two.

These military plans were soon to be severely tested when Jacobite factions in the Highlands, restless since 1715 and 1719, once more rose to their cause in one of the best remembered episodes in Scottish history. The rising of 1745 is a story of romance built around a lost cause, loyalty and gallantry personified in its leader, Bonnie Prince Charlie, and great suffering after defeat. From the military point of view its chief interest lies not in the battles which took place, but in the fact that the rest of the Scottish regiments in existence today were raised from the ashes of this last civil war fought in Britain.

On 25 July 1745 Prince Charles Edward landed in Moidart. At first there was reluctance on the part of some of the Highland chiefs to join the Prince and risk their all in what must have seemed a doubtful adventure. But his youthful enthusiasm, vaunted physical toughness and passionate love of Scotland won the hearts of many doubters. On 19 August at Glenfinnan he raised the Standard and proclaimed his father King James VIII and III. The first to join him were the Camerons and Macdonalds and, with a force of about 900, the Prince marched on Edinburgh. He collected more support along the way, swelling his force to some 3,000 clansmen.

The line of advance of the Jacobite army was from Glenfinnan, through the pass of Corrieyairack following one of Wade's military roads to Dalwhinnie, and then down the route followed by the present A9 road to Perth. Having captured Perth they pressed on where Mar had faltered towards Edinburgh, defeating two regiments of Government dragoons on the way. On 17 September Prince Charles Edward and his Jacobite army entered Edinburgh in triumph.

Meanwhile, the Government forces were in considerable disarray. When the rising started they had practically no Scottish troops in the country, and few English or Hanoverian. Moreover the Commander-in-Chief of the Army in Scotland was now General Sir John Cope. As events will show he was an officer of little ability. To begin with, Cope had hoped to prevent the spread of insurrection outside the Western Highlands, and with this aim he had advanced towards the Corrieyairack Pass. However, when he heard that the Jacobites were increasing in strength he withdrew towards Inverness, thus leaving the route to the south unguarded, and the enemy intact. From Inverness he moved to Aberdeen where he took ship to Dunbar.

As soon as he had landed his troops at Dunbar, Cope advanced on Edinburgh. Prince Charles came out of the city to meet him. The two armies met at Prestonpans in East Lothian on 21 September, only four days after Charles's entry into Edinburgh. Both sides were about equal in numbers. The Jacobite army was little better than a collection of independent clans and individual enthusiasts, but they had the two outstanding military qualities of bravery and determination which in combination made the Highland charge irresistible. They also had an arrogance bred of the clan system and the freedom they enjoyed in their mountain fastness, which simply did not allow them to contemplate for a moment the possibility of defeat.

The Highlanders charged out of the morning mist upon the ranks of the Government troops. Their ranks staggered and broke, and immediately the Highlanders were amongst them, wielding their claymores – their two-handed broadswords – like scythes. The enemy guns were overrun before they could fire with effect, and the English cavalry took to its heels. In ten minutes the battle, whose site is marked by a memorial cairn one mile east of the town of Prestonpans, was over. Cope's army was destroyed. Cope himself galloped from the battlefield, and was the first to arrive at Berwick with news of his own defeat.

After Prestonpans Prince Charles got down to the task of organizing his own idiosyncratically arranged followers into some sort of military cohesion in Edinburgh. Clans were grouped together to form regiments and brigades, and commanders appointed at all levels. This was not an easy task in view of the jealousies and rivalries which existed between the clans and chiefs. The bulk of his force were Highlanders and wore the kilt, their chief weapons being the claymore and dirk, though some also carried French muskets. The Lowlanders supplied most of the cavalry, which consisted of lairds and their retainers. The only artillery to support this untrained collection was a very small number of imported French weapons, and the guns captured from Cope.

The Jacobite victory at Prestonpans brought more volunteers to join Charles's standard, and by October he had collected about 5,000 foot and 300 horse. By now the Government had brought back some more regiments from Flanders, and these reinforcements were sent to Newcastle where General Wade was forming a new army. Every day saw the Government forces grow stronger.

Charles had delayed his departure from Edinburgh in the hope of receiving French reinforcements, but decided by the end of October that he could wait no longer. On 31 October he started his march south. His intention at first was to advance down the east coast route to Newcastle to deal with Wade, but he was dissuaded from this course by his Lieutenant General, Lord George Murray. Instead, after crossing the River Esk, he led his army down the west route through Carlisle. Having captured the city he marched on to reach Derby on 4 December.

Here his troubles began. With no aid from the French, he had looked for reinforcements from English Jacobites but they did not rise, and desertions amongst his Highlanders were weakening the strength of his original force. Government strength kept increasing. Apart from Wade's army of some 8,000 in Northumberland, the Duke of Cumberland was in the Midlands with another army of 10,000. Ahead even more troops were gathering for the defence of London. Finally the news from Scotland completed a gloomy picture. The Campbells and the Whig clans of the north and north-east were gathering in force for the Government, and Edinburgh had been lost. On 6 December a retreat was ordered.

On 19 December Charles reached Carlisle, and the next day crossed the Border back to Scotland where he had a mixed reception. Much of the Lowlands were now openly against him, and the Mackenzies, Sutherlands, Munros, Mackays and Macleods in the north had declared for the Government.

New recruits from Jacobite clans were nevertheless still being rallied to Charles' cause and with an army of some 8,000, Charles advanced on Stirling. At Falkirk his progress was blocked by a slightly larger Government force under General Hawley. Despite the slight advantage in numbers, Charles' Highlanders soon put the Government troops to flight, but he did not follow up this victory. Instead of trying to take Stirling he decided to move on into northern Scotland. His Highlanders were now tired and homesick, and supplies were getting dangerously short. He arrived at Inverness with a dispirited army whose numbers were reduced daily by desertion.

Meanwhile Cumberland had moved his army from Northumberland to Aberdeen, which he now used as a base for his offensive against the Jacobites. Cumberland's army, recently re-inforced by veteran regiments from the Flanders campaign, was well trained and superbly equipped and armed.

At the beginning of April 1746, having completed his prepara-tions, Cumberland advanced towards Inverness. Charles had posted Lord John Drummond at Fochabers on the Spey to patrol the east bank of the river, to allow the option of fighting the Government force along the line of the river. With far fewer numbers, Drummond was quite unable to withstand Cumberland, who forded the river at Garmouth and Fochabers without much difficulty. The speed of his advance meant that Charles had to muster his half-starved clansmen and deploy them on Culloden Moor five miles south-east of the town. Their position could not have been worse. Unable to take to the mountains or make use of some natural obstacle on which to stand and fight, these Highlanders, still at their best in guerilla warfare, were forced to offer pitched battle to a well-trained regular force.

Cumberland took his time to reach them, and on 14 April his army encamped outside Nairn. The site is just south of the road from Nairn to Balblair. On 15 April his army lay inactive, celebrat-ing their commander's birthday in festive style, while the commander himself spent the night in the big house at Balblair.

It was then that the Jacobites launched a night operation which, had it succeeded, might have changed the course of history. The plan was to advance by night in two columns to the enemy's camp where it was hoped the defence would be dulled by the birthday festivities. The advance was to start at 8 p.m. on 15 April, and it involved a ten-mile approach march to the objective on a very dark night. The actual attack on the enemy camp was to be launched at 2 a.m.

Such a night operation would have been difficult with trained and well-fed troops. With the untrained and starving Highlanders it was unachievable. The columns started as planned, and they had got three-quarters of the way when exhaustion and confusion amongst their ranks forced a retreat back to Culloden Moor. There the weary Highlanders sank to the ground to snatch some much-needed sleep in a cold bleak dawn.

Shortly before noon on Wednesday, 16 April the sound of drums heralded the approach of Cumberland's army.

The battle started about 1 p.m. with a heavy cannonade from Cumberland's artillery. The Prince's guns replied but their response was pitiful in contrast. None was larger than a 4-pounder and they were handled by makeshift crews. The accurate and sustained fire of Cumberland's experienced gun crews did dreadful damage to the Jacobite ranks for an hour, and no effective reply was possible. To allow his men to be mown down in this way instead of launching them immediately into a charge was a serious mistake which, together with the choice of such unfavourable ground, made defeat inevitable.

When at last Prince Charles gave the order to charge, the Jacobite clans swept forward like a tidal wave, striking the first line enemy with such force that they broke right through it. But then the discipline and training of Cumberland's regiments, amongst them The Royal Scots, The Royal Scots Fusiliers, and The King's Own Scottish Borderers, began to tell.

The remnants of the regiments of the first line closed their ranks, while the second line stood like rocks to the Highland wave. The Jacobite clans caught between the two lines died in their hundreds. It was then that Cumberland launched his cavalry round the flanks, and the Jacobites' second line gave way. The Jacobite army was utterly broken, and 1,000 of its starving, ill-armed, and untrained Highlanders lay dead upon the field.

Despite this calamity, many Highland clans stayed true to their Prince, sheltering him as he wandered among them for five months as a fugitive before escaping to France. They paid a high price for such loyalty. Cumberland initiated a reign of terror in which many men were hunted down and killed. Highland dress and tartan were both banned. Until 1782, when the legislation was repealed, the kilt was only permitted to be worn in the Army.

But the Forty-Five had one direct result which was to have a lasting effect on Scottish soldiering. It was during the period after the Jacobite rebellion that the martial spirit of the clans, including those who had come out for Prince Charles, was slowly but surely harnessed in the raising of the remaining Highland regiments of the British Army.

The 73rd (later 71st) Highlanders were raised in 1777 in the northern counties by John Mackenzie, Lord MacLeod. An ex-

Jacobite, Mackenzie had been imprisoned in the Tower of London for his part in the Forty-Five. After being released because of his youth he made his way to Sweden, where he rose to the rank of general in the Swedish Army. When the American War of Independence broke out he offered his services to King George III and received a commission to raise the regiment. It was the first clan regiment to be raised under the British Crown, The Black Watch having already been raised from several clans serving in independent companies.

In 1787 the 74th Highland Regiment was raised in Argyll and opened its headquarters in Glasgow in 1788. It was a Campbell regiment, eleven of the original officers being of that name, including the Colonel, Sir Archibald Campbell of Inverneil. It sailed for India by companies, and in 1789 fought alongside the 71st in the second Mysore campaign. Both regiments fought with outstanding gallantry throughout the wars in India between 1780 and 1797. Later they were to join to form The Highland Light Infantry.

Meanwhile another Highland regiment, the 72nd, was raised in 1778 by the Earl of Seaforth, mainly from the Mackenzie estates in Ross-shire and the Isle of Lewis, and then mustered at Elgin. It was soon fighting in the wars in India, and distinguished itself at Mysore, Cuddaldore, Bangalore, Seringapatam and Pondicherry.

The 75th Highland Regiment was raised in 1787 by Colonel Robert Abercromby for service in India. It wore the kilt and was embodied at Stirling. The regiment embarked for India in 1788 where it was also to distinguish itself in the Mysore Campaign and at Seringapatam in 1792 and 1798. In 1794 the fourth Duke of Gordon raised the 100th Regiment (renumbered 92nd in 1798), but from its earliest days the regiment was always referred to as The Gordon Highlanders. He was assisted by his wife, Jane, the beautiful Duchess of Gordon who encouraged recruiting by riding round some of the small villages, fairs and markets of north-east Scotland and, it is alleged, by also giving a kiss to a number of those who joined up. The 75th and 92nd were joined in 1881 to form The Gordon Highlanders.

Two regiments were raised on the outbreak of war with revolutionary France in 1793. The 78th Highlanders was raised in

Ross-shire by Colonel Francis Humberston Mackenzie of Seaforth, and the 79th Cameron Highlanders by Major Alan (later Lieutenant General Sir Alan) Cameron of Erracht. The 79th were recruited mainly from Lochaber and North Argyll, and were first mustered at Stirling Castle before being deployed immediately to Northern Ireland, followed by Flanders and the West Indies. In 1799, the regiment distinguished themselves at the Battle of Egmont op Zee, the one successful action of the Duke of York's Helder campaign.

Finally the 91st Argyllshire Highlanders were raised in 1794 by the Duke of Argyll, and the 93rd Sutherland Highlanders in 1799 by General Wemyss, a kinsman of the Earl of Sutherland. The 91st and 93rd fought against the Dutch at the Cape of Good Hope shortly after being raised. The 91st then went on to fight with distinction in the Napoleonic War and the 93rd similarly in the American War. It was men of the Argyllshire Highlanders who disinterred the body of Napoleon on St Helena, on 25 November 1840, for repatriation to France. Later the two regiments were to be joined to form The Argyll and Sutherland Highlanders.

Such large-scale recruiting from the Highlands was not without its problems. Emigration had reduced the population base from which the Highland regiments had to draw and by the 1790s the well had all but run dry. Successful clan levies relied upon a range of measures, including offering land and bounties, coercion and turning to non-Scots for support.

Meanwhile, all over the world, the older Scottish regiments were fighting the King's enemies. While The Royal Scots and The Black Watch were winning glory in North America (1756–67), The Royal Scots Greys, Scots Guards, and The King's Own Scottish Borderers were fighting the French in Germany in the Seven Years War. The King's Own Scottish Borderers fought with great valour at the Battle of Minden (1759), reputedly the first battle in which the development of firearms allowed formed bodies of infantry to fire aimed shots. The American War of Independence saw the Scots Guards, Royal Scots Fusiliers, Cameronians, and Black Watch giving distinguished service in all the major engagements of that long and bitter struggle.

In 1758, during the war in Canada, The Black Watch was part

of a force sent to capture the French-held fort at Ticonderoga. The French, although numerically weaker, knew that the attack could only come from one direction so had constructed concealed positions and obstacles in the woods. Reconnaissance was inadequate and these were not identified, and the attack was mounted without artillery support. The result was inevitable and disastrous. A few men of The Black Watch actually got through the forward positions and into the fort, only to die there. The Regiment lost 647 men killed and wounded.

On 17 October 1777 The Royal Scots Fusiliers were part of Burgoyne's column that was surrounded by the Americans at Saratoga. Starvation forced their surrender. The regimental history notes: 'save for the officers who were exchanged and the few men who escaped the 200 or so who survived Saratoga vanished into the mist'. The regiment ceased to exist until it was reconstituted in Scotland five years later. In the latter part of the eighteenth century Canada attracted a large number of Scottish settlers. Some came from the disbanding of regiments and some were quasi-military. Others came north from the United States, and many of these were of Jacobite descent. Perhaps some were from The Royal Scots Fusiliers. It was the descendants of these settlers who were to provide the basis of the many Scottish regiments in the Canadian Army that fought in two world wars. They preserved their nationality, traditions, dress and military attributes.

While 1st Battalion 42nd (The Black Watch) was still in North America, a second battalion was raised in 1779. It went to the East Indies two years later, becoming a separate regiment, the 73rd Highland Regiment, in 1786. This regiment also fought in the Mysore Campaign of 1798–99, taking part in the Battle of Seringapatam for which it received a battle honour. The 42nd (The Black Watch), back from North America, fought alongside The Royal Scots Greys and Scots Guards in the operations against the French in the Low Countries in 1793–5.

The 74th, together with the 78th Highlanders, won the rare distinction of being awarded a third colour for their bravery at the Battle of Assaye in 1803 against the Mahrattas.

A British Army under Arthur Wellesley, later Duke of Wellington, met the Mahratta army at a crossing of the Kaitna

River on 23 September 1803. Wellesley had only two British infantry regiments – Highland Light Infantry (74th) and Seaforth Highlanders (78th). His force of 4,500 men was outnumbered ten to one. Once they had crossed the river The Highland Light Infantry formed up and began to advance towards the village of Assaye. Almost immediately they came under fire from the Mahratta guns. Within a very short time eleven officers were killed and seven wounded out of nineteen, and 400 of the 569 other ranks fell. Despite these losses the British line continued to advance and the enemy broke.

In the higher command of all these forces Scotland was more than taking her share. General Sir Ralph Abercromby from Menstrie in Clackmannanshire, the son of a Scottish landowner, commanded the British Army in Egypt at the Battle of Alexandria in 1801. He probably did more than any other soldier of his time to raise the discipline of the British Army. The remarkable work of Sir John Moore, born in Glasgow and educated at Glasgow High School, in training the infantry makes him one of the creators of the British Army. When he was Commandant of Shorncliffe Camp, in Kent, he developed the tactics and training of the new light infantry, including skirmishing and sharpshooting. This led to the formation of the Light Division that fought with such distinction in the Napoleonic War. It was a Scottish general, Sir George Elliot, later Lord Heathfield, who defended Gibraltar in its long siege of 1779–82; and another, Sir David Baird from Newbyth in East Lothian, who commanded at the storming of Seringapatam, and captured Cape Town six years later.

By the close of the eighteenth century Scotland was making a significant contribution to the British Army. In addition to The Royal Scots Greys and Scots Guards, Scotland now provided no less than fourteen infantry regiments. All were to play a major part in the Napoleonic and Imperial Wars ahead.

Chapter Eleven

The Napoleonic Wars

The dawn of the nineteenth century brought with it many changes in the British Army. Some were in organization, and Scots soon found whole new fields opening up in which they could serve.

New spheres of operation included a wealth of supporting arms and services all of which attracted recruits from Scotland. In the Artillery a corps of drivers had been created in 1794 which was a great improvement on the old system of hired teams. From then on Scotland subscribed generously in officers and men to this main supporting arm. Scots were also enrolled into the earliest bodies of Engineers.

At sea many Scots were now serving with the Royal Navy all over the world, and not a few of the great sea captains in this period come from north of the Border. One such was Admiral Adam Duncan, who was born in Dundee, and rose to the highest command in the Royal Navy. In 1797 he obtained a decisive victory over the Dutch fleet at the Battle of Camperdown, for which he was created a Viscount.

Nor should we forget the part played by many thousands of Scots who fought under the East India Company, thus helping to lay the foundations of the Indian Empire. But it was Scotland's part in the wars against Napoleon that will be best remembered because of the many outstanding actions fought by her cavalry and infantry regiments. From the start of the war with revolutionary France in 1793 to the final victory at Waterloo, Scottish troops served in every theatre of war and fought at every battle. Six Scottish regiments took part in the campaign in Egypt under General Abercrombie in 1801, earning the battle honour 'the Sphinx superscribed Egypt'; the Seaforth served as far away as

Cape Town and Java, and The King's Own Scottish Borderers in Martinique.

The Royal Scots Fusiliers found themselves in America and the West Indies. After arriving in Bridgetown, Barbados on 20 May 1793, the Regiment then took part in an abortive attempt to wrest the island of Martinique away from the French. Yellow fever was rife and many men and their families died. The following year the Fusiliers were widely scattered with companies in Dominica, St Kitts, Montserrat and Antigua. They were then concentrated and took part in the successful attacks on Martinique, St Lucia and Guadeloupe. However, it was one thing to take these islands from the French, quite another to hold on to them. Disease, inadequate medical facilities, the absence of reinforcements and general neglect from home took their toll. For two years the regiment fought with great distinction in futile campaigns in Antigua, Dominica and Guadeloupe. When the regiment returned to Scotland in 1796 it was only 119 strong. Regimental histories are full of similar tales of campaigns fought at that time in places far from home. The common theme is the courage and endurance of the soldiers in conditions so appalling that it is hard to reconcile them with locations best known today as holiday paradises.

Many regiments fought in the Peninsula and Belgium, and the names of all the great battles adorn their Colours. There were seventy-two regimental engagements which were rewarded by the grant of a battle honour to be borne on the Colours of their respective regiments.

On 24 December 1808 Sir John Moore began to withdraw to Corunna before Napoleon's much superior army collected to crush him. This retreat ranks high as a feat of arms. It lasted eighteen days and involved the passage of the Galician Mountains in deepest midwinter. The narrow and inadequate tracks through mountains rising to 6,000 feet had to cross numerous deep gorges by ford or bridge. While these obstacles helped to impose delay on the French there was also the constant risk of being outflanked and cut off. On New Year's Day 1809 The Gordon Highlanders (92nd) were marching towards the town of Villafranca 'their clothes torn to shreds, their shoes worn out and feet bleeding, their bodies overrun with vermin, and suffering from extreme cold

100

and hunger'. By the time they arrived in Corunna on 11 January the battalion was in a terrible state. One hundred and ninety men had been lost during the 300 mile march although many of these were to re-join. Having reached the port of Corunna, Moore could not embark his exhausted army but instead had to turn, stand and fight. At last able to confront their pursuers on favourable ground the army took on a new lease of life. The onslaught of repeated French attacks was held off and the troops put safely on to the waiting ships, but not before Moore himself fell mortally wounded and died, surrounded by men of The Black Watch.

Seven Scottish regiments fought throughout this campaign – Royal Scots, Cameronians, Black Watch, Highland Light Infantry, Gordon Highlanders, Cameron Highlanders, and Argyllshire Highlanders. Both Moore's divisional commanders were, like himself, Scots – General Sir David Baird, who lost an arm in the battle, and General Sir John Hope, who assumed command on the death of Moore. General Robert Craufurd, the commander of the famous Light Division, which Moore had created, was yet another Scottish soldier.

For the next six years the British Army under Wellington fought to drive the French out of Portugal and Spain. The Scottish regiments played their part and their Colours bear witness to this – Busaco, Talavera, Fuentes d'Onor, Alamaraz, Cuidad Rodrigo, Badajoz, Salamanca, Vittoria, St Sebastian, Nive, Nivelle, Orthez and Toulouse. The French were driven back into France and then defeated.

On 22 July 1809 the British took up a position outside the Spanish town of Talavera. The advance guard of the French under Marshal Victor arrived on 27 July. His first attack that night was repulsed as was the second attack at dawn on 28 July. He decided to wait for his full force to arrive and in the meanwhile pounded the British centre held by the Guards Brigade, which included 1st Battalion Scots Guards, with his artillery. The battalion suffered the ordeal with courage and discipline. At 2 p.m. the French attacked along the whole front with a two to one superiority. The battalion was drawn up in line. At fifty paces they fired a devastating volley that shattered the French columns and then charged.

As a result they got ahead of the rest of the line and were cut off. They were only extricated after severe fighting in which 321 men were killed or wounded. Most of the latter were to die from gangrene or loss of blood.

When Wellington advanced from the security of the Lines of Torres Vedras in early 1811, and began investing the frontier fortress of Almeida, Marshal Massena marched a strong French force to its relief. Wellington was forced to abandon the siege and take up a defensive position on a ridge astride the French axis of advance. The strongpoint was the village of Fuentes d'Onor, protected by a river, and held by over 2,000 men from the light companies. The remainder of the Army was held back on the reverse slope of the ridge. As Wellington had expected, the French launched a massive frontal assault on the village and eventually forced back the light companies. His reserve was then launched. It consisted of 71st Highland Light Infantry and 79th Cameron Highlanders. In a most spirited and determined action against overwhelming odds the two highland regiments recaptured and held the village. Next day the French again attacked the village. In some of the heaviest house-to-house fighting of the campaign the two regiments, reinforced by 74th Highlanders, charged and counter-attacked repeatedly, and the vital strongpoint was held. Among the 79th Cameron Highlanders' 287 casualties was their Commanding Officer, Lieutenant Colonel Phillips Cameron, son of Sir Alan Cameron of Erracht who had raised and then commanded the regiment.

Wellington wrote: 'I look upon Salamanca, Vittoria and Waterloo as my three best battles – those which had great and permanent consequences'. At Salamanca on 22 July 1812 the British and French armies were about equal, each about 50,000 strong. The 74th Highlanders (later 2nd Battalion The Highland Light Infantry) and 3rd Battalion The Royal Scots played significant parts in the battle.

The Gordon Highlanders fought throughout the campaign and distinguished themselves on many occasions and particularly in the later battles in the Pyrenees. They participated in the action at Maya on 25 July 1813 when a British force of 2,600 held 11,000 of Napoleon's best infantry. This has been described as one of the most brilliant achievements of the Peninsular War. The battalion suffered 367 casualties out of 853 all ranks. It did not take part in the fighting on 28 July but was with Wellington when he attacked and drove back the French at Sauroren two days later. An officer mentions that an order was issued early that morning for all men who could not keep up to be sent to the baggage. He selected three from his company. Two went with apparent goodwill, but William Dougald respectfully told him that he would rather die than leave his comrades. He had been hit three times by spent bullets on 25 July, and though not 'minded at the time', the wounds had become so inflamed by subsequent exertion that on 30 July he could scarcely drag his right leg after him. 'I shall never forget the exertions he made to keep up with his companions, and the admirable manner in which he performed his duty in action till stretched a lifeless corpse on the heights of La Zarza.' Napier in his *History of the Peninsula* wrote: 'the stern valour of The Gordon Highlanders would have graced Thermopylae'.

In early December 1813 the British were approaching Bayonne. A flood on the night of 12 December had destroyed a pontoon bridge over the River Nive. As a result Wellington's right, consisting of 14,000 men under General Hill, was cut off. The French force approaching him was more than three times the size. The village of St Pierre on the high ground between the Rivers Nive and Ardour was the key position. On the morning of 13 December The Gordon Highlanders (92nd) were in the village, in reserve, with the rest of the brigade deployed forward. At 8.30 a.m. as the sun burst through the mist four French divisions attacked Hill's force; one attacked the British in St Pierre and very quickly drove back the forward battalions. It was a critical time in the battle. Had St Pierre fallen Hill would have been defeated and few men would have escaped. The Gordons were ordered forward. As they cleared the village they saw the first column of two regiments approaching up the road. Driving the French skirmishers before them they charged the column; it wavered and gave way. Many French prisoners were taken. Another column approached to press the attack. The Highlanders charged again but this time they were forced back in desperate hand-to-hand fighting. The other battalions had now reorganized and this allowed the Gordons to reform behind the village. They were soon needed as the French threw in their reserves. With the two surviving pipers playing and Colours flying the Gordons again advanced down the road driving all before them. One piper fell but the other played on, encouraging his comrades. The battalion was now very small particularly in comparison with the massed French columns but its advance encouraged the other units and they too pressed forward. Again the French wavered and then began to retreat. By now the bridge over the Nive had been repaired and Wellington was able to reinforce Hill. The battle was won. During it the battalion suffered 184 casualties.

The last great battle with Napoleon at Waterloo saw seven of the Scottish regiments again in action – The Royal North British Dragoons (Royal Scots Greys), Scots Guards, Royal Scots, Black Watch, Highland Light Infantry, Gordons (92nd), and Camerons. Several had fought at Quatre Bras, where they suffered severe losses stemming the French advance before falling back to Wellington's main position at Waterloo. When Napoleon closed up on to this position, and launched his attack on 18 June 1815, all the regiments were plunged into fierce fighting which raged throughout that day.

On the right the Scots Guards and Coldstream Guards held the key tactical feature of Hougoumont Farm with their light companies actually in the buildings. Wellington later wrote: 'the success of the battle of Waterloo turned on the closing of the gates of Hougoumont'. It had to be held at all cost – and it was. With the farm buildings in flames men of 2nd Battalion Scots Guards hung on all day, beating off repeated attacks by 30,000 French. At one point the sheer numbers of French forced the defenders back. The gate to the farm was wide open. Scots Guards reinforcements from the battalion outside the farm moved to assist. In the heavy fighting Sergeant Ralph Fraser, who had enlisted in 1799 and was a veteran of Egypt, Copenhagen and the Peninsula, charged down the lane with his halberd. He met Colonel Cubières, the commander of 1st Infanterie Légère and pulled him off his horse, mounted it himself and galloped back through the Great Gate in time to join the struggle in the courtyard. This diversion and sudden support allowed the light companies of the Coldstream and Scots Guards defending the farm to rally and close the gate, then wipe out those Frenchmen remaining inside. The survivors stood victorious among the ruins of Hougoumont. In the battle the Scots Guards lost twelve officers and 415 rank and file killed or wounded.

Meanwhile, in the centre of the British line Black Watch, Camerons, Gordons and Royal Scots formed part of Picton's Division. At the beginning of the battle they had the Belgian Brigade in front of them, but this broke and fled before the mass attack of thirty-six battalions of French infantry. Now the Scottish regiments, having fired a volley into the densely packed enemy, charged them with the bayonet.

One of the most celebrated examples of the effect of the Highland bagpipes in battle occurred at Waterloo. The 79th Cameron Highlanders, deployed in line, had successfully routed the massed French infantry who attacked them. When the French cavalry approached, the 79th hastily formed into a square. As the cuirassiers tried to break into the square of the 79th Piper Kenneth Mackay, from Reay in Caithness, stepped from the security of the lines of bayonets and played outside the square. The tune that he played to encourage the 79th was 'Cogath no Sith' 'War or Peace – the True Gathering of the Clans'. He knew that this ancient tune would be instantly familiar to the Highlanders, and would rally them at this moment of extreme danger.

From behind the Highlanders, The Royal Scots Greys made a cavalry charge which was to become immortal, although it is viewed with some suspicion in academic circles. The regiment came sweeping down the hill and between the ranks of The Gordon Highlanders, intent on completing the defeat of the enemy infantry. As the regiment passed by, the Highlanders gave a great cheer and surged forward on the tail of their comrades with pipes playing. Legend has it that some of the Gordons charged with them, hanging on to their stirrups. It was during this charge that Sergeant Charles Ewart of The Royal Scots Greys captured the Standard of the French 45th Regiment, crowned with its famous eagle. These trophies are to be seen in the Regimental Museum of The Royal Scots Dragoon Guards in Edinburgh Castle, while the eagle is worn by the Regiment as their cap badge to this day. At the time of the battle Sergeant Ewart from Elvanfoot in South Lanarkshire was forty-five years old, having served in the regiment for more than twenty-five years including the campaign in the Low Countries. He described how his route to the Standard was blocked by three Frenchmen: 'One made a thrust at my groin; I parried him off and cut him down through the head. A lancer came at me – I threw the lance off by my right side and cut him through the chin and upwards through the teeth. Next, a foot soldier fired at me and then charged me with his bayonet, which I also had the good luck to parry, and then I cut him down through the head.' It was a great day for The Royal Scots Greys, but one for which the regiment paid a heavy price with more than half of the 416 men that had taken the field that morning being killed or wounded.

On the morning of the battle The Highland Light Infantry, as part of Adam's Light Brigade, had taken up a position on the right of the line not far from Hougoumont. For over two hours the regiment was exposed to intense artillery fire, and when it moved at last left 127 killed and wounded on the ground. In the course of the battle they repulsed seven cavalry charges, during one of which Wellington, attended only by his trumpeter, took refuge in their square. Later in the day The Highland Light Infantry charged the 'Middle Guard' of Napoleon's Imperial Guard and drove it back. At the end of the day, leading the final advance, it assaulted the reserve position of the Old Guard and captured a battery; then one of the French guns was turned round and discharged at the retreating enemy.

Activity had not been confined to the front during the war. At home the rise of Napoleon and the threat of French invasion had generated a feeling of intense patriotic fervour and martial spirit. This found expression in the raising of volunteer and militia units throughout Britain. In Scotland citizen soldiers were enrolled from every background into all kinds of military units – horse, foot, and guns. Some of them could hardly have been a danger to the enemy, and many must have been quite a danger to themselves. But what they lacked in training they certainly made up for in enthusiasm.

The (de)Fencibles, as their name implies, were established for home defence with six regiments being raised as early as 1759. In England the task of home defence was carried out by the Militia, but in Scotland there was at this time no such body. Memories of the Forty Five were still painfully fresh and volunteer Fencibles were preferable to the creation of a conscripted force of all fit men – allegiances notwithstanding. For this reason Scotland produced six out of the eight Fencible battalions formed in the whole of the United Kingdom in 1759. The first regiment to be raised was the Argyll Fencible Regiment under John, Duke of Argyll. It is interesting to note – in view of the later amalgamation of the regular regiments of Argyll and Sutherland – that the second unit to be raised was the Sutherland Fencibles.

On the outbreak of war with France in 1793 the Fencibles were greatly expanded and no less than fourteen cavalry regiments and forty-four infantry battalions were raised in Scotland out of a British total of thirty-three and sixty-eight. Some of these regiments, raised for service in Britain and Ireland, volunteered for service in Europe, and a few were raised specifically for service overseas. The Fencibles were disbanded when the threat from France receded, most in 1800 and the remainder after the Treaty of Amiens in 1802.

At the same time another force was established, the Volunteers. Whilst Fencibles could be embodied and served outside their county, the Volunteers were recruited solely for service in their county and were part-time. This much more limited commitment attracted those involved directly or indirectly in commerce and the professions.

In addition volunteer cavalry 'yeomanry' regiments were formed on a county basis both for home defence and for internal security. The first of these created entirely from volunteers in Scotland was The Ayrshire Yeomanry raised by the Earl of Cassillis in 1798, and mainly recruited from yeoman farmers. The Yeomanry was given the option of disbandment in 1802 but most chose to continue. A year later, when war resumed, the Yeomanry was greatly expanded.

By 1797 the Government faced a major problem with recruitment in Scotland. It would have been preferable to raise even more units of Fencible volunteers but this plan had to be discarded because the Highlands, from which most volunteers for regular and Fencible units came, had been bled dry. From the time The Black Watch was raised until the end of the Napoleonic war, the Highlands provided no less than fifty battalions of regular infantry in addition to the Fencible battalions. All these were volunteers, and the quality was superb. Well might Pitt the Elder have said in Parliament of the Highland regiments:

> I sought for merit wherever it was to be found and it is my boast that I was the first minister who looked for it and found it in the mountains of the north. I called it forth and drew into your service a hardy and intrepid race of men, who when left by your jealousy became a prey to the artifice of your enemies, and had gone nigh to have overturned the State in the war before the last. These men in the last war were brought to combat on your side; they served with fidelity as they fought with valour, and conquered for you in every part of the world.

With 65,000 Scotsmen enlisted in the British Army, the country was drained of volunteers. This led to the decision to raise ten regiments of Militia, as a quasi-third line for home defence, behind the regular forces and the Fencibles. They were raised under a quota ballot system from men between the ages of eighteen and fifty years old, on a county basis, with the Lords Lieutenant in charge. Men served for three years. Opposition to 'conscription' in the Militia led to numerous cases of abuse in Scotland as elsewhere, particularly at times when the threat was perceived to be low.

After the Fencibles were disbanded the Militia continued until it was incorporated into the regular army. The Volunteers and Yeomanry remained as locally recruited reserve forces, although often much reduced in size and inadequately trained during times of peace when local support was inevitably low. In due course they were to provide the basis of the Territorial Force. The close local connection between the various reserve forces and the counties from which they are drawn has continued to the present day.

There is no doubt that the regular Scottish regiments benefited considerably from the recruitment of these additional forces, and there were many transfers from the Fencibles and Militia to the regular units. Regulars, including those returning wounded or sick, came home periodically with orders to recruit from Fencibles and Militiamen. Their battle stories, no doubt embellished in the local hostelries, persuaded many a young man to enlist.

Throughout this period, regiments of the British Army tended to recruit where they were stationed. Most recruits for the Scottish regiments, however, still came from Scotland, many from the area in which the regiment was originally raised. Family and clan connection were exerting their age-old power on the new focus of the regiment and this was, and still is, immensely strong in Scotland. Recruiting parties had to have the authority of a Beating Order, which defined the towns and villages where they might operate. The Colonel of a regiment would naturally apply for this authority to recruit where his name, or those of his officers, would have influence on potential recruits, and this helped to maintain clan and family links.

With the peace which followed Waterloo came cuts and stagnation, though a new chapter in the story of Scotland's soldiers was soon to unfold in the imperial wars of the nineteenth century.

Chapter Twelve

Crimea and Imperial Wars

With the defeat of the French at Waterloo the British Army entered a long period of peace in Europe. With peace came neglect and the Scottish regiments were no exception. From 1815 until the outbreak of the Crimean War most of them reverted to their peacetime establishment and suffered from a general lack of interest on the part of Government and people. Regiments may have lost their public prominence but the decision to keep them substantively in existence was to prove critical over the next 100 years.

There were, however, numerous small campaigns overseas during this period in which Scottish troops took part. The Royal Scots were in action against the Pindaris in Central India in 1817, winning the Battle Honours 'Nagpore' and 'Maheidpoor'. The 72nd (later Seaforth Highlanders) and 75th (later Gordon Highlanders) took part in the Kaffir or Frontier War in 1834 and the Cameronians, 73rd (later The Black Watch), Highland Light Infantry and Argylls served in the further operations against the Kaffirs in South Africa between 1846 and 1853. All these regiments won battle honours for these engagements.

Like other soldiers in the British Army, Jocks were asked for courage and a willingness to give their lives for their country on battlefields in many parts of the world. On 26 February 1852, however, a calamity occurred at sea which demanded a very different kind of sacrifice.

At 2 a.m. the troopship *Birkenhead* struck a rock and sank off the coast of South Africa. She was carrying 638 passengers, including 479 soldiers under the command of Lieutenant Colonel Alexander Seton, Highland Light Infantry. About half the soldiers belonged to the 73rd (later The Black Watch), Highland Light Infantry and Argyllshire Highlanders. The rest of the passengers included women and children of the soldiers' families.

As the troopship sank the women and children were lowered into the only serviceable boats, while the troops stood quietly on parade on the decks, knowing that if they tried to board the boats themselves, they would be sure to swamp them and send the women and children to the bottom. These were not all battle-hardened soldiers, bonded through years of campaigning, but included many raw young recruits from different regiments. For them there was not the adrenalin of battle, a job to be done to occupy their mind. They had time to think, to reflect and to be afraid.

Captain Edward Wright of the 91st (Argyllshire Highlanders) was in command of the draft for his regiment's reserve battalion. He was to be the senior surviving officer of the disaster. In his report he wrote: 'Every man did as he was directed and there was not a murmur among them until the vessel made her final plunge.' Even after the ship had sunk, there were extraordinary tales of heroism, such as that of Ensign Russell, recently commissioned into The Highland Light Infantry. Russell had been picked up by one of the boats but insisted on making room for an injured man he had noticed struggling in the water. Within a few minutes of slipping over the side, Russell was seized and devoured by sharks. Most of the men perished in this tragedy but their steadiness and selfless discipline won the undying admiration and respect of the world. It was this incident that established the principle of 'women and children first' and the heroism so impressed the King of Prussia that he ordered a full account of the incident to be read out at the head of every regiment in the Prussian Army.

It was not until 1854, however, that Scots were once more launched into war on a grand scale. In the Crimean War most of the Scottish regiments fought in all the major engagements, and they carry on their Colours the names of these great battles. The bungling performance of many of the generals in this conflict left

111

the soldiers in a series of impossible combat situations. They were forced to shoulder the heavy burden of poor leadership and, in so doing, demonstrated immense fortitude and courage.

In the first battle of the Crimea, at the Alma on 20 September 1854, no less than six Scottish regiments were in action. The Scots Guards won renown for their stand at the critical moment of the battle. Having fought its way up the heights overlooking the Alma River, the regiment had almost reached the Great Redoubt at the summit when it was fiercely counter-attacked by the Russians. First two battalions of the Kazan Regiment attacked the Guards from both flanks, firing volley after volley. Then, over the top of the Great Redoubt, charged four battalions of the Vladimir Regiment. The Scots Guards were now almost entirely surrounded by hordes of Russians, and the situation was desperate.

The Colour Party, with Lieutenant Lindsay carrying the Queen's Colour and Lieutenant Thistlethwayte the Regimental Colour, stood firm, and round it the companies rallied. This was the turning point of the battle, as it is certain that without this stand by the Scots Guards the other British regiments advancing up the hill would have been overwhelmed. The Scots Guards, having quickly reorganized their ranks, started to advance again up the slope, now with the Grenadiers on the right and the Coldstream on the left. Forty yards from the Great Redoubt the order to charge was given and, with a ringing cheer, the Guards swept forward on to their objective.

For their heroic stand with the Colours, Lieutenant Lindsay, Sergeant James McKechnie (from Paisley in Renfrewshire), Sergeant John Knox (from Glasgow) and Private William Reynolds (from Edinburgh) of the Scots Guards all received the Victoria Cross, the first to be awarded this new decoration – the highest for gallantry.

While this tremendous struggle was taking place in the centre of the British line, an equally stirring feat of arms was being carried out by the Highland Brigade on the left. The brigade consisted of Black Watch, Camerons, and Sutherland Highlanders. It was commanded by Sir Colin Campbell, a man of humble parentage, born in Glasgow, who later was to rise to the rank of field marshal and to be made a peer for his part in quelling the

Indian Mutiny. He served in several regiments during his career but in only one Scottish regiment – The Royal Scots Fusiliers in Barbados in 1818 as a captain at the age of twenty-six.

The Highland Brigade was also fighting uphill. Its objective was the Lesser Redoubt on the high ground to the left of the Great Redoubt being attacked by the Guards. The Highlanders started up the slope at a rapid pace with the regiments in echelon, The Black Watch in front. This proved to be a wise formation when the battle developed. As The Black Watch approached the top of the hill they were attacked on the left flank by two battalions of the Sousdal Regiment. The Russians however were themselves taken in the flank by the Sutherlands who came up on the left of their comrades in The Black Watch. Another two Russian battalions were then thrown in to deal with the Sutherlands but they were similarly taken in the flank by the Camerons, who had come tearing up the hill even further round to the left. All three Highland regiments then carried the crest with the bayonet. The cheers of the victorious Highlanders swept along the line and were taken up by the Guards on the neighbouring heights, with bonnets and bearskins raised in triumph.

The Battle of Balaklava on 25 October was to see one regiment of Highlanders win further lasting fame. At a critical moment in the battle the 93rd Sutherland Highlanders found themselves the only British regiment in the path of a tremendous Russian thrust to Balaklava, threatening the main supply base of the British Army. On their right and left were some hastily formed Turkish units. Under the eagle eye of Sir Colin Campbell, the Sutherlands, only 750 strong, were quickly formed in line only two deep to take the shock of the 1,000 strong enemy cavalry charge. *The Times* correspondent W.H. Russell was standing on the hills above and it was from his report on the 'thin red streak tipped with a line of steel' that the Sutherlands earned their famous nickname of the 'Thin Red Line'. The Turks met the charge of galloping horses and the yells of their Cossack riders boldly, but were driven back having suffered considerable loss. The Sutherlands stood alone to face the enemy. With superb discipline the Highlanders waited until the horsemen were nearly on them before firing a withering volley into their packed ranks. They had recently been issued with the Minié rifle and this made a significant difference to the accuracy and effectiveness of their fire. The Russians staggered and then recoiled. One more volley, and they retreated in disorder.

Commenting on the battle, soldiers of the Sutherlands said:

Sweeping towards us they made the ground quiver under their proud and agile feet, their appearance as they approached our line was imposing in the extreme. (Robert Sinclair later from Aberdeen.)

Our company was in the centre of the line, we were thoroughly prepared for the Russians and in order to be in readiness each man had placed cartridges between the buttons of his coat. (Charles Gray from Grantown.)

Being in the front rank and giving a look along the line it seemed like a wall of fire in front of the muzzles of our rifles. (Donald Cameron from Aberfeldy.)

A Russian Hussar officer wrote:

On advancing your regiment rose out of the ground and fired a volley at us, we were made to rein up or swerve before we received your second volley. When we were inclining to our left a wing of your regiment changed front and fired a volley into our flank. Almost every man's horse in the ranks was wounded. I myself had a bullet through my arm and one breaking my thigh.

A few Turks who had fled from the field of battle inadvertently passed through the camp of the Highlanders where, according to observers of this action, they met a new and terrible foe. A powerful and angry wife fell on them with a heavy stick, chastising all who came near her. Even the grimmest battles have their funny moments. Balaklava was no exception, and apparently the regiment enjoyed this one.

In the same battle The Royal Scots Greys took part in the charge of the Heavy Brigade which has been reckoned as one of the most

1. Traprain Law – East Lothian. Site of large Celtic hill fort 300-200 BC.

2. Mousa Broch,
   Shetland.
   *Photograph by
   Charles Tait.*

3. Aberlemno Stone – Battle of Dunnichen or Nechtansmere.
Crown Copyright: Royal Commission on the Ancient and Historic Monuments of Scotland.

4. Urquhart Castle, Inverness-shire. A fortress since the twelfth century, of great tactical strength and strategic importance.
Crown Copyright: Historic Scotland.

5. Dunnottar Castle, Kincardineshire. Fourteenth century Royalist stronghold in the Civil War. *Crown Copyright: Historic Scotland.*

6. Caerlaverock Castle, Dumfriesshire. Thirteenth century castle of great strength – triangular shape based on the gatehouse. *Crown Copyright: Historic Scotland.*

7. Threaves Castle, Kircudbrightshire. Fourteenth century stronghold of the Black Douglases. *Crown Copyright: Historic Scotland.*

8. Dunstaffnage Castle, Argyll. MacDougall stronghold captured by Bruce in 1308. *Crown Copyright: Historic Scotland.*

9. Stirling Castle – home of The Argyll and Sutherland Highlanders. *Crown Copyright: Historic Scotland.*

10. Edinburgh Castle – A fort has stood on the rock since earliest times. The present castle originated in the twelfth century but it was much extended in the fifteenth and sixteenth centuries. *Crown Copyright: Historic Scotland.*

11. Bothwell Castle, Lanarkshire. Mainly thirteenth century and principal English
stronghold in Western Scotland during the wars of independence.

Crown Copyright: Historic Scotland.

12. Sir Robert Douglas of Glenbervie, Colonel of the Royal Regiment of Foot, killed at
the Battle of Steenkirk, 24 July 1692. *The Royal Scots.*

13. Fort George. Eighteenth century fortress built by William Skinner at Ardersier; still in military use.

14. The Black Watch at Fontenoy 1745. Painting by Skeoch Cumming.

Trustees of The Black Watch Museum.

15. The King's Own Scottish Borderers at Minden 1759. Painting by Gordon Ellis.
Regimental Headquarters The King's Own Scottish Borderers.

16. The Third Guards at Talavera 1809. Painting by CCP Lawson.
Headquarters Scots Guards.

17. The Black Watch at Bay, Quatre Bras 1815. Painting by WB Wollen.

18. Scotland for Ever. The Charge of The Scots Greys at Waterloo.

19. Piper Kenneth Mackay,
    79th Cameron Highlanders
    at Waterloo. Painting by
    Lockhart Bogle.
    *Trustees of The Highlanders
    Museum.*

20. The Loss of the *Birkenhead* 1852. Painting by Thomas Hemy.
    Trustees of The Black Watch Museum.

21. The Scots Guards at the Alma 1854. Painting by Lady Butler.

Headquarters Scots Guards.

22. Forward the 42nd. The Black Watch at the Alma. Painting by Robert Gibb 1888.

Photograph by Dr. WH Findlay.

23. The Thin Red Line. 93rd Sutherland Highlanders at Balaklava. Painting by Robert Gibb RSA. *Trustees of The National Museums of Scotland.*

24. Scots Greys in the Charge of the Heavy Brigade at Balaklava 25 October 1854. Painting by Felix Philippoteaux. *Headquarters The Royal Scots Dragoon Guards.*

5. The 78th Highlanders at Lucknow 1857. Painting by Chevalier Louis W Desagnes. It depicts Assistant Surgeon VM McMaster and Surgeon J Jee attending the wounded and Lieutenant and Adjutant HT MacPherson. All three were awarded the Victoria Cross for this action.   *Trustees of The Highlanders Museum.*

6. Black Watch at Tel-el-Kebir 1882. Painting by Alphonse Marie de Neuville.
                    Trustees of The National Museums of Scotland.

27. No Surrender, The Black Watch at Magersfontein 1899. Painting by Frank Feller. *Trustees of The Black Watch Museum.*

28. The Royal Scots Fusiliers at Battle of Mons 23 August 1914 – Defence of Jemappes Bridge. Painting by Gilbert Holiday. *The Royal Highland Fusiliers Museum.*

29. 2nd Battalion Scots Guards digging trenches near Ghent, 9 October 1914.
Photograph courtesy of the Imperial War Museum, London (IWM Q57168).

30. Brief interlude before the fateful hours of Wytschaete – 1st Battalion The London Scottish. *Photograph The Daily Mail.*

31. The London Scottish at Messines, Hallowe'en 1914.
Painting by R Caton Woodville. *Trustees of The London Scottish.*

32. Horses of The Royal Scots Greys out of the line 1914.
Headquarters The Royal Scots Dragoon Guards.

3. Men of 2nd Battalion The Argyll and Sutherland Highlanders in the Bois Grenier sector in June 1915 wearing some of the first gas masks.

Photograph courtesy of the Imperial War Museum, London (IWM Q48951).

4. Piper Laidlaw KOSB – winning Victoria Cross in France 1915. Painting by Samuel Begg. *Regimental Headquarters The King's Own Scottish Borderers.*

35. The Scottish Horse bivouacking on the beach at Lala Baba, Suvla Bay, 3 September 1915. *The Scottish Horse.*

36. 6th Battalion The Queen's Own Cameron Highlanders at the Battle of Loos, 25 September 1915. Painting by Joseph Gray. *Trustees of The Highlanders Museum.*

37. 1st Battalion Scots Guards in Big Willie trench at the Battle of Loos, October 1915. *Photograph courtesy of the Imperial War Museum, London (IWM Q17390).*

38. The Queen's Own Cameron Highlanders in a trench dugout at Contalmaison, September 1916. *Photograph courtesy of the Imperial War Museum, London (IWM Q4133).*

39. George Russell of 16th Battalion The Royal Scots, Contalmaison 1916.
Photograph Jack Alexander, McCrae's Battalion Archive.

40. 12th Battalion The Argyll and Sutherland Highlanders in Macedonia. Rehearsal –
advancing by short rushes, February 1916.

Photograph courtesy of the Imperial War Museum, London (IWM Q31789).

41. 8th Battalion The Black Watch resting by the roadside, Contalmaison Wood, Battle
of Transloy Ridges 18 October 1916.

Photograph courtesy of the Imperial War Museum, London (IWM Q4360).

42. Lance Corporal William Angus VC, The Highland Light Infantry, and Sergeant Thomas Caldwell VC, The Royal Scots Fusiliers, both from Carluke in Lanarkshire. *The Royal Highland Fusiliers Museum.*

43. 4th Battalion The Gordon Highlanders in 51st Highland Division, crossing a trench at Ribecourt, Battle of Cambrai 20 November 1917. *Photograph courtesy of the Imperial War Museum, London (IWM Q6278).*

44. Battle of St Quentin, 23 March 1918. The South African Scottish on the Moislains to Bouchavesnes Road.

Photograph courtesy of the Imperial War Museum, London (IWM Q8594).

45. 2nd Battalion The Black Watch reach Beirut, 10 October 1918. 7th (Meerut) Division marched ninety-six miles from Haifa to Beirut in eight days.

Photograph courtesy of the Imperial War Museum, London (IWM Q12407).

46. 'Sans Peur' 2nd Battalion The Argyll and Sutherland Highlanders cross the causeway into Singapore 1942. Painting by Peter Archer.

The Argyll and Sutherland Highlanders Museum.

47. Grant tank of The Royal Scots Greys, El Alamein, 17 July 1942.

Photograph courtesy of the Imperial War Museum, London (IWM E14550).

48. Sergeant Victor Mutch MM from Govan and Sergeant Joseph Stephenson MM, 2nd Battalion Scots Guards, who knocked out five German tanks near Medenine, 12 March 1943.
Photograph courtesy of the Imperial War Museum, London (IWM NA1107).

49. 5th Battalion The Queen's Own Cameron Highlanders in 51st Division coming ashore in Sicily 1943.
Photograph courtesy of the Imperial War Museum, London (IWM NA4194).

50. Men of 6th Battalion The Royal Scots Fusiliers going up the line on Hill 113, Normandy 15 July 1944.

Photograph courtesy of the Imperial War Museum, London (IWM B7428).

51. 7th Battalion The King's Own Scottish Borderers, Arnhem.

Photograph Airborne Museum 'Hartenstein', Oosterbeek.

52. 25-pounder gun of 151 (Ayrshire Yeomanry) Field Regiment in action near Asten, Holland, 22 September 1944.
Photograph courtesy of the Imperial War Museum, London (IWM BU1085).

53. Crab Flail Tank of The Lothians and Border Horse coming ashore at Walcheren, 2 November 1944.
Photograph courtesy of the Imperial War Museum, London (IWM B11631).

2nd Battalion The Argyll and Sutherland Highlanders in 15th Scottish Division move up for attack on Tilburg, 27 October 1944. *Photograph courtesy of the Imperial War Museum, London (IWM B11391).*

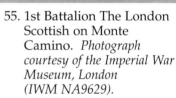

55. 1st Battalion The London Scottish on Monte Camino. *Photograph courtesy of the Imperial War Museum, London (IWM NA9629).*

56. 6th Battalion The Gordon Highlanders advance to Rome. *Photograph courtesy of the Imperial War Museum, London (IWM NAI6007)*

57. 6th Battalion The Highland Light Infantry in 52nd Lowland Division advancing
    towards Breberen, Holland 21 January 1945.
            Photograph courtesy of the Imperial War Museum, London (IWM B13927)

58. 7th Battalion Seaforth Highlanders in 15th Scottish Division cross the Rhine 24
    March 1945. *Photograph courtesy of the Imperial War Museum, London (IWM BU2092)*

59. 1st Battalion The Gordon Highlanders in Malaya 1951. On the right is Private Alexander Gray from Greenock who died of wounds received in an ambush on 27 May 1951. *The Gordon Highlanders Museum.*

60. 1st Battalion The Argyll and Sutherland Highlanders, Battle for Hill 282 in Korea. Painting by Peter Archer. *The Argyll and Sutherland Highlanders Museum.*

61. Men of 1st Battalion The Black Watch waiting to return to the front after a brief rest following the fierce fighting at The Hook, Korea 1952. *Illustrated London News.*

62. Recapture of Anduki airstrip, Seria, Brunei by 1st Battalion Queen's Own Highlanders 1962. Painting by Terence Cuneo.
Reproduced with permission of The Cuneo Estate.

63. 2nd Battalion Scots Guards at Battle for Tumbledown, Falkland Islands 1982.
    Painting by Terence Cuneo.   *Reproduced with permission of The Cuneo Estate.*

64. 1st Battalion The King's Own Scottish Borderers at Derryard, Northern Ireland
    1989.   *Regimental Headquarters The King's Own Scottish Borderers.*

65. Sergeant Tom Gorrian from East Lothian of 1st Battalion The Royal Scots in Iraq 1991. *Photograph by Mike Moore.*

66. A Challenger 2 tank of The Royal Scots Dragoon Guards on the outskirts of Basra 2003. Captain Alex Matheson and Trooper John Cassidy (gunner) from Rutherglen. *Photograph by Tony Nicoletti, Daily Record, Glasgow.*

successful cavalry-versus-cavalry charges in history. Without hesitation the regiment took on a huge body of stationary Russian cavalry, who outnumbered them by nine to one, and broke them by the sheer momentum of their charge. For their bravery in this action Sergeant Major John Grieve and Private (Trooper) Henry Ramage of The Royal Scots Greys received the Victoria Cross. Of Grieve's actions Charles Dickens wrote in his journal:

> When he cut off a soldier's head at a blow, and disabled and dispersed several others, he had no very exciting motives of self-devotion. Pay, promotion, or popularity could not well enter his head, for he knew the rules of the Service about rising from the ranks, and he knew too, that the British public rarely asks the names of the poor privates and non-commissioned officers who fall. What John Grieve did, then, was an act of the purest and most unselfish heroism; but I daresay, when the Queen pinned on the Cross to his breast in Hyde Park, he felt he was more than rewarded for what to him was a very ordinary matter-of-fact bit of duty.

The Royal Scots Fusiliers had spent the night before the Battle of Inkerman in the trenches and were tired after their night duty. Most of the army had Minié rifles but they were armed with old-fashioned smooth bore muskets and with damp powder that caused continual misfires; and the mist on that morning of the battle, 5 November 1854, was very thick. When the guns starting firing, signalling an attack, the regiment charged down the hill. As they came out of the mist they were confronted by the Russian columns. In the ferocious fighting that followed they held the Russians long enough for others to deploy then went on to hold 'The Barrier' for six hours against tremendous odds. This feature was the hinge on which hung the whole British position and the Fusiliers fought stubbornly to defend it. In doing so, however, they lost their colonel and a third of their strength, killed or wounded. Inkerman was a soldiers' battle in which the infantry fought at close quarters. The British victory was almost entirely due to the courage and determination of the Jocks, and their English and Irish counterparts, as they fought hand-to-hand with the Russians. Ultimately it was the resolve of the Russians that was to break first. Sergeant James Clarke, originally from Perth and later Ayr, wrote in his diary:

It was now about 11.30 am but the enemy showed no signs of giving up the struggle and our Fusiliers, though hungry, weary and wet had not the least intention of giving up one inch of ground. There was not a man in our gallant band who would not have rather died at his post than surrender to any number of Russians.

On arriving in camp, our ration of rum was issued; this and some hard biscuit served the majority of us for our evening meal.

No sooner was the Crimean War finished than most of the Scottish regiments were in India, helping to quell the Indian Mutiny, one of the darkest chapters in the annals of the British Army. Native troops who had fought side by side with their British counterparts had turned on them, and massacred soldiers and their families.

The Seaforth Highlanders, who had been taking part in a small expedition under Sir James Outram in Persia, in which they had won the Battle Honours 'Koosh-ab' and 'Persia', were hurried back to India. Very soon they were to take part in Sir Henry Havelock's march on Cawnpore through the appalling heat of midsummer, to try and rescue the women and children held prisoner by the mutineers.

The people they were marching to rescue were the families of the British garrison at Cawnpore, who had been treacherously betrayed and put to death by the mutineers under Nana Sahib. The relief force had little information about the survivors, only that they were in the hands of merciless fanatics, and that their men had been slain.

For ten days the Seaforth with detachments of two other regiments marched 126 miles across the burning plain, fighting four battles along the way. Before the gates of Cawnpore, Havelock's tiny column destroyed a much larger force of mutineers and then burst into the city, only to find that Nana had ordered the murder of all the women and children two days before. This was surely one of the grimmest episodes in the mutiny, and one of the most tragic sights the regiment ever encountered.

Sergeant William Mitchell of the Sutherlands was there and wrote:

> . . . most of my men visited the slaughterhouse where the European women and children had been murdered. The floors were covered in blood, torn dresses, children's shoes and locks of severed hair. Every man of the regiment was determined to risk his life to save the women and children in the Residency at Lucknow.

The (75th) Gordon Highlanders' action at Badli-ki-Serai in 1857 helped to stem the number of Indian rulers about to support the mutiny. The regiment attacked a ridge on which the mutineers were well entrenched with guns. Exposed for 1,200 yards to destructive fire by round and grape shot, they suffered great loss but took the position by storm. The action was witnessed by the Raja of Jheend. He wrote to the Raja of Patiala saying he knew the difficulties the British were in but he saw the rush of the white soldiers at Badli-ki-Serai in the face of heavy fire, yet there was no hesitation or halting or seeking cover. 'They went straight. The nation that could produce such men was sure to succeed in the end whatever the adverse odds might be at the commencement.' Now with Cameronians, Black Watch, Seaforth, Camerons, and Sutherlands they took part in the relief of Lucknow.

The 1,700 British troops of the garrison at Lucknow and their families were besieged in the Residency by about 60,000 mutineers. A 1,500 strong column under General Havelock was sent to their relief. Having crossed the Ganges, the column fought a series of engagements before reaching the Residency where they were themselves besieged. The (78th) Seaforth Highlanders were in the relief column. Colour Sergeant Stewart McPherson of the regiment was awarded the Victoria Cross 'for daring gallantry in the Lucknow residency on 26 September 1857 in having rescued, at great personal risk, a wounded private of his company who was lying in a most exposed position under heavy fire'. The reinforced garrison was then able to hold out for six weeks until relieved by a larger force but it was then decided that the Residency was untenable and it was abandoned.

The 93rd Sutherland Highlanders had been on route to China in 1857. When they reached Simonstown on 9 August they were told of the mutiny and diverted to India. On arrival they joined the force sent to relieve the Residency in Lucknow arriving there on 9 November. The battle that followed lasted for a week – hand-to-hand fighting, house by house, street by street. The biggest problem was the large fortified palaces. Private David Mackay, from Lyth near Wick in Caithness, was one of the six Sutherlands to be awarded the Victoria Cross on 16 November. The citation records his 'personal gallantry in capturing an enemy's colour after most obstinate resistance'. Mackay, a veteran of the Thin Red Line at Balaklava, was to be seriously wounded later that same day. Colour Sergeant James Monro from Nigg in Cromarty and Sergeant John Paton from Stirling were similarly decorated for their bravery.

All the regiments that took part carry the Battle Honour 'Lucknow' on their colours. The Black Watch and Seaforth each won eight Victoria Crosses in the mutiny, and the Sutherlands seven, six of them on that one day.

Meanwhile The Royal Scots were seeing service in China, first in the attack on the Taku Forts in 1859, and then in the capture of Peking the following year. This operation was really the first of the many 'small wars' in which Scottish regiments took part between the Crimea and the Boer War. The Cameronians served in the Abyssinian Expedition of 1867, the first campaign in which British troops were armed with a breech-loading rifle with its much higher rate of fire. The Black Watch fought in Ashanti in the bloody campaign of 1873–4, and King's Own Scottish Borderers, (92nd) Gordons, and Seaforth Highlanders took part in the Afghanistan, Chitral and Tirah campaigns on the North-West Frontier of India between 1878 and 1897. The Royal Scots Fusiliers also served in the Tirah operation, having previously distinguished themselves in the Burma campaign of 1885.

During the Second Afghan War 1878–80 the Seaforth fought

an outstanding night action at Peiwar Kotal. They and The (92nd) Gordon Highlanders then took part in the epic march from Kabul to Kandahar for which a special medal was struck. Three hundred and twenty-three miles were covered over poor tracks in twenty-three days. During the march they had to contend with the severe heat and frequent sniping attacks. The day after they arrived in Kandahar they attacked the Afghan positions. The Gordons under Major (later Field Marshal Sir George) White led the final successful charge.

It was in the Tirah campaign at the Battle of Dargai that The Gordon Highlanders won fame for their capture of the heights. The frontier tribes, mainly Afridis and Orakzais, had made several attacks on British posts. If the tribes combined they could have put almost 50,000 fighting men in the field so it was decided to mount an expedition against them. The force, Tirah Expeditionary Force, consisted of two divisions. 1 Gordons was in 2nd Division. The advance was held up by an enemy force holding the village of Dargai set on a high rocky ridge which dominated the only road leading into Tirah. On 18 October 1897 the village was taken but, because the water supply was some distance away and the heights above the village would have to be held, the decision was taken to withdraw. The enemy subsequently re-occupied the heights with a force of several thousand tribesmen. On 20 October the heights were assaulted. The attack started at 10 a.m. It was preceded by concentrated artillery fire but this had little effect because the tribesmen hid in the clefts in the rocks. The three leading battalions were unable to make progress so 1 Gordons was brought forward. The Commanding Officer addressed his highlanders: 'The General says this hill must be taken at all costs – The Gordon Highlanders will take it.'

In his dispatch to the Adjutant General in India the commander of Tirah Force reports:

The Gordon Highlanders went straight up the hill without check or hesitation. Headed by their pipers and led by their Commanding Officer this splendid battalion marched across the open. It dashed through the murderous fire, and in forty minutes had won the heights. The first rush of the Gordons was deserving of the highest praise, for they had just undergone a very severe climb and had reached a point beyond which other troops had been unable to advance for over three hours.

The battalion reached the summit and the enemy that had held up a whole brigade fled. Because of the speed of their attack the Gordons' casualties, thirty-three in total, were surprisingly low. Piper George Findlater from Turriff in Aberdeenshire was shot through both feet. Although unable to stand he continued to play under heavy fire, encouraging the battalion forward. Private Edward Lawson from Newcastle carried Lieutenant Dingwall who was wounded and unable to move, out of heavy fire, and then returned and brought in another private, although he was twice wounded in doing so. Both these Gordon Highlanders were to receive the Victoria Cross.

Towards the end of the century attention became focused on Egypt, the Sudan, and South Africa. In the Egyptian campaign of 1882 the Scots Guards, and all the Highland regiments except the Sutherlands who were in South Africa, fought in the Battle of Tel-el-Kebir. In this action a British force of 13,500 under General Sir Garnet Wolseley routed an Egyptian army of 25,000 after a night attack.

The campaigns in the Sudan which followed saw much bitter fighting against the Dervishes, and Scottish regiments took part in them all, The Royal Scots Greys providing a detachment of the Heavy Camel Corps. In the expedition up the Nile to Khartoum, the fierce attack on the Dervish position in the Battle of the Atbara, and in the final triumph at Omdurman in 1898, all these regiments fought with distinction.

Most of the imperial wars of the nineteenth century were small wars, in regard to the number of troops involved, but they did a great deal to develop the character of the regiments and the individual soldiers in them. This operational service should have done more to develop tactics and equipment. Instead it produced a degree of complacency which was only shattered when faced by a much better equipped and tactically aware enemy in South Africa. Many Scottish soldiers were to die because of this complacency.

The Boer War was an imperial war, but it could hardly be called small. Before it was successfully concluded the greater part of the British army had been committed, and with it all the Scottish regiments. It divided itself into three phases. First there was the Boer invasion of British territory, and the British efforts to drive them back. The British then needed to advance to occupy the Boer capitals and territory. The last phase, the most difficult and costly, was the campaign to break the Boer resistance in the open field.

The problems involved in fighting the Boers were very different from those encountered in previous campaigns. For the first time in nearly fifty years Britain was confronted by a European foe, and a clever one. The Boers showed themselves expert in the art of guerrilla warfare, by far the most suitable to employ in South Africa. Above all, the Boer was a good fighter, an excellent horseman, and a first class shot.

But the British Army rose to meet the challenge. In the course of operations new organizations were developed, new tactics evolved, and even new units raised. Khaki gradually replaced scarlet tunics, new equipment was invented and some infantry found themselves mounted.

With the exception of The King's Own Scottish Borderers and Camerons who arrived in South Africa after the other regiments, The Royal Scots Greys, Scots Guards, and all the Scottish infantry regiments fought right through the three years of the Boer War from start to finish (1899 – 1902).

In the first attempt to relieve Kimberley the Scots Guards, Highland Light Infantry, and Argylls won the Battle Honour 'Modder River' for their part in forcing the passage of that river at considerable cost. The Black Watch, Gordons, and Seaforth in the Highland Brigade under General Wauchope, suffered heavy casualties in the disaster at Magersfontein, so named after the main hill dominating the approach to Kimberley, which rises 200 feet from the plain.

The Boers had placed their main trenches about 100 yards from the base of the hill. These were probably the best prepared trenches up to that date – all were well camouflaged and many had overhead cover. Although the British had had about ten days to carry out a reconnaissance of the Boers' positions, they failed to identify the trenches or the wire fencing in front of them. For the men of the Highland Brigade who were to lead the attack, conditions before the battle were dreadful enough. During the day they had had to contend with hot winds, flies and driving sand which filled food and drink, eyes, ears and mouth. The approach march to Magersfontein was made during a very dark night in heavy rain. At first light on 11 December 1899 when the Boers opened fire the two leading battalions, Black Watch and Seaforth, were caught in the open. For much of the day they were completely pinned down. The heat was intense. As more than one man recalled, the worst aspect was painful blistering on the back of the knee, an area not usually exposed to sunburn. Later in the day the Highland Brigade was withdrawn. This failure of reconnaissance had cost The Black Watch seventeen officers and 311 other ranks and the Seaforth eleven officers and 200 other ranks.

Of all the accounts of the battle that of Private James Williamson from Montrose, serving in The Black Watch, deserves to be reproduced in full:

I got wounded at Magersfontein after waiting for so long in Africa for a start, but I am glad it is all up with me now, since I saw what like the General in command was, we were led up in four columns to the trenches and got no command off anyone, only to charge on our own tin pot way and to my sorry I was in the front company. We pulled up the barbed wire and rushed on the Boers but were soon away from them again. We extended out to the left then lay down, previous to this I got my helmet knocked off, and couldn't go after it, the bullets were coming down on us like hail stones, so we had to stick there, about 30 yards from the trenches, as soon as I lay down I got a mauser bullet through my left foot which made me wilder so I started firing back but my luck was out that day, for they peppered at me as if I was the only man firing at them. I got one through left leg severing my mussle (sic) then I got another in the back but kept on the fire as long as I was able to hold the rifle, then I got one in the right shoulder, it made me drop the rifle but I managed to pick it up and fire again, but not for long, for I got another in the right leg so I thought it was the last, but no I got another in the right arm that broke it, so I was done for, I had to lie and witness the fight all day, and then at night until 9 o'clock next morning I lay watching the Boers taking away their dead. They would have taken me but they saw I was no use to them, so they allowed three of the Highland Light Infantry to come over for me.

Private James McFarlane from Perth was also in The Black Watch. He had served seven years from 1888 to 1895 before working for Pullars, the cleaners in the City. As a reservist, he was called up for the Boer War. Writing to his sister after Magersfontein he says: 'I escaped safe only a few bullets through my pack. We fought all day, the British on the bare plain and the Boers entrenched on a big hill. We had to retire at dark after about 30 hours hot work. I was fairly done up we never had a drop of water all the time.'

The Gordons had another battalion, its 2nd, in the defence of Ladysmith, where they distinguished themselves by their valour and by the initiative they displayed in the siege. Throughout the siege the number of men unavailable for duty because of sickness was extraordinarily low, an indication of the discipline and morale maintained in the battalion. The Royal Scots Fusiliers and Cameronians were given the Battle Honour 'Relief of Ladysmith' for their part in the lifting of that siege, and The Royal Scots Greys won another Battle Honour for the Relief of Kimberley. The Royal Scots Greys also took part, with The King's Own Scottish Borderers, Black Watch, Gordons, Seaforth, and Argylls in the defeat of Cronje at Paardeburg.

The 6th (Scottish) Battalion of the Imperial Yeomanry contained companies of Ayrshire and Lanarkshire Yeomanry, Lothians and Border Horse, Fife and Forfar Yeomanry and Queen's Own Royal Glasgow Yeomanry. The Lovat Scouts provided two companies of Imperial Yeomanry. Lord Lovat believed that the Highland stalker, equipped with spyglass and rifle, could match the fieldcraft of the Boers. The intelligence the Lovat Scouts gathered, acting as observers and snipers, was a major factor in reversing the early disasters in the war. The Scottish Horse produced two regiments – one was recruited from Scots living in South Africa and the other from Scotland and Australia. The latter regiment while guarding a column west of Pretoria repulsed an attack by a Boer force seven times its size. Only six of the seventy-nine men of the Scottish Horse were unwounded at the end of the action.

During the war in South Africa twelve Victoria Crosses were awarded to Scottish soldiers. Of these no less than six were gained by Gordon Highlanders, a truly remarkable record. This regiment also produced one of the outstanding soldiers of the period. Hector MacDonald came from Mulbuie in Rosshire. As a colour sergeant during the Second Afghan War he was mentioned in dispatches on 16 October 1879 for taking command of a small party of Gordon Highlanders and Sikhs and beating off a much larger Afghan force. He again showed extraordinary courage and leadership a few days later at the Battle of Charasiah. As a result of these actions he was commissioned, much at the instigation of Lord Roberts, the Commander-in-Chief. Thereafter he fought in India, Afghanistan, Egypt, Sudan and South Africa. He commanded the Highland Brigade as a major general in South Africa after Magersfontein. It was a tremendous achievement to rise from the ranks to be a general officer, particularly at that time. But he was a very good soldier and commander, one who understood his soldiers. Because he took his own life, amid lurid allegations about his sexuality, his achievements were never fully understood or appreciated.

The lessons learned from the Boer War and the dawn of the twentieth century saw many reforms and changes in Army organization which affected the Scottish regiments. Under Cardwell's reforms in 1870 short service had been introduced in to the Regular Army, with six years with the colours and six with the reserve. A depot system under which regiments were brigaded was also introduced.

In 1881 a number of regiments were linked together, to form new regiments each of two regular battalions. They were:

26th and 90th – The Cameronians (Scottish Rifles)
42nd and 73rd – The Black Watch
71st and 74th – The Highland Light Infantry
72nd and 78th – Seaforth Highlanders
7th and 92nd – The Gordon Highlanders
91st and 93rd – The Argyll and Sutherland Highlanders

The Militia battalion, by now much reduced, became the third battalion of each regiment and the Volunteers were also linked, becoming the territorial units of the regular regiments in 1908. Both Militia and Volunteers had been allowed to run down between Waterloo and the Crimea, but in 1859 a war scare led to the raising of ten artillery Volunteer batteries and sixty-seven Volunteer rifle companies in a very short time. The driving force of this movement came from the people of the cities, towns and villages of Scotland, who demanded the right to raise volunteers, and to have them recognized as military units of the Crown. After nearly fifty years of neglect the citizen soldier was back by popular demand.

Most important, each regular regiment was officially allotted an area from which it drew recruits, and in which it had its depot. Except for some recent changes this organization has remained to the present day.

After the Boer War it was clear that the hasty putting together of units and staffs to form brigades and divisions was not good enough, and between 1903 and 1914 two important changes were made in the higher command of the forces. First, the Regular Army units were organized into established brigades and divisions, and the Militia battalion of each regiment became a special reserve unit to provide reinforcements for the regular battalions of the regiment. Secondly, the Yeomanry and Volunteer units were organized into territorial brigades and divisions forming the Territorial Force. It was on this structure that Scotland's contribution in the two World Wars was to be based.

In the north most units were organized into the Highland Division (Territorial Force) and south of the Forth-Clyde line most units were organized into the Lowland Division (Territorial Force). The units of each division were raised and trained at a very large number of drill halls scattered throughout the divisional district, the infantry being located in the regimental area of their parent regular regiment. This increased enormously the tie between regular and volunteer, and strengthened the regimental connections with counties.

The regular battalions of the Scottish regiments fitted into the general Army organization of brigades and divisions at home and abroad, with one battalion of each regiment always at home while the other served abroad.

Most of this last reorganization of the Army was the work of two Scotsmen – Viscount Haldane, who was Secretary of State for War during this period, and General Sir Douglas Haig (later Field Marshal The Earl Haig) who was responsible for training and organization in the War Office. Much of the detailed work was done by General Sir Spencer Ewart late The Queen's Own Cameron Highlanders, from Langholm in Dumfriesshire, the senior Staff Officer responsible for these functions at the time. As a result of their efforts, the British Army was, in spite of its small numbers, far better constituted and prepared than ever before. With the major conflict ahead this was just as well.

Chapter Thirteen

First World War

Before the outbreak of the First World War, the peacetime establishment of Scottish infantry regiments had numbered twenty-two regular battalions. When the call to arms came in 1914, Scotland's response on land and sea was phenomenal. With a total population of only 4½ million, it raised 200,000 men in 226 battalions from Shetland to the Borders, a roll call that does not include those who joined the rest of the Army, Royal Navy and Royal Flying Corps. Jocks served in every battle of the war. The vast majority of the soldiers in these units were volunteers who answered the call to join Kitchener's new Armies. They were some of the finest fighting material Scotland ever produced. The conditions in which they all fought were appalling, their bravery was extraordinary and their sacrifice enormous.

At the outbreak of war Scotland was providing one regular cavalry regiment, The Royal Scots Greys, and the Scots Guards and ten infantry regiments each with two battalions. They were The Royal Scots, The Royal Scots Fusiliers, The King's Own Scottish Borderers, The Cameronians (Scottish Rifles), The Black Watch, The Highland Light Infantry, Seaforth Highlanders, The Queen's Own Cameron Highlanders, The Gordon Highlanders and The Argyll and Sutherland Highlanders. Their regimental recruiting areas are shown on the map at the back of the book. However, regiments recruited men wherever they could find them, and have continued to do so. In the infantry regiments one battalion was based at home and the other abroad. Reinforcing them when mobilized was the Territorial Force. Most of these units were in Scotland's two Territorial Force divisions. With a few exceptions infantry battalions came from the same regiments as the Regular Army battalions. The exceptions such as the Glasgow Highlanders, London Scottish, Tyneside Scottish and Liverpool Scottish were affiliated to one of the regular regiments. But this was not to be enough and a New Army would have to be raised. Again the same principles were applied. Infantry battalions were recruited within existing regimental recruiting areas and proudly bore the names of their regular and territorial counterparts.

As part of Britain's expeditionary force, described by the Kaiser as Britain's 'contemptible little army', all the regular battalions were mobilized on the outbreak of war. They took the field in the Regular Army divisions in which they happened to be serving. One of the first battalions in action was 1st Battalion The Royal Scots Fusiliers in the 3rd Division. The battalion had returned from South Africa in March 1914 and crossed to France on 13 August. It was immediately deployed forward to hold the Jemappes sector of the Condé Canal. Bridges were barricaded, trenches cut in the canal bank and houses loop-holed. On the night of Saturday, 22 August 1914, they and the rest of the II Corps of the British Expeditionary Force went to sleep, unaware that eight German divisions, four times their number, were marching inexorably against them. Sunday, 23 August started with mist and rain and then cleared to a lovely August morning. A German cavalry patrol approached and was engaged. One man was killed. By 10.30 a.m. the German guns had opened in earnest and this was quickly followed by the main infantry attack. By now the heavy shelling had set the houses ablaze. Thanks to the accuracy of the rifle fire of the Fusiliers, the attack was brought to a temporary standstill. Even so, faced with greatly superior numbers and with both flanks under threat, the battalion was forced to withdraw. Their war had started. The Jemappes bridge was destroyed by Lance Corporal Charles Jarvis Royal Engineers from Fraserburgh. For this and other acts of bravery during the battle he was awarded the Victoria Cross.

All the Scottish regiments fought in the first battle of the war at Mons when, against overwhelming odds, they tried to stem the advance of the German army. Here, and later in the First Battle of the Marne and the First Battle of Ypres – the first five weeks of which were among the most critical of the war – they bought the vital time the country needed. That time was paid for with terrible loss of life of men from every rank. None could easily be replaced.

There were to be numerous acts of outstanding bravery by Scots in the war. One of the earliest occurred on 14 September 1914. At Verneuill the 2nd Battalion The Highland Light Infantry came into action for the first time since Mons. They had been involved for only one hour when Private George Wilson spied a couple of Germans and informed his officer. The officer was incredulous and took up his glasses to take a closer look but he was immediately shot dead. Wilson quickly avenged his killing by taking aim and shooting the two Germans. He then advanced about 100 yards and saw eight more of the enemy. He charged them at once making noises as though accompanied by a strong group. The Germans were taken in and they immediately surrendered, and in doing so gave up two prisoners from the Middlesex Regiment. Wilson went further forward and came across the scores of wounded and dead who had previously been part of the attacking force that had been caught by German machine-gun fire. George Wilson was so incensed by the terrible massacre that he virtually went berserk and, together with a volunteer from another regiment, he set out to destroy the German machine-gun position. After only 100 yards Wilson's colleague was shot dead by the machine gun. Wilson took steady aim and killed the machine gunner, and then wiped out the whole enemy position, eventually getting to within ten yards of the gun. At this point the German officer in charge of the Maxim emptied his revolver in the direction of Wilson, but he missed and Wilson immediately bayoneted him. But even then Wilson was not satisfied; turning the machine gun round he fired 750 rounds at the enemy. Throughout this time he was under heavy shellfire which eventually forced him back to his own lines where he promptly fainted. When he came round he discovered that no one had thought of retrieving the Maxim so he set off again to bring it back. It took two more trips to carry back the remaining two and a half cases of ammunition as well. He still had one more task to carry out and this was to fetch the body of his colleague who had been shot seventeen times.

This extraordinary story is reproduced almost verbatim from the citation. For his courage George Wilson from Edinburgh was awarded the Victoria Cross. Many more such stories were to come.

In a letter to his sister two weeks later, Wilson wrote:

Yesterday, you will be surprised to hear, we caught four hens, and I volunteered to take them to a farm under fire to cook them. We are getting shelled with shrapnel something terrible. I was knocked blind for about three hours. The Germans got into the trenches of B Company of my regiment, and they had a proper Saturday night fight with hands and head. We lost seven and three wounded, but the Germans lost thirty and fifty-three taken prisoner. If we could do that every night the war would be over by the New Year.

At Ypres in October 1914 some of the regular battalions were virtually annihilated in the fierce fighting to hold the salient. The 2nd Battalion The Royal Scots Fusiliers (2RSF), recruited from the small towns, villages and farms of Ayrshire, had recently returned from Gibraltar. It started the battle nearly 1,000 strong. These men were part of the 7th Division which had held a two-mile front for ten days against a force of two army corps that outnumbered them six to one. It was a grim baptism for what was to follow at Ypres. In the first week of the desperate battle to hold their sector of the British ring astride the Menin Road, they lost eight officers and 500 men. The enemy were beaten back and the ring held. Describing the battalion then, Captain Bruce of The Royal Scots Fusiliers who was serving in the brigade machine-gun section wrote: 'With ten days growth on their faces, caked in mud and worn out with want of sleep, it was difficult to imagine that they were the same battalion that had marched into Ypres on the 14th of the month'. There followed a lull of three days, which was then shattered by the main German attack. On 28 October, 2RSF was ordered forward to fill a gap on the Kruseick Ridge. The position was a weak one with little cover and the battalion was under constant fire. When the main attack came 2RSF was totally surrounded by vastly superior numbers of the enemy and, as orders from the Brigade Commander to retire never got through, the Fusiliers had to fight it out. They continued to do so, buying vital time, until engulfed in the German tide; when the enemy was finally held on the divisional front, on 31 October, all that remained of the battalion were two officers and thirty men.

The 2nd Battalion The Gordon Highlanders (2 Gordons) was also in the 7th Division. Like many of the battalions in the division, 2 Gordons had also been stationed overseas at the outbreak of war, in Egypt. The battalion took up its position on the right flank unaware, like everyone else, that the Germans were about to commit four fresh army corps to one of the great offensives of the war. These troops were the flower of the youth of Germany, thousands of them volunteers from the educated middle classes. They were pitted against men such as Drummer William Kenny. Kenny had enlisted in the Gordons in 1898 at the age of eighteen, and had seen action in the Boer War, as well as service in Egypt and India. In the first week of the battle, Kenny, who had already been commended for his actions in saving some machine guns and conveying urgent messages over fire-swept ground, rescued five men in succession under heavy fire. For these actions he was awarded the Victoria Cross. As a comparatively old soldier his actions were all the more remarkable. He was obviously a survivor since he served right through to the end of the war.

By 27 October the battalion had been fighting for over a week. They had suffered casualties but they were fewer than other battalions in the brigade. The men were tired but in good spirits. The Germans mounted major attacks on 29 and 30 October. In front of one platoon alone 240 enemy dead were counted. The line was held but now casualties were mounting. So far the battalion had escaped the main onslaught. The critical day was 31 October. It was at this point in the battle that 2 Gordons had their finest hour. By 2.30 p.m. the battalion had already taken part in a series of counter-attacks to re-take ground seized by the Germans. It was severely depleted and was ordered to prepare a new defensive position in the rear of the line. But the Germans again attacked and once more threatened to break through. The 2 Gordons were again ordered forward. Less than 100 strong, in a single line and with a tremendous cheer, they swept through the breaking line encouraging those who remained to join them. The Germans turned and ran. They were pursued, large numbers were killed, and most of the lost ground was re-taken. During the First Battle of Ypres the battalion lost twenty-three of its twenty-six officers and over 600 men, more than three quarters of its strength.

The Scots Guards had two operational battalions. Both were quickly mobilized for France in August 1914 and both participated in the First Battle of Ypres. The 2 Scots Guards had been stationed in the Tower of London when war broke out. Following mobilization it too joined the 7th Division and arrived in Belgium on 6 October. Two weeks later it was heavily involved in the almost continuous fighting around the village of Kruiseik, southeast of Ypres. Like the other battalions, it faced sustained German attacks in great strength which inevitably penetrated the thinly held British line. Counter-attacks had to be launched by reserves. In this ebb and flow of battle groups of men were isolated, and killed or captured. Such was the fate of much of the battalion. By 27 October it had been reduced to 472 all ranks, less than half those who had landed three weeks earlier. For the survivors this was just the prelude to the main attacks over the next four days. Again the battalion played its part in holding the line but in doing so lost a further 140 men

On 25 October the 1st Division had been deployed north of the Menin road. In this division was 1 Scots Guards, so both battalions of the regiment were fighting side by side within a few miles of each other. The 1 Scots Guards was deployed in the area of Gheluvelt. When the main German attacks started on 29 October they were in overwhelming strength and they continued the next day. On 31 October, that fateful day for these men and for - thousands of others at Ypres, Gheluvelt fell. The fighting was desperate and all the reserves were committed. Gheluvelt was re-taken. More German divisions, including the Prussian Guard, were committed. The battalion was reduced to holding a strongpoint in a ruined farmhouse near Gheluvelt Wood. The weather was atrocious with snow and rain, and glutinous mud. But the line was not broken. By 16 November the battalion had done its job but it had ceased to exist. When the roll was called, there was one officer and seventy-three other ranks able to continue.

Both battalions served in France throughout the war and participated in all the major battles. In those five years the regiment lost 111 officers and 2,730 other ranks killed, the equivalent of three battalions. During that time five Victoria Crosses were awarded to men of the regiment.

One of these went to Private James Mackenzie from Maxwelltown in Kircudbrightshire, who was serving in the 2nd Battalion Scots Guards during the Battle of Ypres. Shortly after it, on 19 December, the battalion was at Rouges Bancs to the north-west of Neuve Chapelle. During the severe fighting and under very heavy fire Mackenzie rescued a wounded man from in front of the German trenches. He was killed later that same day performing a similar act of gallantry. Another Victoria Cross was awarded to Sergeant John McAulay from Kinghorn in Fife serving in 1 Scots Guards. He had already been awarded the Distinguished Conduct Medal and twice mentioned in dispatches. On 27 November 1917 at the Battle of Cambrai he assumed command of his company when all the officers had become casualties during an attack. The objective was held, thanks to his reorganization of the company under very heavy fire. Noticing a counter-attack developing on his exposed left flank and, with the help of two men, he repulsed it, killing some fifty of the enemy. He also carried his mortally wounded company commander to a safer place, again under heavy fire. Twice he was knocked down by a bursting shell but, nothing daunted, he continued on his way, killing two Germans who tried to intercept him. McAulay survived the war and became a policeman in Glasgow.

For much of the First Battle of Ypres The Royal Scots Greys occupied trenches and fought as infantry, as did the majority of cavalry in the Cavalry Corps on the British right. Their horses were held saddled close behind the positions and, with only the minimum number of handlers to spare, this caused serious problems when they came under artillery fire. Troopers had to abandon everything they knew to adjust to trench warfare and rapidly became familiar with their bayonets, using them far more frequently than their swords. Despite their comparatively small numbers they caused large numbers of casualties among the waves of advancing Germans by the accuracy of their rifle fire. Their last action of note was at Wytschaete where C Squadron continued to pour volley after volley into the advancing infantry, long after the order had been given to withdraw. Indeed, the last two troop commanders only stopped when their commanding officer physically intervened to restrain them. The Germans were in such great strength that the Cavalry were hard pressed – but help was coming.

The 1st Battalion The London Scottish contained many professional men from the City of London. Like all the Territorial battalions, it had expected to be employed on home defence initially. If mobilized, it was to be given six months' training. The reality was to be very different. Within six weeks of the outbreak of war the battalion was in France. For the next two months it was broken up into small groups carrying out rear area duties. On 28 October it was concentrated at St Omer and then moved to Ypres in thirty-four London double-decker buses. The battalion disembarked from its strangely familiar transport on 30 October and for two days marched and countermarched. Then at 8 a.m. on 31 October, Halloween, it was ordered to support the 4 Cavalry Brigade fighting as infantry on the Wytschaete – Messines Ridge. This brigade, which included The Royal Scots Greys, was on the extreme right of the British Expeditionary Force and was astride the second of the two German axes. This second axis aimed to turn the whole Ypres salient. The battalion, the first Territorial infantry in action, advanced on to the ridge, all the time suffering casualties from the German artillery fire. By dusk it was in position and throughout the night of 31 October/1 November, it faced numerous infantry attacks in overwhelming strength and constant heavy artillery bombardments, all pitilessly lit by a full moon in cloudless skies. The battalion, among whose numbers were raw recruits, had received no further training since mobilization. They had no transport apart from three London buses that had bizarrely accompanied them to war, much to the annoyance and consternation of their civilian drivers. There was very little artillery support and no machine guns. The rifles, with which the men had been supplied, had defective magazines, which meant each round had to be loaded separately. With no sleep and very little food for the previous three days, this battalion was flung into one of the most desperate fights of the war. Its commitment with little training and inadequate equipment shows just how serious the situation was. In the battle the battalion suffered 394 casualties. Private Eric Wilkins recalls: 'I shall never forget the experience of the night of October 31, the rifle fire was terrific and farmhouses, barns etc were burning all round us.'

His brother was wounded and captured in the battle, and subsequently died of his wounds. Many others were killed, including Private James Ross, a London Scottish rugby player capped several times for Scotland. There were also many instances of bravery. At a critical stage Lance Corporal Latham led fifty men of his company in a bayonet charge against 1,000 Germans. They broke and ran. Describing the battle in a letter to his parents, Sergeant Lance Hall wrote:

Part of No 4 Section to the left was nearly overwhelmed. They shot down Germans by the hundreds. Poor Purvis was killed and then as they ran out of ammunition Latham organized a bayonet charge. He ran four men through himself. Little Conway, a boy of 18, got three and then they bolted. Little Phelps who is with Swifts in the Market got enveloped by a howling mob of dozens of Germans. From the centre came a cry 'Where is the Scottish, I want the Scottish' and little Phelps cut his way out.

Later in the same letter he goes on:

I have not had the chance to write to Auntie Kathleen to thank her for the chocolate, do you mind letting her know why.

It was actions such as this that enabled the battalion to hold its position against the German onslaught, long enough to prevent a breakthrough that would have resulted in the loss of the whole Ypres position. And Latham was but one of the London Scots.

The Regular Army fought on for the first year of the war, giving the country time to mobilize its military strength. In doing so many of its magnificent battalions were all but obliterated in this deadly conflict, but they handed down their traditions to the units which still bore their names, and their example to the new units which followed in their footsteps.

On the outbreak of war the two Territorial Force divisions of Scotland, Highland and Lowland Divisions, were immediately mobilized (the numbers, 51st and 52nd, were allocated on arrival in France). The 51st Highland Division moved at once to Bedford which was its war station in the mobilization plan. Here it remained, training in very unsuitable country, until it went to France. The arrival of some 20,000 Highlanders in the peaceful countryside of Bedfordshire caused some sensation, not to say apprehension, among the local inhabitants. So many wild Scotsmen had not been seen in the south of England since Bonnie Prince Charlie's abortive invasion of the Forty-Five. By the time they left for France in May 1915, they had won the hearts of the good people of Bedford. In a farewell letter the local Mayor said:

> The people of this Borough will never forget the visit of the Highland Division . . . I need hardly say how much we will miss you. The friendships formed during the last nine months will last for many years to come. We shall watch for news of the Division as if they were our own people.

During its time in Bedfordshire the Highland Division had not only to train, but also to re-equip. As a result of the parsimonious policy of the Government in providing equipment for the Army in peacetime, there was a scramble to find equipment on mobilization. Improvisation was the order of the day and, luckily, it is an art in which the British soldier excels. The Highlanders were no exception and they were especially creative in their efforts to find suitable chargers for their mounted officers. When 100 polo

136

ponies were sent to England as a present by the Zaminders of Madras, they were not regarded by most authorities as suitable material for infantry chargers. But the Highland Division promptly took them, with the result that their senior officers and staffs went to war on mounts that were fit, well fed and superbly agile.

Shortly after arriving in France the Highland Division was in action at Festubert, but the first offensive operation in which it was employed entirely was the Battle of the Somme in July 1916. It was here that the division lost over 3,500 officers and men. They were to be locked into this bitter trench warfare for the next two years, but in one aspect of this type of fighting, some members of the division became expert. In the ranks of the Highland Territorial battalions were a number of stalkers and gillies, and their unique experience meant they were excellent material from which to produce snipers.

In the Battle of Ancre in November 1916 the 51st Highland Division was ordered to capture the key enemy position at Beaumont Hamel. The attack was carried out by 6 Black Watch, 5 Seaforths, 7 Gordons and 8 Argylls in the front line under appalling weather conditions. It had rained so much that the country had become waterlogged, and the heavy artillery bombardment had reduced the ground to pulp. Roads and tracks were lost in mud that had the consistency of glue. Despite this the Highlanders staggered on in mud over their ankles and sometimes up to their waists. Jocks stopped to pull each other out of water-filled shell-holes in the middle of the assault, and all were weighed down by the sheer effort of trying to move one foot after another in conditions that were the stuff of nightmares. Captain Sutherland of 5 Seaforth, whose men had been largely recruited from the northern counties of Caithness and Sutherland, described what his battalion had faced:

The Germans had two years to convert the ruined village into a stronghold. The village and trenches stood high on a spur. In front of the village were three main trench systems, deep dug outs, wire entanglements, machine-gun posts and trench mortar emplacements. The buildings in the village had been strengthened with reinforced concrete, and there were subterranean passages between them. From 17 October it rained turning everything into a quagmire. The morning of 13 November was dark and misty. At 5.45 am a mine was exploded. This signalled the opening of the artillery barrage on the German front line. Then over the top went the infantry, not doubling, not even walking but wading knee deep, sometimes waist deep through a morass of sticky mud and water. Occasionally men would disappear into shell-holes. The battalion led the attack on one sector of the village. They were held up by machine-gun fire and uncut wire. Each defensive line was taken at the point of the bayonet. The battalion took 600 prisoners and suffered 292 casualties, then held for 36 hours until night of 14/15 November against repeated counterattacks.

In this, the Battle of Beaumont Hamel, the fighting reputation of the Highland Division was truly established.

In April 1917 the division confirmed its reputation in the assault on Vimy Ridge at the Battle of Arras. Together with the Canadians, their task was to capture this position of great natural strength and tactical value held by first-class troops. The attack was launched with 6 Gordons and 6 Seaforth on the right, and 4 Seaforth and 9 Royal Scots (who had joined the division since mobilization) on the left. 8 Argylls, 5 Seaforth, 4 Gordons and 7 Argylls were detailed as the second wave to take the furthest objectives. After intense fighting all objectives had been achieved and Canadians and Scots stood victorious on Vimy Ridge. One factor in this success was the raids carried out by the division beforehand to gain information and to weaken the enemy's defences. The first, on 5 March, was carried out by 300 men of 6 Gordons. It was meticulously planned and as a result achieved its objectives. Twenty-one prisoners were taken and many dugouts destroyed. Much information was gained, not least that the Bavarian Infantry Regiment facing them was a formidable adversary. Further successful raids were mounted by 8 Argylls and 6 Black Watch.

The Highland Division fought right through the rest of the

Battle of Arras, sustaining heavy losses but adding to its fine reputation. When units were not in the line they were in billets in Arras, where they made themselves as comfortable as possible, with the help of the friendly inhabitants. The massed pipe bands of the division, consisting of over 100 pipers and ninety drummers, played on several occasions to the delight of the Jocks and astonishment of the local populace.

The Third Battle of Ypres saw the Highlanders again fully committed. In the two attacks carried out by the division in this battle the Germans, in spite of the strength of their positions and of the fierce defence they had put up, were unable to stop the Jocks from reaching all their objectives. It was after this battle that the Germans announced that they considered the 51st Highland Division the most formidable division on the Western Front.

The Seaforth Highlanders had seven battalions in the battle (2, 4, 5, 6, 7, 8 and 9), The Gordon Highlanders nine (1, 2, 4, 5, 6, 7, 8/10 and 9) and The Cameron Highlanders four (1, 5, 6 and 7). More than 14,000 Highlanders fought from just these three regiments. The 7 Camerons were in support when the Germans counter-attacked on 1 August. Such was their offensive spirit that, rather than remain in the comparative safety of their own trenches, they headed up over the top to drive the Germans back. Sergeant Alexander Edwards from Lossiemouth was serving in 6 Seaforth. He was a cooper and a caddy at the golf course, and had joined up at the beginning of the war. Having located a machine gun in a wood, he led some men against it, killed the team and captured the gun. Later when a sniper was causing casualties Edwards crawled out to stalk him, and although badly wounded went on to kill him. He continued to lead his men in the battle that day and on the following day when he was wounded twice more. The citation for his Victoria Cross notes how 'his high example of coolness and determination engendered a fine fighting spirit among his men'. Sergeant Edwards was not to return to Lossiemouth as he was killed at Arras in 1918.

Despite difficulties at the top over infantry-tank cooperation, the division nevertheless fought brilliantly through the Battle of Cambrai in November 1917 and the attack on the Hindenburg

Line. In all the attacks made by its battalions, the objectives were secured, and the division advanced 14,000 yards into the enemy position, capturing some 3,500 unwounded Germans. When the German offensive was launched in March 1918 they showed that they were as good in defence as attack; the enemy were held but in doing so they suffered 5,000 casualties.

The second German offensive in April 1918 saw the Highland Division endure its most desperate ordeal in the whole course of the war. Severe casualties suffered during the first German offensive meant that replacements were required. Those who came as reinforcements were mostly young men of eighteen and nineteen with no war experience, and battalions were seriously undermanned. When the Portuguese divisions holding the line in the Battle of the Lys were overwhelmed, the division was thrown in to stem the tide. Of all the units which fought against all the odds in this battle, perhaps one could be singled out for special mention. The 4th Battalion Seaforth Highlanders, in action for five days and repeatedly attacked, did not yield an inch of ground and inflicted heavy losses on the enemy. The line was held and the battalion relieved. Its reinforcements were not so fortunate. Out of necessity these reinforcements, numbering some 200 men, had been put in the line. They had not even joined their battalion and many were only boys who had arrived in France for the first time. They had fought for many hours, holding on to their positions despite numerous attacks to drive them in. Orders to withdraw never reached them and they became isolated, but still they continued to fight on until completely surrounded and overwhelmed.

The division next moved back to the Arras area and into the line with the 15th Scottish Division on the right and 52nd Lowland Division on the left. For the first time three of Scotland's Territorial and New Army divisions were shoulder to shoulder, holding a sector of the front from the River Scarpe on the south to the Lens on the north. This accidental convergence of Jocks was not to last and, two months later, the Highland Division was moved again to the French front in Champagne where it took part in the counter-attack of July. At the end of these operations a special honour was awarded to 6 Black Watch – the French Croix de Guerre. This was in recognition by the French of the seven days of furious fighting in July 1918 during which the battalion, in spite of exhaustion and heavy losses, successfully stormed a wood heavily fortified and stubbornly defended by the enemy. The ribbon of this decoration is worn on the shoulder by Territorial officers and soldiers of The Black Watch serving in Perth to this day.

August and September 1918 found the 51st Division yet again in the Arras sector, where it distinguished itself in the capture of Greenland Hill, the main tactical feature in the enemy position. Its capture was vital to the planned British offensive that was about to unfold to its south. In his message after the battle the Commander of the Canadian Corps, under whose command the division had fought, said: 'That your division was able after all the continuous fighting this year to take and keep the strong position of Greenland Hill testifies in the strongest possible manner to the fact that the fighting qualities of the 51st are second to none in the Allied armies.'

Finally the division took part in the general offensive of October 1918 which led to victory and the German surrender.

The story of the 52nd Lowland Division, mobilized for war at the same time as its Highland sister division, is very different. Its war station was in Scotland and its role was home defence. In a very short time it was deployed with the divisional headquarters at Bridge of Allan and its brigades at Stirling, Falkirk and Dunfermline. These brigades contained the Territorial battalions of The Royal Scots, Royal Scots Fusiliers, King's Own Scottish Borderers, Cameronians, and Highland Light Infantry.

For nine months the division trained, absorbed new recruits and prepared itself to face the enemy. Like the Highlanders they need much re-equipping to become fit for operations. It had been known in April 1915 that the division was to proceed overseas, and everybody assumed it would be to France or Flanders. But on 7 May the destination was announced – Gallipoli. On top of all its other new equipment the division now received a mass of stores suitable for the Near East, including sun helmets and extra water carts. Military service wagons replaced some highly irregular transport pressed into service at the beginning of the war. The only civilian vehicles kept in the units were the strongest and lightest officers' mess carts which, being horse-drawn, turned out to be of great value afterwards in the desert. As the *History of Fifty-Second Division* records: 'It was quite usual to meet a homely milk-cart or butcher's trap being pulled round a sand hill by a wicked-looking mule, urged on by a verbal accompaniment in the unmistakable accent of some part of the Lowlands'.

On 18 May 1915 the Lowland Division began to embark for the voyage to Gallipoli, but a terrible disaster occurred to one battalion on its journey south to the port. A train carrying 500 officers and men of 7 Royal Scots crashed into a stationary train near Gretna on the Border. Before the survivors of this accident had time to realize what had happened, the north-bound London express smashed into the middle of the overturned troop train. The whole wreckage then caught fire. Three officers and 207 men died in this accident, and five officers and 219 men were injured.

By 8 June the whole division was at sea, bound for the Mediterranean in ten troopships. The units of the division were closely identified with their recruiting areas in the Lowlands. Many walks of life and all parts of the south of Scotland were represented. Professional men, clerks, mechanics, shop assistants, teachers, and students filled the ranks of 4 Royal Scots from Edinburgh and the Highland Light Infantry battalions from Glasgow. 7 Royal Scots were recruited from the coal miners of the Lothians, from Leith, Musselburgh and Dalkeith. The Cameronians came from the small farms and mines of Lanarkshire and one battalion of the regiment was raised in Glasgow. From the Borders and Galloway, Cunningham, Kyle and Carrick there were coal miners and factory hands, farmers and tradesmen in the uniform of The King's Own Scottish Borderers and The Royal Scots Fusiliers. 5 Argylls, although belonging to a Highland regiment, were part of the division, recruiting the men of Renfrewshire, with a leavening of Highlanders from the Western Isles.

Most of the Lowland Division had been landed at Gallipoli by the end of June. There they came under command of a distinguished Scottish soldier, General Sir Ian Hamilton, a Gordon Highlander who had served with his regiment on the North-West

Frontier of India and in the Egyptian Campaign. The division soon found itself under Turkish fire as it was concentrated in a small bridgehead within range of the enemy guns. However, it was not long before the Lowlanders were in the line alongside the 42nd Lancashire Division and 29th Division, and indeed mixed up with them. Their baptism of fire was so devastating that it is amazing that any military formation could survive. But survive it did.

On 28 June 1915, 156 Brigade, consisting of two battalions of Royal Scots and two battalions of Cameronians, was launched into its first attack on the strong Turkish positions dominating the British beach-head at Cape Helles. The Turks were tough fighters and strongly entrenched; the ground to be crossed entirely exposed. The odds could not have been worse.

At 11.00 a.m. the order to attack was given and, as one man, the long khaki line of Lowlanders sprang forward into the open, followed a few seconds later by the supporting waves. As they did so, a tempest of machine-gun and rifle fire burst on them, the bullets whipping up the dust into a sand storm. The Turkish shrapnel came down like hail. Men started to fall as soon as they left their trenches, but the attacking Royal Scots and Cameronians never faltered. The orders were no stopping, no firing – the bayonet was to do the job.

The first Turkish line was captured after a fierce bayonet fight, and the garrison killed or taken prisoner. Then the remnants of these battalions, 4 Royal Scots with less than sixty men, charged the second Turkish line, passing through a leaden storm which cut them down in heaps. By now every officer had been killed or wounded. The attack eventually ground to a halt, simply because there was no one left to advance. 8 Cameronians caught the full withering fire from the start of the attack, and in a few minutes nothing was left of this battalion but one officer and a few men. 7 Cameronians, the reserve battalion, fared no better when it was committed. In less than twenty-four hours these four battalions had suffered over 1,300 casualties. The dried grass and scrub over which the attack had been made caught fire; in the inferno that followed, many men lost their lives trying to save wounded comrades from further suffering or death.

143

What sort of men were these who attempted the impossible? They were not the well drilled, highly disciplined, professional soldiers of the Regular Army. They were the part-time citizen soldiers, reinforced by the ordinary man in the streets of Edinburgh, Lanark, Hamilton and Glasgow, welded together by the bonds of the regimental family. There can be few troops in the world outside the ranks of the British Army who would have attempted the task given to The Royal Scots and Cameronians, and it is not what they achieved, but the fact that they even tried, which will be remembered.

After this dreadful battle the remnants of these battalions hung on to the captured ground and repulsed enemy counter-attacks. Gallipoli has been described as a 'disease-ridden place, where myriads of pestiferous flies torment the living; where the supply of water is lamentably inadequate; where men's throats are parched by heat, dust and breathing a foul atmosphere; where the Turks have all important points ranged to a yard; and which possesses every possible military defect'. It was an appalling place but, in that curious way in which soldiers meet misfortune, the Jocks were invariably cheerful. In fact the worse the conditions, the better the morale became. In his book *Gallipoli to Baghdad*, Dr William Ewing, Chaplain to the Forces, recalls: 'The close life of the trenches, and the long strain of constant vigilance, especially after the fierce experiences of action many have come through, have to some extent affected the physique of the men. But you may walk from one end of the lines to the other and never see a gloomy face or hear a grumbling word.'

This typifies the Scottish soldier's resilience in adversity.

In the middle of July it became the turn of the men of Ayrshire, the Borders, Glasgow, and Renfrew. Attacks on the Turkish positions were made by The Royal Scots Fusiliers and King's Own Scottish Borderers of 155 Brigade, and The Highland Light Infantry and Argylls of 157 Brigade. Throughout August and September the division suffered from disease and endless enemy bombardment.

The rest of the year saw the Lowlanders stuck in the same place but under changed weather conditions. Instead of frightful heat they now had to contend with cold and rain. In October the infantry was reinforced by The Ayrshire Yeomanry and The Lanarkshire Yeomanry, fighting on their feet as infantrymen. The Ayrshire Yeomanry's first major action was the division's attack on the Turkish trenches on 15 November 1915. The assaulting parties had to cross 100 yards of open ground. Supported by mines, artillery and machine guns they did this very quickly and were able to achieve complete surprise. Then came the task of consolidation in the very shallow Turkish trenches. Torrential rain had filled them with water and movement became very difficult. The Turks tried to counter-attack but were driven off by the fierce fire of the yeomen. For the next six weeks until the withdrawal the regiment was in and out of the line supporting the, by now, very weak infantry battalions of the division in dreadful conditions of wet and cold.

The division hung on in Gallipoli until the evacuation in January, and when it departed it left behind 70 per cent of its officers and over 50 per cent of its men. During the withdrawal the Lovat Scouts fought a very successful rearguard action at Suvla Bay. The strategic objectives of the campaign and the tactics employed during it have been argued over ever since. No doubt the arguments will continue. For those who took part the futility of the campaign was very obvious. The withdrawal represented a failure to achieve objectives, appalling loss of life, and defeat. But none of the blame for this could be laid at the feet of the soldiers of the division. They could not have done more.

From Gallipoli the Lowland Division moved to Egypt where units had a chance of recovery, re-equipping and re-training. It was here that the Jocks made the acquaintance of the camel, which took over a great deal of the work from wheeled transport. Seventy were attached to each battalion. The 5HLI's history records the initial charm of the stately motion, the less endearing qualities such as the unpleasant smell and vicious temper, and then the appreciation of an animal that would carry its burden through shell-fire that horses and mules would not endure. All appealed to the Jocks.

The Lowlanders were then launched once more against the Turks. With the Australians and New Zealanders the division took a leading part in the advance across the Sinai Desert. After a long and bitter battle before Gaza it fought its way up the coast of Palestine with Allenby's army, its regiments distinguishing themselves at Jaffa and the passage of the Auja.

Three years after landing at Gallipoli the 52nd Lowland Division sailed for France to take part in the final and biggest battles on the Western Front. The division had fought in all kinds of country, and under all conditions of intense cold and heat. It had suffered grievous losses, but what was left of it was tough and hardened by long service. It arrived in France in April 1918 and took part in the Second Battle of the Somme from June to August. The bravery shown by 6th Battalion The Highland Light Infantry (6HLI) was characteristic of numerous separate unit engagements undertaken by the soldiers of the Lowlands in this battle. In the assault on the Hindenburg Line the battalion had gone into action on 24 August with twenty-three officers and 750 men. For three days they struggled to get through the dense wire obstacles and sophisticated defences, only succeeding on 27 August after continuous heavy bombardment and machine-gun fire. At the end of the battle six officers and 223 men remained. But, together with the other Lowland battalions, they had succeeded in tearing a gap nearly four miles wide in the German position. It was during this battle that Lieutenant MacIntyre of the Argylls, serving as adjutant of 6HLI, won the Victoria Cross for his bravery in attacking enemy machine-gun posts and pill-boxes.

Finally the Lowland Division took part in the Second Battle of Arras and the advance to Mons. The Battle for Moeuvres in September 1918 was particularly ferocious. The capture of Moeuvres was vital to the British. Until they had taken this fortified village they could not continue the process of rolling up the Hindenburg Line. It was, therefore, of equal importance to the Germans. During the eleven days of fighting the village was continually drenched with poison gas and bombarded by high explosive and shrapnel. By 17 September the division had taken the village. The Germans promptly counter-attacked and retook their positions. One post of 5HLI under Corporal David Hunter was cut off. With only what remained of one day's ration, their

146

iron ration, and a bottle full of water, Hunter and his six men found themselves in a small trench in the open, cut off by the German advance. They had no information and no orders but they managed to hold on for four days. During the last seventy-two hours both the German barrage and the British barrage had each passed over them twice. Several times parties of the enemy had approached the trench but each time Hunter had driven them off. It was a tale of survival, one that required sustained courage and inspirational leadership. Corporal Hunter from Dunfermline was awarded the Victoria Cross and his six men received the Distinguished Conduct Medal. The advance to Mons continued, leading to victory in November 1918.

Apart from the 51st Highland and 52nd Lowland Divisions, Scotland provided three other divisions – the 9th Scottish, 15th Scottish and 64th (2nd) Highland Divisions. The 64th Division was formed in 1914 as an entirely new formation, containing the second-line Territorial units raised in the Highlands. It remained in Britain as a training and reinforcement organization. The 9th Scottish went to France and fought along-side the 51st Highland in the Battle of Arras. The 15th Scottish also fought in France and Flanders.

The 9th and 15th Scottish Divisions had a quite different begin-ning and history from the Territorial divisions. They were raised in 1914 as New Army formations made up entirely of the new volunteers who came forward in answer to Kitchener's appeal. They were also different in that they were made up of both Highland and Lowland units, every Scottish regiment subscribing to their orders of battle. Their stories of fighting on the Western Front are very similar.

The 9th Scottish Division was the senior division of the New Armies and the first to go on active service, arriving in France on 15 May 1915. The division's first battle was at Loos in September 1915. The objective of 26 Highland Brigade included a major redoubt and the German main trench beyond it. 7 Seaforth led on the right with 5 Camerons on their left. At 6.29 a.m. on 25 September the two battalions climbed out of their trenches and formed up behind a dense screen of phosphorous smoke. Although 7 Seaforth had many casualties they succeeded in taking all their objectives. For 5 Camerons it was to be a very different story. The battalion was commanded by the Chief of Clan Cameron, Donald Cameron of Lochiel. His recruiting appeal to Highlanders in Edinburgh, Glasgow and elsewhere had been an astonishing success. Every tram in Glasgow bore a large poster reading 'Join Lochiel's Camerons' and he quickly recruited enough men to form four battalions. They included two complete companies from the Glasgow Stock Exchange, one company from Glasgow University and high schools, and many men from Glasgow police and trams. The calibre of the men prompted one brigadier general to comment ruefully, 'The finest material I have ever seen'.

The battalion had been delayed for about ten minutes by gas hanging in the front trenches. As the advance began they came under very heavy enfilade fire from their left flank. The first two lines of the battalion were almost annihilated. Yet there was no hesitation, the remainder kept going until they too had captured their objectives. When they stopped at 7.45 a.m. the battalion that had started with 820 officers and men, had been reduced to seventy-two. That evening they were relieved and returned to their original trenches. The relieving brigade had great difficulty in holding the positions that had been taken. On the morning of 27 September thirty men of 5 Camerons were sent up to re-inforce the Redoubt. Seeing that German bombers were working up a trench towards it, Corporal James Pollock from Tillicoultry in Clackmannanshire climbed out of his trench, walked along the top, and bombed the Germans from above. For all of this time he was under very heavy machine-gun fire. He maintained his position for over one hour, forcing back the German bombers, until he was severely wounded. Pollock was awarded the Victoria Cross for this action but for him it had been a long two days.

At the Battle of the Somme in July 1916 the division suffered appalling casualties yet succeeded in taking its objectives. The 27 Brigade (11 and 12 Royal Scots, 6 KOSB and 9 Cameronians) had 2,114 casualties out of 3,000 men who started the battle. Throughout the war it was often easier to take an objective than to hold it. The remnants of 26 Highland Brigade were holding

148

the village of Longueval on 18 July when they saw a force of German infantry, four times their strength, emerging from Delville Wood, the scene of earlier fighting. So unexpected was this meeting that both sides hesitated, then the Highlanders of 8 Black Watch, 7 Seaforth and 5 Camerons charged. The Germans wavered and then fled into the wood. It was an extraordinary feat by these Highlanders, reminiscent of an earlier age, but it saved Longueval.

The division took part in the offensives at Arras and Passchendale in 1917. In the great German offensives in 1918 the division fought with great distinction during its retreat to Moislains. Then it was moved to Flanders. On 16 April it was on familiar ground to the very few surviving regular soldiers – the Messines Ridge. Wytschaete fell to the Germans and 7 Seaforth was tasked to retake the village. The Highlanders' charge was irresistible and took them right through it. The division then fought off numerous German attacks but succeeded in holding the ridge. Two battalions, 12 Royal Scots and 4KOSB, were almost completely overwhelmed and destroyed. In an Army Order Sir Douglas Haig, the Commander-in-Chief, noted that: 'It was mainly due to the stubborn resistance of the 9th Division that the Army was now in a position to hold on to the present line. If the 9th Division had not held on there would have been no alternative but to retire a long way back.'

The actions were all the more remarkable because the division now consisted of many eighteen and nineteen year olds. These men took the division through the successful capture of Meteren and the final advance in 1918. On 28 September the Corps Commander reported:

The 9th Division was specifically selected to carry out the attack on the left flank of the British Second Army and to cover the right flank of the Belgian Army attack. The objectives given were rather more distant than those we have attempted hitherto in Flanders but, not only were all the objectives gained, you broke through the enemy's line to a depth of nine miles. In 1917 it took our Army over three months to get only half that distance, and at great cost. The

9th Division has done it and a great deal more in twenty-four hours.

On 15 October 11 Royal Scots attacked Hill 40, north-east of Courtrai. The enemy were surprised by the time of the attack and initially all went well. Then they came under machine-gun fire from a wood to their left flank. This held them up albeit only for a few minutes; but it was enough for two enemy machine-gun groups on Hill 40 to recover and open fire. The battalion took cover. Seeing the situation Corporal Roland Elcock rushed forward with his Lewis gun, killed the two-man crew of one gun, then turned it on the other gun and knocked it out also. The attack was then able to continue and Hill 40 was taken. Elcock, who had earlier been awarded the Military Medal, received the Victoria Cross.

The other New Army division, 15th Scottish Division, was assembled together as a division at Aldershot in September 1914, and went to France in July 1915. Its first big battle was also at Loos in September of that year, where it too suffered 6,000 casualties. It was here that 6th Battalion The Cameron High-landers (6 Camerons) fought with conspicuous bravery and determination. Led by Lieutenant Colonel Angus Douglas-Hamilton, himself a reservist, the Camerons charged the enemy four times when the troops on the right and left had fallen back. On the last charge Douglas-Hamilton led the fifty men who remained and he was killed at their head. For his bravery and leadership he was posthumously awarded the Victoria Cross, the first of six won by the division in the war. The village of Loos had been successfully captured and part of Hill 70 taken.

The story of 7th and 8th Battalions The King's Own Scottish Borderers (7 and 8 KOSB) is special. These battalions had been raised and trained together and, in many respects, they acted as one. On 25 September 1915, 7 KOSB was to lead the assault with the 8 in support. They had breakfast at 3.30 a.m. then moved to the forward trenches. The coal mining landscape was a cheerless sight at any time. It had been raining heavily and although the downpour had stopped before the attack, the ground was heavy and very slippery. There was also a thick ground mist that morning, compounded by gas and smoke. Because of a change in the direction of the wind some of the British gas drifted back in a dense cloud about two feet off the ground. Men already smothered in their smoke helmets had to make a choice: become half choked through want of air or wholly choked trying to get it. At 6.30 a.m., heavily laden, they had to climb out of the fire trench and get through the wire. It was a critical moment when even the bravest would have faltered. Forty year old Piper Daniel Laidlaw from Little Swinton in Berwickshire stepped up to the task and consequently his place in Scottish military history. He described his action thus:

> On Saturday morning we got orders to raid the German trenches. At 6.30 the bugles sounded the advance and I got over the parapet with Lieutenant Young. I at once got the pipes going and the laddies gave a cheer as they started off for the enemy's lines. As soon as they showed themselves over the trench top they began to fall fast, but they never wavered, but dashed straight on as I played the old air they all knew 'Blue Bonnets over the Border'. I ran forward with them piping for all I knew, and just as we were getting near the German lines I was wounded by shrapnel in the left ankle and leg. I was too excited to feel the pain just then, but scrambled along as best I could. I changed my tune to 'The Standard on the Braes o'Mar', a grand tune for charging on. I kept on piping and piping and hobbling after the laddies until I could go no farther, and then seeing that the boys had won the position I began to get back as best I could to our own trenches.

For this conspicuous bravery, Laidlaw was awarded the Victoria Cross.

Although wounded that morning, Laidlaw, like the rest of his surviving comrades, would have remembered all too well what happened next. The battalion swept forward to Hill 70, advancing nearly two miles before being stopped. That night they dug in, and again it rained very heavily. They held the position until relieved on 27 September. Their success was achieved at the cost of 675 casualties out of 970 all ranks. This included all twenty of the officers, the maximum allowed to participate. All but three were casualties in the first 1,000 yards.

The other regiments had shown equal determination to take their objectives, and had paid as heavy a price. The 9th Battalion The Black Watch (9 Black Watch) lost all but two of its twenty-two officers in the Battle of Loos, 25 – 27 September 1915. In total the battalion suffered over 680 casualties in the battle and their dead lay so thick in front of the enemy wire that it was difficult to step between them. In spite of this, the survivors had swept on into the German position. The diary of Lieutenant Colonel J. Stewart DSO, who was second in command of 9 Black Watch, describes the battalion's part in the battle:

Just after 6.30 (on 25 September) our 1st line left the parapet. Alas casualties began directly we showed ourselves. The enemy's machine guns got to work and our men dropped right and left, but they never wavered for a second, on they went line after line, into and over the German front line trenches, on into the second and third lines and bang into Loos itself, nothing stopped them.

There was no sensational charging, they kept in touch in distance and marched solidly across the hay field.

Eric Wilson passed down, hit by a bullet through the shoulder, our only officer left. We then heard that all the remainder had either been killed or wounded crossing the field.

Arrived at Hill 70 at about 10 am.

Just think, the remnants of a battalion who went into action over 900 strong to be relieved by half a company. We got our men together, and found that there were about ninety-five and two officers including myself.

9 Black Watch were relieved by 21st Division at 1.30 a.m. on 26 September but their respite was not to be a long one. Unable to hold

the German counter-attack 21st Division broke, so the battalion was again called forward and held the line until 28 September.

9 Black Watch in 15th Division was only one of six battalions from the regiment that took part in this battle. They included both regular battalions; 2nd Battalion The Black Watch also had heavy casualties, over 350 in total. 4 Black Watch, the Territorial battalion from Dundee, was in the same brigade as 2 Black Watch and fought side by side with it. Four hundred and forty officers and men of 4 Black Watch took part in the attack. Of these 249 were killed or wounded. Sixty-seven Dundee men were killed in the battle.

The 15th Scottish Division went on to fight throughout the Battle of the Somme in August and September 1916 and at Arras in April 1917. All the battalions suffered enormous losses at Arras, and by the end of the battle the division was down to half its strength. Some battalions, like the Gordons, were down to less than 100 officers and men.

In the Allied offensive of 1917 the division took part in the attack on Frezenberg in the Battle of Ypres. Again the Scottish regiments suffered heavily, and although reinforcements arrived from home there was neither the time nor the opportunity to absorb them properly. By now a large part of the officers and men had had little training and even less experience. But, as so often in this war, they had no choice but to learn very quickly. They fought through the German offensive of 1918, at the Marne, and the final advance to victory. Through it all these 'new' battalions conducted themselves in accordance with the highest traditions of the Scottish regiments to which they belonged.

Not all the Territorial and New Army battalions served in the Scottish divisions. The 15th and 16th Battalions of The Royal Scots were in 34th Division. Their finest hour came in the advance to Contalmaison during the Battle of the Somme on 1 July 1916. These two battalions, recruited almost entirely from Edinburgh and boasting an unusual number of professional footballers, were on the right of the division. Their line of attack was overlooked by the village of La Boiselle. The village and its fortifications extended into no man's land like a peninsula. From it machine guns could enfilade the attack and they were to do so with devastating effect.

The German position had three lines of trenches and was bristling with barbed wire that had been erected five feet high and more than thirty yards deep. The British artillery began shelling on 25 June and there was to be no respite for six days. On 1 July the bombardment rose to a crescendo and the very earth shook. At 7.30 a.m. on that breathless and blue skied morning the battalions went over the top with bayonets fixed. The artillery fire had been ineffective against both German guns and the machine guns, and many men were killed before they were clear of the trenches. Despite this, the battalions continued to advance, heads bowed against the hail of bullets and shrapnel as if it were a deluge of rain. They secured their first objectives, including Wood Alley, vital to the attack of the division on their right. Lieutenant Colonel Sir George McCrae, like all commanding officers in the brigade, had been forbidden to lead his battalion, 16 Royal Scots, when it attacked. He went forward that evening and coordinated the operations of the two now exhausted battalions and others. Positions were consolidated then extended around Wood Alley and a series of counter-attacks were beaten off. By dawn on 3 July the position was completely secured and that evening, they were finally relieved. Some men had penetrated much further. 2nd Lieutenant George Russell of 16 Royal Scots was a twenty year old banking apprentice from Howe Street in Edinburgh. He had enlisted in the battalion as a private and had only recently been commissioned. He led a group of thirty men right into Contalmaison itself, the final objective, and was shot in the head and killed within 200 yards of the church. All told, it had been an incredible achievement but one for which these Edinburgh battalions paid a very high price. 15 Royal Scots lost eighteen officers and 610 men, and 16 Royal Scots lost twelve officers and 460 men. One thousand and eighty soldiers from one regiment gone in thirty-six hours.

5 Cameronians was also at the Battle of the Somme in 33rd Division. The battalion detrained at Amiens on 9 July 1916 with 1,067 all ranks. On the evening of 19 July it was ordered to take High Wood. They formed up at about midnight with 1 Cameronians on their left. By 3.25 a.m. the battalion was within fifty yards of the wood. Enemy artillery fire – mainly shrapnel – had been very heavy and it had turned High Wood into a blazing

inferno of uprooted trees and wire. Into this went the battalion taking out dug-outs and machine-gun posts one by one. Having lost the wood the Germans immediately counter-attacked and the suddenness of their retaliation almost overwhelmed the two Cameronian battalions. But the Jocks held on for four days and nights until relieved on 20 July. In this battle, the battalion lost thirty-six out of forty officers and over 700 men.

12th Battalion the Argyll and Sutherland Highlanders (12 Argylls) was formed in Stirling in September 1915. In 1918, while most of the Army was fighting in France, this battalion was serving in 26th Division in Macedonia where, in September, it took part in the Battle of Doiran. Several unsuccessful attacks had already been made against the very strong Bulgarian positions on the hills above Doiran. On 19 September a further attack was mounted by 77 Brigade consisting of 12 Argylls, 8 RSF and 11 Cameronians. The battalions had the Greeks on their left and the French on their right. The Scots were able to advance, 12 Argylls even reaching its objective but, as neither flank made any progress, they did so against the full brunt of concentrated artillery fire and the fire of some seventy-five machine guns. The order to withdraw never reached the battalion and they pulled back only on the order of their commanding officer. The battalion started the battle over 500 strong. When it returned only three officers and 147 other ranks were present. 12 Argylls was awarded the Croix de Guerre for its actions that day. The citation states:

It boldly attacked an enemy position formidably organized and defended by concentrated machine gun fire. It stormed the position, killed or made prisoners all its defenders, and heroically resisted counter-attacks in spite of the loss of its Commanding Officer (who fell mortally wounded), and of the heavy casualties which it suffered.

Private George Wilson, a Lewis gunner, was awarded the Military Medal for his part in the battle. His finger was blown off but he continued to fire his gun until it was destroyed by artillery fire and he was severely wounded a second time.

Scotland also produced seven regiments of yeomanry – The Ayrshire Yeomanry, The Lothians and Border Horse, The Lanarkshire Yeomanry, The Lovat Scouts, The Queen's Own Royal Glasgow Yeomanry, The Fife and Forfar Yeomanry and Scottish Horse. All the regiments began the war as divisional or corps cavalry and were mainly used for reconnaissance or flank protection. Parts of the Royal Glasgow Yeomanry and Lothians and Border Horse continued in this role for much of the war. However, as the need for cavalry reduced and the demand for infantry increased, many were re-roled as infantry units and later became battalions of Scottish infantry regiments. Almost all the Scottish yeomanry regiments served as infantry in Gallipoli, the Scottish Horse alone providing a brigade of three regiments. After Gallipoli, The Ayrshire and Lanarkshire Yeomanry, who fought together in 52nd Division, were joined together in 1917 into 12th (Ayrshire and Lanarkshire Yeomanry) Battalion The Royal Scots Fusiliers and sent to 31st Division in France. On 30 October 1918, in almost the last battle of the war, Sergeant Thomas Caldwell from Carluke in Lanarkshire was in command of a Lewis gun section engaged in clearing a farm house when they came under intense fire from another farm. Caldwell was awarded the Victoria Cross for single-handedly capturing this enemy position and taking eighteen prisoners.

No story of the Scottish soldiers' part in the First World War would be complete without a mention of the part played by those Scots who joined up in Scottish regiments formed outside Scotland. Many thousands of exiled Scotsmen served in The London Scottish, The Liverpool Scottish and The Tyneside Scottish.

Few women served anywhere near the front line in the First World War. Those that did had to overcome the resistance of the military establishment. Two that deserve particular mention are Grace Smith and Muriel Thompson, both from Aberdeen. Smith joined the First Aid Nursing Yeomanry (FANY) in 1907 and, by the outbreak of war, was one of its senior members. In September 1914 she persuaded the War Office to grant her a military pass and was soon driving a Belgian ambulance in Antwerp picking up the wounded from the trenches under fire. Captured by the Germans, she then escaped and was back in charge of a small team of FANYs at Calais during the First Battle of Ypres. During the first five days 8,000 wounded were evacuated through the port. Rows of wounded, sick and dying men lay patiently waiting for places on the few hospital ships. It was icy cold, there were not enough blankets, there was nothing to eat, and there was no one to care for them. They did the best they could. She and her team were then sent to an old school that had been taken over by the Belgians as a makeshift hospital. Again the conditions were dreadful. They stayed there for two years undertaking the hardest and most revolting tasks with little equipment. For her service Smith was decorated by the Belgians with the Order of Leopold and by the French with the Croix de Guerre.

Thompson joined the FANY as a driver in 1915. On 29 March she was personally decorated by King Albert for evacuating Belgian soldiers under fire. On 18 May 1918 her team was called to Arques following a bombing raid. The target included an ammunition depot. Further bombing raids were in progress and shells were exploding. Despite this Thompson and her team continued to tend to the casualties. For this action Thompson was awarded both the Military Medal and the Croix de Guerre.

Nor should we forget the immense number of Scottish kinsmen who served in Australian, New Zealand, South African and Canadian forces. The 1st Canadian Division included battalions from several Canadian Scottish regiments. Amongst them were The Royal Highlanders, 48th Highlanders, and Canadian Scottish (a composite battalion made up from four Canadian Scottish regiments). More were to come with further Canadian divisions. They included the Seaforth Highlanders of Canada and Cameron Highlanders of Canada. In the Second Battle of Ypres, in the early dawn of 23 April 1915 The Royal Highlanders were attacked. A great cloud of gas drifted down upon their lines, and through the yellow mist came the steady thresh of the German shells. As Arthur Conan Doyle wrote in his history of the campaign:

The ordeal seemed mechanical and inhuman, such an ordeal as flesh and blood can hardly be expected to bear. Yet with remarkable constancy The Royal Highlanders and their neighbours, The 48th Highlanders, held on to their positions,

157

though the trenches were filled with choking and gasping men. The German advance was blown back by rifle fire, even if the fingers which pulled the triggers were already stiffening in death. No soldiers in the world could have done more finely than these volunteers.

Regiments of Scots came from all over the empire to fight in France, the Middle East and in other campaigns. At the Battle of Amiens in August 1918 there were seventeen Canadian and five Australian Scottish units.

When orders arrived that hostilities would cease at 11 a.m. on 11 November 1918, the 4th Battalion The Royal Scots Fusiliers stood on the same battle ground where 1st Battalion The Royal Scots Fusiliers had fired the first shots of the war on 23 August 1914. It had been four long and dreadful years in the military history of Scotland.

The exact number of Scots who gave their lives in the war is not known. Many lie in military cemeteries close to where they fell. They are remembered on war memorials in towns and villages throughout the land and there can have been few families and communities in Scotland that did not suffer the pain of loss. It is estimated that near on 740,000 British men lost their lives in the First World War. The names of more than 148,000 Scots are commemorated in the Scottish National War Memorial in Edinburgh Castle.

Chapter Fourteen

Second World War

With the end of the First World War came demobilization and reduction of the forces to their peacetime establishment. The Regular Army returned to its pre-war size and shape in many of its old stations. The Territorial Force was disbanded, although the Territorial Army was raised in 1920 in its place and based in local drill halls up and down the country. The New Army formations and units disappeared.

A new force had, however, been born during the great conflict of 1914–18 which was to continue and grow in the subsequent years. Early in the war the Royal Flying Corps had been raised and one of its earliest members was a Royal Scots Fusilier, Hugh Trenchard. He later became the first commander and 'father' of the Royal Air Force, and ultimately Marshal of the Royal Air Force Lord Trenchard. To this Scottish officer must go the credit for not only having the foresight and imagination to fashion and develop the Air Force as a separate service but also the determination to do it in the face of much opposition. Following his lead, very large numbers of young Scotsmen joined the Royal Air Force on its formation, and they have continued to do so ever since.

Apart from contributing handsomely to the regular Royal Air Force, Scotland mobilized its three auxiliary air squadrons on the outbreak of war. These 'Territorials of the Air', based on the three major cities, were 602 (City of Glasgow) Squadron; 603 (City of Edinburgh) Squadron and 612 (County of Aberdeen) Squadron.

602 Squadron operating Spitfires fought in the Battle of Britain

and later, after D-Day, crossed to France and later moved forward into Belgium.

It was aircraft of 603 Squadron, also operating Spitfires, that shot down the first Luftwaffe raiders over Britain on 16 October 1939, during an attack on the Forth Bridge and the Rosyth Naval Dockyard. The squadron then moved south to fight in the Battle of Britain. In 1942 it was en route to the Middle East on the United States aircraft carrier *Wasp* when the squadron was diverted to Malta and fought in the battle for its defence.

612 Squadron operated first Ansons, then Whitleys before finally converting to Wellingtons. It conducted coastal patrols from bases in Iceland, Northern Ireland and the south of England. Operational areas included the Western Approaches, the Bay of Biscay and the Dutch Coast.

As in the First World War, the Royal Navy was not short of Scotsmen. From Scotland's long coastline came many recruits, some with proven experience of the sea in the deep water trawlers which went out from Aberdeen, Peterhead and Fraserburgh; and others who had lived with the sea in their soul on the many islands of Orkney, Shetland, and the Hebrides. One such Aberdeen trawler became HMT *Clythness*. Amongst its crew was Leading Seaman 'Jock' Cargill from Gourdon in Kincardineshire. He received the Distinguished Service Medal for his courage in fighting a serious fire in the engine room when the ship was on patrol; an action made more remarkable by a man who had been awarded the Military Medal while fighting with The Black Watch in the trenches in the First World War, and the Titanic Medal for his part in rescuing survivors from that ship. Every ship in the Royal Navy had its share of Scots and they served in every theatre.

The years between the wars saw the Regular battalions of the Scottish regiments taking their part in keeping the King's Peace around the world wherever the British flag flew. One of these was 2nd Battalion The Highland Light Infantry, deployed after the Great War to Russia (Archangel) in 1919, then to Ireland. By 1920 it was stationed in Egypt from where it took part in campaigns in Palestine, keeping law and order between Jews and Arabs, and in Turkey between the Turks and Greeks. In 1924 it was in India where it stayed until 1938. This service included internal security duties such as the Cawnpore riots and a record period of six years on the North-West Frontier. The battalion was in Palestine when war broke out.

Many other battalions have similar stories. They were short of equipment but their soldiers were well trained and had considerable operational experience. This was to prove invaluable.

The Territorials, back in their home locations, did their drills and attended their annual training camps. The economic blizzard which struck the nation in the 1930s kept the military purse-strings tight but, as before in similar bleak periods, Scotland kept its regiments and their traditions lived on, albeit in units sometimes at greatly reduced strength. Mechanization had arrived and Jocks whose fathers had learnt to handle horses, mules and sometimes camels, were now learning to control motor transport. They must have been hazardous times on the roads of Scotland.

The two Territorial divisions, 51st Highland and 52nd Lowland, re-formed in Scotland after 1918 and suffered like the rest of the Army from lack of funds and new equipment, but they certainly never lacked volunteers. Moreover, the standard of keenness and efficiency was very high. The battles of the 1914–18 war had given these divisions a tremendous confidence in themselves, and the individual units had fighting records of which they could be proud. Recruits to carry on these traditions were not hard to find in the Highlands and the Lowlands, and regimental associations which kept the old regulars and volunteers together did much to keep the torch aflame. The volunteer in the Territorial battalion and the regular coming from the same regimental area had become cemented into a strong regimental family. As a result, the ties of each regiment with the civilian population of their own community became even stronger.

On the outbreak of the Second World War all the regular units of Scottish regiments were again mobilized in the regular divisions in which they had been serving at home and abroad. Thereafter they served in every theatre of war from Singapore to France, and in every type of formation – British and Indian, armoured and infantry. Wherever they went they added fresh laurels to their names.

The Royal Scots Greys fought in the Middle East, North Africa,

Italy, and north-west Europe, and always with that same élan and spirit which marked the regiment at Waterloo and Balaklava. It was a Royal Scots Grey, Lieutenant Colonel Geoffrey Keyes MC, aged only twenty-four, who typified this spirit by his daring raid on Rommel's headquarters in North Africa.

11th Scottish Commando was one of the special units formed early in the war. In June 1941 many in the unit were killed in an attack on a Vichy held bridge in southern Lebanon. Those who survived found their way into the Middle East Commando. It was they, under the command of Geoffrey Keyes, who were landed by submarine on the evening of 13 September 1941 on the coast of Libya on a secret mission – to kill Rommel. After numerous problems they reached their target on the night of 17/18 September and launched the attack. The information they had been given proved to be inaccurate and Rommel was not there. The explosives were also defective. Nevertheless Keyes decided to continue. During the attack he and many others were killed. Keyes was posthumously awarded the Victoria Cross.

On 4 September 1943 The Royal Scots Greys left North Africa in sixty landing craft, equipped with new Sherman tanks, to take part in the invasion of Italy. Sergeant Bill Cross was among them. He had joined the regiment in 1934 at the age of fifteen from the General Gordon School and was snapped up as a trumpeter. His career with the regiment followed some remarkable twists of fortune. The Royal Scots Greys were stationed at Hounslow in 1937 but shortly afterwards moved to Palestine, with their 700 grey horses, where the regiment was employed on internal security operations. In 1941 they found themselves at war with the Vichy French in Syria. Cross was taken prisoner and later, after he had re-joined the regiment, had the indignity to have to take part in a guard of honour for Marshal Petain. The regiment was then converted to tanks, the last cavalry regiment to be converted, and moved to Egypt where it fought throughout the North African campaign. Cross was wounded shortly after Sidi Barrani and lost sight in one eye. But he was back with his third tank named 'The Fighting Haggis' in time for Salerno.

After a week at sea in open landing craft, the regiment arrived off the Italian coast early on the morning of 9 September 1943. Its task was to provide support for 56th London Division in its first battle. In the run in to the beach the landing craft carrying Cross and his troop was hit about 150 yards from the shore. He recalls what happened next:

We'd been a bit seasick on the way over but it wasn't too bad, living in The Flying Haggis was almost like living in a caravan. We were all old sweats by that time and because we'd already been blooded in the desert, we knew what to expect. It wasn't like that for everyone. Many of the infantry were in their first fight. As we came in to the beach, we had the tank engines running and everyone was inside. These were aircraft engines, mind, with 90 octane petrol. It was like sitting in a bomb. The German shell blew the side off the boat and everyone had to get out fast. There's not much room for storage inside a Sherman so all our kit was packed up on the outside. We lost everything when we had to swim for shore. When we got to the beach we were still under fire from an 88mm gun in a farmhouse. We picked up what we could from men on the beach and got on with it. Everyone was fighting by then, even the cooks. It was complete chaos, and we were very angry. By the end of it, I think the squadron only had three tanks able to fight.

'A' and 'C' Squadrons had landed in the first wave and were quickly in action against a well-prepared German defence that included 16 Panzer Division. They were delayed by boggy ground in which eight tanks got temporarily stuck. However, they were freed in time to engage the German tanks that were seriously impeding the infantry's advance. In one action 'A' Squadron engaged the enemy from a flank. Sergeant McMeekin, from Stranraer, took out four tanks in rapid succession. This was despite his tank being hit and the lap gunner being killed. For this action he was awarded the Military Medal.

For a week the regiment was split up supporting the infantry forward in close country against strong opposition. There were numerous examples of skill and courage. The report of 'C' Squadron leader on one such action is typical:

We set off and had only gone about half a mile when Sergeant Munro got his first Mk IV Special at 800 yards across two fields and before the Germans had seen us. His next shot was also a long one – another Mk IV Special, this time at about 1000 yards. After that things happened very fast. At almost point blank range, Sergeant Munro brewed up a half-track towing an anti-tank gun, knocked out a 75mm anti-tank gun and its crew, and then a smaller one, I think a 37mm, all in quick succession.

For this Sergeant Munro was also awarded the Military Medal. The regiment suffered nearly 100 casualties, a high proportion of its tank crews. Providing support to all three brigades and keeping up the momentum of the advance required detached squadrons and troops to operate for extended periods. Tanks had to be maintained in the rare pauses in the battle, so everyone was short of sleep. It was a testing time particularly for the junior commanders. The regiment rose to the challenge and played a major part in the defeat of the Germans at Salerno.

After Italy the regiment fought in north-west Europe. Cross was with them when they linked up with the Russians on the Baltic coast. So ended the remarkable odyssey of this regiment's war. Cross remains convinced that it was the history and traditions of his family regiment, and the humour of its many Glaswegian soldiers, that underpinned it and held it together in good times and bad.

The Scots Guards served throughout the war in Guards formations. The two battalions of the regiment were increased to five, and they fought in Norway, North Africa, Italy and north-west Europe. Their discipline and courage were recognized by the additional Battle Honours of Tobruk, Medenine, Anzio, and Rhineland.

The story of the 3rd Battalion Scots Guards deserves special mention. Having been reformed in 1940 it was told a year later, much to everyone's surprise, that it would be converted to tanks. Some had reservations that Scots Guardsmen would not adapt easily to armoured warfare because they were too tall for the cramped conditions inside a tank or because they would not be able to master its technicalities. In the event they adapted exceptionally well. Everyone understood the support requirements of the infantry and all ranks were always determined to provide the closest possible support until an objective was secured.

This was certainly proved during the Battle of Caumont in July 1944. Five miles south of the town lies a great ridge running east to west. The Germans hoped to hinge their left flank on the ridge allowing an orderly withdrawal. If the Allies could take the ridge the hinge would be broken, and they would be able to break out of the Normandy beach head and overrun the whole of Northern France. 3 Scots Guards, as part of 6 Guards Tank Brigade, supported 15th (Scottish) Division throughout the battle, specifically the 2nd (reconstituted after Malaya/Singapore) Battalion The Argyll and Sutherland Highlanders. The ground they faced could not have been more daunting. The approach was over the Bocage farm land, small arable fields surrounded by high banks built of earth and stones and topped by thick hedges. This was interspersed with solid stone farmhouses and hamlets that made excellent strong points. The ridge itself was a defensive position of great strength and provided excellent long range observation of an attack. Amongst the defenders was a unit of 2nd Panzer Division with 88-mm self propelled guns, *Jagd Panthers*, against which the Churchill tanks were powerless. For two days the battalion fought its way forward with the infantry. Inside each tank the crew had to contend with the appalling noise and the smell. This was all made worse by the terrain. Each tank had to climb repeatedly up near vertical banks, exposing its vulnerable underside to short-range anti-tank weapons. Following the briefest of pauses on the top, the tank dropped down on the other side with a bone-wrenching crash. Guardsman Richard Kershaw was a wireless operator/gunner. He had enlisted as a boy soldier before the war, joined the battalion on its formation, and served with it throughout the long years of preparation, conversion to tanks and intensive training for the invasion of Europe. Deep inside his tank he had little knowledge of events outside apart from what he could glean from the wireless. He remembers the seemingly endless firing of the tank's main armament and machine gun throughout the many hours of the battle, with the rattle of the enemy's machine-gun fire on the tank's hull providing a constant reminder of the bigger threat from their 88-mm guns. The battalion fully deserved all the praise it was given for its part in this critical battle.

In the war against Japan, the losses suffered by regular battalions were considerable. 2nd Battalion The Argyll and Sutherland Highlanders fought a magnificent rearguard action against the Japanese before the fall of Singapore. The battalion had arrived in August 1939 and was part of the mobile reserve in Singapore. At that time military theory held that the jungle was impassable. The Highlanders took a different view and, for two years, the battalion focused their training on jungle fighting in small groups, honing their resourcefulness, speed of reaction and aggression. It was as well that they did so.

When the Japanese landed the battalion was moved north. But it was not until 17 December 1941 that they first met the enemy – at Tiri-Karangan. By then everyone was very tired. The rain was torrential and they faced an enemy in overwhelming strength with total air superiority. The subsequent story is one of a series of tactical successes due to the training and determination of all ranks, but the battalion was continuously outflanked and forced to withdraw southwards down the peninsula. The end came at the Battle of the Slim River on 13 January when a bridge demolition failed. Japanese tanks got across the river and broke up the battalion. Reduced to 250 men, 2 Argylls were the last to cross the causeway into Singapore on the morning of 1 February with pipers playing. Privates John Bennett and Douglas Stewart, who had been cut off from the main body, were to remain in the jungle for the next four years helping to instruct the guerrillas. Bennett relates becoming isolated from the remnants of the battalion, his capture by the guerrillas, then being used by them as an instructor. His four year story is one of extraordinary courage and determination. He emerged from the jungle near Segamat in September 1945. The Highlanders set an example of how to fight the Japanese in the jungle that others were to follow. The cost was very high. 2 Argylls started with 880 all ranks. Two hundred and twenty-three men were killed and at least 162 men were wounded; 187 men subsequently died in prisoner of war camps. These grim statistics, more than half the battalion, take no account of the suffering of all but a few who became prisoners during the retreat and when Singapore fell.

Men of the Royal Scots captured in the fall of Hong Kong, and 2 Gordons, captured with the Argylls in the fall of Singapore, were also to suffer appalling hardship and brutality as prisoners of the Japanese. The courage and resilience of all these men in the face of such adversity was so extraordinary as to be beyond comprehension. In any story of the Scottish soldier they should not be forgotten.

The 1st Battalion Cameron Highlanders and 1st Battalion Seaforth Highlanders both played a part in the defeat of the Japanese in Burma. 1 Camerons was evacuated from France in 1940 and spent the next two years on home defence in the United Kingdom. It was sent overseas in 1942 to India and joined 2nd Division. It was not, however, until April 1944 that the battalion was deployed to Burma where the immediate task was to relieve Imphal and Kohima, both threatened by the Japanese.

1 Camerons was focused initially on Kohima most of which was in Japanese hands. On 14 April, in a well planned attack, the battalion took a hill reported to be held by an enemy company. Unbeknown to the Camerons it had been reinforced by a further company during the night before the attack. However, so well organized and determined was the attack, with highly effective artillery support, that those Japanese who were not killed broke and fled – an unusual event in the Burma campaign. Then, on the night of 2 May, the Camerons took the key point in the Japanese defence, Point 5120.   To take this high feature the battalion had to infiltrate through the Japanese positions. Everyone was very lightly equipped and wearing gym shoes. At midnight they set off by companies in single file, climbing forever upwards. It was a dry night with the stars providing just enough light for those in the column to maintain contact as they moved in complete silence through the Japanese positions. When dawn came they found themselves on the summit with views across the Kohima valley. Opposition had been minimal. The Japanese had been completely surprised. But they soon recovered and counter-attacked, infiltrating through gaps in the defences. Ground was lost and

retaken but the battalion managed to hold on to much of the feature. In the middle of the month it rained, torrential rain. One diary records: 'Living in water-logged slit trenches, their clothes soaked, their boots sodden, their food when they get it often cold and mushy'. The wounded faced a three-hour journey on stretchers each carried by four local tribesmen along narrow muddy paths with precipitous climbs and descents. The battalion had 283 men killed and wounded in the battle but Kohima was relieved and by 31 May the Japanese had withdrawn. The taking of Point 5120 was a remarkable achievement against an enemy who was rarely caught off guard, and reflected the discipline and training of the battalion. Company Sergeant Major Thomas (Tommy) Cook from Leith was awarded the Distinguished Conduct Medal and Lance Corporal David Hendry from Edinburgh the Military Medal for their bravery during the battle. Hendry led his men in a bayonet charge of the Japanese weapon pits, accounting for several Japanese with his own bayonet.

1 Seaforth arrived in Burma two years before the Camerons in March 1942 and served in 23rd Indian Division. For the next two and a half years the battalion was employed on long range patrol operations up to the River Chindwin. Operating in small groups they built up the intelligence on this huge area and the Japanese within it which was to be invaluable when major offensive operations were mounted in 1944. But the difficulties of such operations were enormous. Groups operated many miles from any support with maps that were very sketchy; they were always wet and in the monsoon season the ground was flooded which made the going even more difficult. Malaria was rife and there were no antidotes. Only the very best could have survived the conditions but the Seaforth did much more.

Meanwhile other battalions were fighting in the Middle East. After Palestine 2nd Battalion The Highland Light Infantry (2 HLI) served in Egypt and Eritrea in 1940 and Iraq and Cyprus in 1941. By 1942 it was serving in the Western Desert in 5th (Indian) Division. Dick Bromley Gardner, then the Carrier Platoon commander, recalls a very experienced and closely-knit battalion with many long serving soldiers. After so many years in India and the Middle East the vocabulary of the Glaswegians

168

contained numerous words of other languages. In the last week of May 1942 the battalion was deployed in a defensive box south-east of Tobruk. On the afternoon of 4 June they received orders for the offensive next day known as the Battle for the Cauldron. The battalion's objective was to capture and hold a low ridge called Bir El Tamar, believed to be held by about 100 German tanks with some infantry in support. The attack would be made during the night of 5 June. 2 HLI, lorried infantry, would be supported by a squadron of I Tanks (Matildas). They would lead, followed by the 2 HLI carriers and lorries. Once they were on the ridge an armoured brigade would join them to destroy the remaining enemy tanks and defeat any counter-attack. It seemed straightforward but it was not to be. 2 HLI started to move forward to the start line at 8.30 p.m. It was a dark night with no moon, compounded by the dust of so many vehicles. Navigation, always difficult in vehicles in the desert, became even more so but they managed to form up and cross the start line on time at 3 a.m. Although the Germans may not have been able to see their attackers, they could certainly hear them and defensive fire was immediate and heavy – artillery, tank and machine-gun fire. The battalion's supporting tanks got split up and separated from their infantry. As the sky began to lighten they found themselves just short of their objective but, after a short pause to regroup, continued the assault on foot. By 5.30 a.m. the battalion had taken its objective and began to dig in to the very hard ground, all the time under heavy fire. The Germans were mainly on the reverse slope of the ridge and were quick to counter-attack. 2 HLI should by now have been joined by the armoured brigade. Some tanks could be seen to their rear but did not come to their support. There were few radios and communication was mainly by runner. Messages to the tanks went unheeded. The battalion was unsupported when faced by the German armoured counter-attacks – in the open, with no tanks and very little artillery. Time and time again it was overrun yet managed to reform and fight it out as best it could. That evening the Brigade Commander ordered the battalion to withdraw and, after dark, in ones and twos, men made their way back. One platoon was trapped in a position from which no withdrawal was possible. Surrender was out of the question. Private Campbell was one of six men last seen charging a tank; he was firing his Bren gun from the hip. The carrier platoon played a vital role in maintaining communication with the companies and in evacuating wounded, all the time under direct and indirect fire against which they had almost no protection.

The battalion lost ten officers and 221 men that day. The regimental history laconically records that this was comparatively low considering it was a major battle lasting nine days, and goes on to compare it with losses in one day at Assaye (418), Toulouse (141) and Festubert (382). Many more would have been lost had it not been for the actions of men such as Sergeant Hugh Gateley. When his company withdrew he stayed behind and brought in the wounded and stragglers, all the time under heavy fire. At one stage, and with complete disregard for his own safety, he stood on a sangar waving his balmoral to direct men back. When his company commander and another officer were wounded he crossed 1,000 yards of open ground, all the time under machine-gun fire, to report the situation, and returned to the position with the stretcher bearers to evacuate them. Later that day the truck he was travelling in was hit by shellfire and several men were wounded. Disregarding his own wound he ensured the others were evacuated before reporting again for duty. For his actions that day Gateley was awarded the Distinguished Conduct Medal. It is difficult to exaggerate the appalling situation in which the battalion found itself. Others failed but these men did not; they achieved what was asked of them despite the lack of support, a tribute to an excellent battalion and the soldiers in it. Their problems were still not over. The depleted battalion remained intact but again the German tanks attacked. For four days they, along with the rest of the Army, were pushed back before the Germans were eventually held.

After the Western Desert 2 HLI was withdrawn to Lebanon and converted to a ski battalion. From there the battalion was sent to the island of Vis in the Adriatic where its new skills would have been of little use in its raids on the Dalmatian Coast. But later it served in Italy, Greece and Austria.

The story of the Royal Scots Fusiliers in 1942 was perhaps the strangest of all. Concerned about a possible Japanese invasion of Vichy-held Madagascar, the loss of the naval base at Diego Suarez and the consequent threat to the sea route around the Cape, a British force was dispatched to capture the island. In this force were both 1st and 2nd Battalions of The Royal Scots Fusiliers (RSF). They sailed from Liverpool in March 1942. David Coutts, a platoon commander in 2 RSF, recalls that no one knew their destination for most of the voyage; in fact the battalion was en route to Burma. The decision to send the force to Madagascar was taken much later and the men only knew where they were going when they reached South Africa. The landings on 5 May achieved total surprise which was fortunate as there had been no time for any training or rehearsals. Coutts's first objective was a lighthouse from which artillery fire was being directed at the ships. For a time they were held up when the French officers rolled grenades down the stairs but eventually they and their Senegalese soldiers surrendered. The French had adopted a static defensive line covering Antsirane. This was taken after two days of fighting and the force went on to take the rest of the island. The two RSF battalions lost thirty-nine killed and over ninety wounded in this brief campaign.

The 2 RSF later took part in the Italian campaign in the 5th Division. The Germans made maximum use of the numerous rivers to hold or delay the Allied advance. One such river flowing west into the Mediterranean was the Garigliano. It is fast flowing and not fordable in a flood plain which is up to two miles wide. Near its mouth there are dangerous currents. Seasonal rains had compounded the problems. In the assault over the river the 2 RSF was on the left of the division, on the coast. The plan was for the battalion to be embarked in DUKWs, amphibious wheeled vehicles, and landed on the beaches some 2,000 yards behind the German lines. Their objective was Monte Argento. After dark on 17 January the battalion embarked and set off. Problems started almost immediately. Many of the American crewed DUKWs lost direction in the darkness; a combination of poor navigation, the current, and the difficulty of seeing the guiding lights. As the remaining DUKWs approached the beach they were betrayed by the phosphoresence of the sea and came under heavy shellfire. For those who made it to the beach and tried to move forward the confused situation was made worse when they found themselves in a large minefield. Peter Nicholson, then a platoon commander, recalls how his platoon of twenty-eight men had eleven casualties in the minefield. Eventually a lane was cleared through it by the battalion's pioneers using their bayonets. They pressed on despite very heavy artillery and mortar fire. Dawn on 18 January found the battalion held up by wire on a rocky ridge with little cover some 800 yards from the top of Monte Argento. There they remained all day. One company that had gone astray in the landing had many casualties when they were caught in the open trying to re-join. Following up this success the Germans counter-attacked. The numbers were small but many of the Fusiliers' weapons were blocked by sand. One attack was eventually halted when Fusilier Bonner fired a PIAT at the German officer leading it and killed him.

The Brigade Commander ordered the Fusiliers to 'capture the mountain by next morning at all costs'. For the first time in the operation the battalion was given artillery support. By 1 a.m. the mountain was in their hands although the fighting continued for several days. In the two days of 17 and 18 January the battalion had suffered 140 casualties. Training, courage and leadership undoubtedly played their part but so did the stubborn determination of these men – reminiscent of the qualities shown at Inkerman nearly a century earlier.

The 51st Highland Division was the first of the Scottish Territorial formations to go into action, and the beginning of 1940 saw it once more in France. Shortly after its arrival there, three of its Territorial battalions were replaced by three regular battalions of the same regiments – The Black Watch, Seaforth and Gordons – who had already had experience in the Maginot Line.

When the British Expeditionary Force (BEF) fell back towards the Channel ports before the German onslaught in May 1940, the Highland Division was called upon to make its greatest sacrifice. It had fought a rearguard action down the French coast, protecting the left flank of the French army. The bulk of the Division finally made a last stand at St Valéry-en-Caux. With the rest of the BEF evacuated from Dunkirk, and the French army having surrendered, they were completely on their own. At first there was a chance that ships would be able to come to St Valéry to take them off, but this proved impossible. The German Panzers under Rommel pressed ever closer until, their ammunition exhausted, the remains of the Highland Division were overwhelmed. On 12 June General Fortune, the Divisional Commander, ordered what was left of his units to surrender, and with them he went into captivity.

The sense of loss in Scotland was very great and there was not a village in the Highlands and Islands which did not mourn for some soldier of this division.

But the 51st Highland Division was not dead. The 9th Scottish Division which had been recruited from the Highlands as a second line formation, was renamed the 51st Highland Division, and all its brigades took on the old numbers. The lost regular battalions of The Black Watch, Seaforth and Gordons were raised again.

The new Highland Division reformed in the north-east of Scotland with its headquarters at Aberlour in Banffshire, and brigades at Dingwall, Elgin and Banchory. In April 1942 it moved south to Aldershot, and in June it embarked on a nine week voyage round Africa to Egypt, calling in at South Africa where it got a rapturous welcome.

From then on its story is the story of the 8th Army. At El Alamein on 23 October 1942 the battalions of the new division went into the attack for the first time, advancing with all the determination and courage of their predecessors of the old 51st, and their forefathers at Waterloo and the Alma. With each battalion marched its pipers playing the music which has stirred the blood of Scotsmen from the days of the 'Fiery Cross'.

Three battalions of The Black Watch (1st, 5th and 7th) served in the division and took part in the battle that was to be the turning point of the war in North Africa. 5 Black Watch spent the day before the battle under cover in camouflaged trenches. Private Sid Lunn had joined the battalion when it was at Forres in 1941. He recalls the events leading up to the battle; the move to the south of England; the journey on the troopship *Empress of Australia* in 1942, packed like sardines, everyone thinking they were going to India; the stop in Cape Town and the hospitality they received there; their arrival in Egypt in August 1942; acclimatization and intensive training at Mena camp near the Pyramids and later in the forward areas; and then digging the trenches from which the attack was to be launched.

Once it was dark they moved forward of the British wire. Then the artillery barrage started. The battalion's diary records simply that the noise was deafening. Then at 10 p.m. the advance began with bayonets fixed. It was a clear moonlit night dimmed by smoke but further lit up by Monty's moon, the reflection of searchlights. The company pipers could just be heard playing above the noise of the battle. Piper Duncan McIntyre from Glasgow, reputed to be the quietest man in the battalion, was hit during the assault but continued to play until he was hit again and killed. Lunn remembers crossing the British minefields with some misgivings – they had been briefed that they were mainly anti-tank mines. Then there was an area of level ground before it rose to the German positions on the ridge. As the ground began to rise Lunn was thinking what he would do when he met his first German – would he fire his rifle or use the bayonet? He was not to find out because he was hit in the back by mortar shrapnel. Others kept going, the German wire was cut and just after midnight the battalion had taken all its objectives. They should then have been joined by their tank support but this took much longer than expected to move through the gaps in the minefields. So they had to face counter-attacks by German tanks without them; many of the battalion's 250 casualties occurred at this stage in the battle. Lunn returned to the battalion in time for the invasion of Sicily to find that his platoon sergeant, section commander and half his platoon had been killed that day – many friends who had made the long journey from Forres with him.

Private Johnny Cleveley who was attached to the medical officer, was killed two days later. One section had secured a captured 88-mm gun but several men had been wounded in subsequent fighting. Cleveley was told to wait until darkness to go forward and treat them. He clearly had other ideas and was seen walking forward to the gun in broad daylight, with his first aid pack on his shoulder. Others called on him to wait but he did not stop or waiver. He was last seen bending down to someone near the gun but was then lost to sight. When he was found he had been killed by a sniper's bullet. Each of the three wounded men had been treated and they survived their wounds.

The 5th Battalion Cameron Highlanders was also at El Alamein. Its story is very similar. Part of the battalion was responsible for securing and controlling the gaps in the minefields. During the attack, Cameron pipers could be heard playing *The Inverness Gathering* as they led their companies forward. 'B' Company's piper was Donald Macpherson from Skye. After they had captured their objective, the Company Commander, hearing the ferocious cries of The Black Watch coming up behind them, and fearful that they might be mistaken for the enemy, instructed Macpherson to play *The Pibroch of Donuil Dubh*. It may have been the last time he played – as soon as The Black Watch had passed through, Macpherson was killed by a direct hit on his trench.

5 Camerons was then withdrawn for the next phase of the battle. In the early hours of 2 November the attack started, supported by a murderous barrage. All the companies reached their objectives and when morning came saw a sight long awaited, the British tanks coming through the minefields. During the battle Lance Corporal James Mightens from Glasgow engaged a German tank single handed, shooting the commander dead and then hurling a grenade in to the turret and killing the crew. For this he received the Military Medal.

The incidents of valour are too many to record here – sufficient to say that the Highlanders captured all their objectives at the point of the bayonet. When news of the great victory reached Scotland, messages of congratulations flooded in to the division from crofts and castles, from workers and clan chiefs. Every man and woman in the land experienced a surge of pride, and a feeling that St Valéry had been avenged.

After Alamein the Highland Division took a prominent part in the advance to Tripoli, and afterwards – while advancing 1,850 miles across the desert from Alamein – fought in all the battles until the final surrender of the Germans at Tunis. A typical engagement was the attack upon the enemy position at the Wadi

Akarit on 6 April 1943, when 7 Argylls was given the task of breaking in and forming a bridgehead for the other battalions of its brigade. The Germans had constructed a very strong defensive position in the Tunisian hills protected by minefields and deep anti-tank ditches. Led by their indomitable Commanding Officer, Lieutenant Colonel Lorne Campbell, 7 Argylls crossed the start line at 5.15 a.m. The wadi and anti-tank ditches were scaled with rope ladders. All the objectives were taken; the battalion then hung on in spite of fierce enemy counter-attacks. Sergeant Dell Porchetta recalled: 'Twelve hours of solid fighting, much of it with the bayonet'. Colonel Campbell's record says: 'the most memorable feature of the battle was the shelling and sniping which began soon after we had crossed the start line and continued almost without a break from dawn to nightfall with an intensity which we had never encountered before and, in my case, since'. The battalion captured 700 prisoners and much enemy equipment. One hundred and fifty-nine Argylls were killed or wounded in the battle. For his bravery that day Lorne Campbell was awarded the Victoria Cross.

The Highland Division next saw service in Sicily in July and August 1943. By the end of that campaign, within a year of its arrival in Egypt, it had suffered some 7,000 casualties. It was here that the division said farewell to General Douglas Wimberley, who had commanded it for over two years. This great Cameron Highlander had trained it and led it in battle all through North Africa and Sicily, and a great deal of the credit for its outstanding performance must be his.

During the campaign in Sicily two battalions of The Gordon Highlanders (1st and 5th/7th) fought side by side in the battle to take the town of Sferro. On the night of 16 July 1943 the advance started into the Catanian plain with 1 Gordons leading. With the carrier platoon in front, they advanced rapidly and, finding the opposition from the Hermann Goering Division light, they quickly seized their intermediate objective. When 5/7 Gordons' turn to lead came they too advanced with skill and determination. German resistance, though, was strengthening. By now the battalion was beyond artillery support and had almost no knowledge of the enemy's positions. Nevertheless the momentum was maintained and both battalions took turns to lead the advance.

Just before midnight on 19 July, 1 and 5/7 Gordons attacked Sferro fighting side by side. The approach involved crossing an unexpectedly deep gully, flat stubble fields devoid of cover, and then a railway line with burning railway wagons on it. When they finally reached the town it proved to be much larger than expected. There was inevitable confusion but by dawn on 20 July the town had been taken, whereupon the Germans mounted a determined counter-attack. This was beaten off, albeit with great difficulty. One company was almost surrounded and the story is told that a German officer called on them to surrender. He did so three times. There was no reply. Then suddenly from what remained of a trench, now only a crack in the ground, came a Buchan voice: 'Surrender? Surrender! Well you come and get us, you frightened fucker!' Needless to say, there was no surrender and the battalions dug in to hold the town. Their task was made even more unpleasant and difficult by the heat, the flies and the impossibility of moving in daylight without attracting fire. This was a soldiers' battle throughout, typified by Private John Hyland of 1 Gordons whose task was to gather information and give early warning of enemy raids. He did so by lying out all day in the blazing heat, about 200 yards in front of the main enemy position, disguised as a stook. For this act of courage and resourcefulness he was awarded an immediate Military Medal. Similarly Private Alexander Wilkie, from Coatbridge, of 5/7 Gordons was in a platoon providing flank protection when it came under very heavy fire from an armoured vehicle. There were several casualties and the platoon became scattered. Twice Wilkie went back under heavy fire to collect men and equipment left behind. He too was awarded the Military Medal.

From Sicily this battle-hardened division came home to take part in the north-west Europe campaign. On the morning of 2 September 1944 the Highlanders entered St Valéry just over four years after they had left, and the Divisional Commander deployed the brigades in the same locations in which they had fought in 1940. The old 51st Highland Division had indeed been avenged.

From there the Highland Division shared in all the hard fighting which brought about the collapse of Hitler's armies in the west – through the Ardennes, and the Reichswald Forest, to ultimate victory on 8 May.

On 23 March 1945, 51st Highland Division (with 15th Scottish Division) spearheaded the British attack across the River Rhine. One of the leading battalions of 51st Division was The Highland Light Infantry of Canada, under command for the first phase of the operation. On 24 March it attacked the town of Speldrop. Although by now the Germans knew that their cause was hopeless, they fought on to the bitter end. They still held a number of strong points, and were supported by tanks, while the approaches to the town were so well covered by anti-tank weapons that the British tanks could not enter. The battalion had the most desperate fight all night and suffered many casualties before they could clear the town. They were then sent into the attack on the town of Bienen, and again succeeded, this time after two other battalions had failed. By the time it came out of action on 27 March the battalion was severely depleted. There were numerous examples of bravery. Sergeant Frederick Jarman, although wounded, cleared a strong point in Bienen – for this action he was awarded the Military Medal.

Of all the divisions of the British Army, none had a more remarkable history in the Second World War than the 52nd Lowland Division. Its story could not be more different from that of its sister division from the Highlands. Trained for mountain warfare, it found itself fighting on the flattest bit of Europe, and below sea level. Its movements were so extraordinarily confusing that the enemy might well have thought some cunning master plan of deception and misdirection was in play. In fact there was a significant element of deliberate deception, since under Plan Fortitude North, the aim was to convince Hitler that an invasion of Norway was imminent, thereby keeping German divisions deployed there that might otherwise have been used elsewhere.

Mobilized in September 1939 in Scotland, the division moved down to Dorset in April 1940, and on 7 June sailed for France on its first strange adventure. It went as part of a British force to try to stiffen French resistance, a last desperate bid to keep the French in the war. They were sailing towards France just as the rest of the British Expeditionary Force were leaving it.

The division which landed at Cherbourg had one brigade of Royal Scots from Edinburgh, and King's Own Scottish Borderers from the Borders, one brigade of Royal Scots Fusiliers from Ayrshire and Cameronians from Lanarkshire, and one brigade of Highland Light Infantry from Glasgow. It also had the 5th Argylls as divisional troops. All its units were Territorial Army, and remained so to the end of the war.

The attempt to support the French proved hopeless. France collapsed, and the 52nd Lowland Division was nearly lost like 51st Highland at St Valéry. But, by no less a miracle than that at Dunkirk, the bulk of the Lowland Division was evacuated safely from Cherbourg in the teeth of the enemy. The 5 KOSB, who played a prominent part in trying to stem the tide of the enemy advance, were the last battalion in action. As it turned out, they were the last British battalion to fight on French soil until the Normandy invasion three years later.

Back in Britain the Lowland Division first concentrated in the Home Counties, and then moved to Scotland where it deployed in a home defence role against possible sea, and – later – airborne invasion. In April 1942 it moved into the Cairngorms and started to train as a mountain division, and for attack rather than defence. This was the turn in the tide, and from then on all the emphasis was on offensive operations.

The Lowlanders thus became the Army's expert mountaineers, trained to ski, use mule transport, and live and operate in conditions of intense cold and high altitude. It certainly fooled the enemy, whose intelligence was convinced it was bound for Norway, and valuable troops were contained in that country as a result. Then the division was dispatched to the area of Loch Fyne, where it switched to training in combined operations, with all the new techniques of assault landings to be learned. If this further confused the opposition, the next move must have caused them to tear their hair. In July 1944 the over-trained Lowland Division became an airborne division, and changed all its training and equipment once again.

In the end the division did none of these things. It went to war as an ordinary infantry division, and into action below sea level. It is difficult to know who could have been more surprised – the Germans or the Jocks. At least for the latter, it put an end to waiting. After years of intensive preparation for practically every possible role, they were at last to fight the enemy.

Troops of the Lowland Division, having crossed the Channel, went into action for the first time up the axis Eindhoven – Nijmegen, as part of 30 Corps, in the great battle towards Arnhem. Then in October 1944 the whole Division was launched in an attack across the nine mile wide estuary of the Scheldt to capture the Walcheren peninsula in southern Holland. This involved not only the use of assault craft and amphibians to cross the river, but also to conduct the offensive operations on the other side, as most of Walcheren was now under water as a result of the destruction of the dykes by the Royal Air Force. Borderers, Scots Fusiliers, Cameronians, Royal Scots, and Highland Light Infantry all fought with distinction in this most successful operation.

The 1st Battalion The Glasgow Highlanders, a Territorial unit of the HLI, particularly distinguished themselves in the capture of the Causeway which connects Walcheren to South Beveland. The Royal Scots and King's Own Scottish Borderers encountered fierce resistance in clearing the ancient town of Flushing, and the mountain artillery found itself using its 3.7-inch pack guns in the streets. The guns were dismantled to get them inside buildings, and then reassembled in upstairs rooms to fire out of the windows, one of the few methods of fighting not foreseen during the long training in the Cairngorms.

At 9.30 p.m. on 2 November 7/9 Royal Scots was ordered to assault the Grand Hotel Britannia in Flushing. This objective was to be achieved by dawn the following day. The hotel stood on a wide embankment which formed part of the sea wall west of the town. The Royal Air Force had blown a hole in the sea wall so the ground on the land side was flooded. Intelligence indicated that the water was around two feet deep and the hotel was held by fifty men. The attack was to start at 3.15 a.m. The battalion came under heavy fire long before this. The seemingly innocent hotel had in fact been turned into a fortress of cunningly constructed trenches, pill boxes and gun emplacements. As it contained the headquarters of Flushing Garrison, there were not fifty but 600 men in the position. The water into which the Royal Scots plunged was much deeper than expected, sometimes as much as five feet deep, swirling at up to five knots and icy cold. Many men, particularly those who had been wounded, were swept away. Navigation was very difficult on a dark night with the moon obscured by cloud. Men held on to each other to keep their footing, thankful for their Mae West life jackets. Step by step they fought their way forward, clearing positions as they went. Casualties mounted. There was much confusion, particularly when the hotel caught fire. Everyone was wet and cold. Many officers were killed or wounded, including the commanding officer who went forward to take direct control of the battle. This infuriated those nearby and provoked an instant and ferocious assault. The end came at dawn when a large bunker was taken. In it was the commander of Flushing Garrison and he promptly surrendered. This battalion, trained in mountain warfare, met the enemy for the first time on the flat plains of a flooded island in a gruelling and relentless battle. They succeeded in taking the hotel despite the appalling difficulties. It was a tribute to their training in the Highland winters and an ability to make do in the face of extreme hardship. The battalion went on to take Middleburg, and German resistance in Walcheren ceased.

After a spell in the line on the lower Maas, the Lowlanders took part in the winter offensive through southern Holland in appalling weather. The division was the first British formation to establish its headquarters on German territory, and then drove on to the Rhine at Wessel, battled its way across that river, and then across the Dortmund-Ems canal, to final victory at Bremen.

Like its predecessor in the First World War, the 15th Scottish Division was created on the outbreak of war and new battalions raised for it. But this time it was formed by duplicating 52nd Lowland Division, each unit of that division reproducing itself. Nevertheless it soon took on the traditions and spirit of its ancestor.

Starting life scattered all over the Lowlands, the new division moved first to the Borders in the winter of 1939, and then to the south of England in 1940. From then until it crossed the Channel in the Normandy invasion, it trained in various parts of the country. The organization of the division changed as battalions came and left. When it landed in Normandy its battalions covered the whole range of Scottish regiments – Royal Scots, Scots Fusiliers, King's Own Scottish Borderers, Cameronians, and Highland Light Infantry from the Lowlands and the middle belt of the country, Seaforth, Gordons, and Argylls from the north and west Highlands. Part of its armoured support was provided by 3 Scots Guards mounted in Churchill tanks.

In its first great battle on the River Odon it distinguished itself against Hitler's crack Panzer divisions, taking the full weight of the German attacks on the Normandy beachhead. From then it took a leading part in the break-out from the beachhead, the advance into Belgium, the Rhineland battle, the crossing of the Rhine, the advance to the Elbe and the final victorious advance to the Baltic.

To it fell the honour of spearheading the assault over the three great river obstacles in the path to ultimate victory – the Seine, the Rhine, and the Elbe. The crossing of the Elbe presented particular problems. The river at the time in April 1945 was 300 yards or more wide and with a current of one and a half knots. The south side of the river from which the assault would have to be mounted was flat, marshy and intersected by canals. There were only two approach roads suitable for the amphibious vehicles and bridging. On the enemy side the ground was very different. It rose steeply from the river bank some 100 feet, almost like a cliff. The Germans on its top could view the preparations for many miles. It was a daunting prospect. Success would need all the experience and expertise of the division. Fifty minutes after midnight on 25 April 1945 the artillery bombardment started. The leading battalions would have had a grandstand view from their waiting areas. Across the river only a few hundred yards away the enemy positions were being pounded. Although it was the middle of the night the beams of searchlights reflected off the cloud provided an artificial daylight. At 2 a.m. the first wave that included 8 Royal Scots and 6 RSF entered the water in their Buffaloes. Within minutes they were across. The artillery fire lifted to the top of the cliff and the two battalions began the ascent. The division had secured another crossing of a major river, a tribute to meticulous planning, teamwork and discipline. It was a record second to none in front line performance.

Apart from the purely Scottish formations, and the regular battalions serving with other formations already mentioned, there were Territorial battalions like the 1st Battalion The London Scottish for much of the time in 56th Division, 8 Argylls who served in 78th Division and 7 KOSB from Dumfriesshire and Galloway who were in the Airborne Forces at Arnhem.

The 1st Battalion The London Scottish went overseas in 1942 and joined the Persia and Iraq Force in Kirkuk. It then fought in the Sicily campaign. On 2 February 1944 the battalion embarked in American landing ships for the sixteen hour journey to Anzio where it arrived at critical time in the battle. 3 Infantry Brigade, holding a salient, had been cut off. 6 Gordons, who had been holding the neck, had lost three of their four companies. The situation was critical. 1 London Scottish mounted its attack on 4 February in heavy rain that gave way to squalls of sleet and snow. It retook the vital ground, and re-established contact with 3 Brigade, allowing it to be withdrawn. Above all it gained valuable time at a pivotal moment. During the attack excellent fire support had been provided by the Scottish Horse (Yeomanry medium gunners). For the next month the battalion was used to plug gaps in the defence or to retake ground lost to the Germans. Split up into company groups or smaller, they fought on for a month. They were short of everything, including sleep, and few men had any idea of what was happening. It was a time of dogged perseverance. By the time the battalion was withdrawn from the beachhead on 11 March, 483 were dead, wounded and missing. In his book *The Battalion* Keith Spooner, then a signaller, recalls:

The battalion we had known, war-created upon its Territorial Army base, was largely gone now. It would in due course be brought up to strength again, but for continuity of spirit would depend on those who were left. Many of the best

183

had gone now, as is so sadly and often the case, for they are the ones less heedful of self-preservation.

For 7th Battalion The King's Own Scottish Borderers (7 KOSB), the war lasted only nine days. Arnhem was the first and last battle of the war for this Territorial Army battalion from Galloway. By the end of 1943 7 KOSB was an air landing battalion in 1st Airborne Division. They took off from airfields on the Wiltshire/Gloucestershire Border at about 10 a.m. on 17 September 1944. A continuous chain of flimsy gliders packed with men and equipment trundled slowly eastwards. One of these men was nineteen year old Private Howard Lee. He and his platoon had made three flights during training, all in one afternoon. He remembers vividly the roller coaster effect caused by the towing aircraft's slipstream. But in training the glider pilots could manoeuvre. On route to Arnhem the number of aircraft made this impossible. Everyone had breakfast before take-off but it was not long before some were very sick. The four hour flight seemed endless. At the key moment the tow was slipped; for those inside there was then silence as the sound of the tug engines faded and the glider descended. In training the glider had circled, now it was going straight down. Lee says it was like floating on the air. Everyone was silent as they prepared for the landing. Then came a tremendous crash. Lee's glider was one of the first to land. As it hit the ground the front wheel collapsed so the tail rose up. Following his training Lee was first out with the Bren gun to give covering fire. He fell nearly ten feet and with all the weight he was carrying was lucky not to break his legs. But all the men of his platoon landed safely. Of the fifty-six gliders carrying the battalion, forty-six made it to the landing site. By 1.30 p.m. the battalion, 740 strong, had landed and was being assembled, assisted by a piper, Lance Corporal Willie Ford from Selkirk playing *Blue Bonnets*. Their task was to secure the dropping and landing zones for the follow-on forces. From the outset they faced heavy German counter-attacks. By 20 September the battalion had been reduced to 270 men but still the attacks continued. Much of the fighting was close quarter street fighting by men who had had no sleep, little food and continuous action for a week, often against SS troops with artillery support. There was no respite. For a further forty-eight hours this continued. Private Howard Lee recalls,

> My platoon was covering the cross roads near the White House. Most of us were behind a wall. We had made a hole in it for the Bren gun. We could hear the German armour moving about. Sergeant Rae (from Gretna Green in Dumfriesshire) was killed by a sniper. He was our platoon sergeant and had really looked after us. We were all very hungry so he had gone out under fire and brought back food from one of the containers. We were also very tired having had no sleep since we landed. Corporal William McDade (from Glasgow) relieved me on the Bren gun and I went back to a slit trench to get some sleep. Just a minute later a mortar bomb hit the wall in front of our position and instantly killed Corporal McDade and Lance Corporal Sidney Cross. I was covered in earth but uninjured.

During the withdrawal to the river Private Lee was wounded in the leg by a grenade and captured. He was held in Stalag 11B initially and then worked in a lead mine until the end of the war. When the battalion was finally withdrawn across the river, only four officers and seventy-two men remained. The remainder of the battalion had been killed or captured, many of those taken prisoner being wounded.

Scotland's six Yeomanry regiments made a significant contribution in the war. The Lothians and Border Horse, and Fife and Forfar Yeomanry, each provided two tank regiments. They fought in France with the BEF, in the Western Desert, Italy and northwest Europe in armoured and infantry formations. 1 Fife and Forfar Yeomanry was re-equipped with Crocodile flame-throwing tanks in 1944 and supported 51st Highland Division in Holland. The Ayrshire Yeomanry provided two field artillery regiments. 152 (Ayrshire Yeomanry) Field Regiment supported 6th Armoured Division in Italy. 151 (Ayrshire Yeomanry) Field Regiment supported 11th Armoured Division. It landed in Normandy on 13 June 1944. The OP parties of The Ayrshire Yeomanry were in Sherman tanks and the guns towed 25-pounders. Also in the 11th Armoured Division was 2 Regiment of The Fife and Forfar Yeomanry. The key day for The Ayrshire Yeomanry was 26 June, when 15th Scottish and 11th Armoured Divisions attacked Cheux. In the advance the reconnaissance parties, riding in jeeps, became caught up in the many tank battles fought at close range. No sooner had the guns taken up their new positions than they were called to help fight off counter-attacks coming from one of the flanks. The guns were in almost continuous action that day, hindered throughout by heavy rain and German snipers around and sometimes even within the gun areas.

The Scottish Horse provided two medium artillery regiments in Italy and north-west Europe. The Queen's Own Royal Glasgow Yeomanry (QORGY) provided two anti-tank regiments. The 64 (QORGY) Anti-Tank Regiment fought with 78th Division in North Africa, Sicily and Italy. On 3 October 1943 the division attacked the town of Termoli on Italy's east coast. The town was initially taken by two commandos but it was essential that the division linked up with them before the Germans counter-attacked. To do this they had to cross the River Biferno over which all the bridges had been destroyed. Eight of QORGY's anti-tank guns were got across the river by raft and were pushed forward with a reconnaissance squadron. They were expecting to be faced by a German parachute battalion but when the counter-attack came they soon realized they were facing a Panzer division. All the crew of one anti-tank gun except one became casualties. The reconnaissance squadron that the yeomen were supporting was ordered to withdraw. The remaining gunner refused to leave his gun and, helped by a trooper from the squadron, covered the withdrawal by firing round after round at the approaching tanks. Both men were killed but the enemy withdrew.

On mobilization the role of The Lovat Scouts was 'mounted Scouts, to provide mobile troops for reconnaissance and protection'. In May 1940 they were sent to occupy the Faroe Islands, a Danish possession of strategic importance in the North Atlantic. Later, in 1944–45, they fought in the Italian campaign, specializing in mountain patrolling and long range operations behind enemy lines. They ended the war in Salonika – by coincidence where they finished the First World War.

There were also a large number of Scots who joined the Commandos and the Airborne Forces as individuals. Amongst them were Lord Lovat, Chief of Clan Fraser of Lovat, who became a commando leader, and General Urquhart who commanded the Airborne Division at Arnhem. Many, like Brigadier Bernard Fergusson, later Lord Ballantrae, fought in the jungle with the Chindits through the Burma campaign, under one of the greatest Scottish soldiers of all time, Field Marshal Lord Wavell.

Wavell was commissioned into the Black Watch and rose to be Commander-in-Chief Middle East and later of India. However, despite reaching high rank he retained two qualities; a real affection for the soldiers he commanded, in particular the Jocks of his own regiment; and an ability to think the unthinkable.

As in the First World War large numbers of Scots from the Dominions fought side by side with the regiments from Scotland. The 48th Highlanders, affiliated to The Gordon Highlanders, mobilized and arrived in the United Kingdom on 17 December 1940 as part of 1st Canadian Division. It fought in Sicily and Italy. In the Battle of the Gothic Line on 16 September 1944, 48th Highlanders was ordered to break through to Rimini some five miles ahead. Much of the ground to be covered was flat and open and they were faced with very heavy machine-gun, tank and artillery fire. Nevertheless the battalion fought its way forward, only to be driven back into a gully. Next day it resumed the attack. One company was deluged by fire but persevered to its objective. Sergeant Stuart Montgomery led the charge to complete the task and threw seventeen grenades to clear a strongpoint before personally repelling a counter-attack. All the time the battalion was under well directed artillery fire from an observation post on the high ground to a flank. A month later Sergeant Ernest Smith of the Seaforth Highlanders of Canada was awarded the Victoria Cross for repelling an attack by German tanks and infantry armed only with a PIAT and Tommy gun.

With the surrender of Germany and then Japan, the Second World War came to an end. Jocks had participated in every campaign and had made a major contribution to the nation's victory on land, sea and in the air. Many men had not seen their homes for six years. Once again victory had been at a high price. More than 57,500 Scots are commemorated on the National War Memorial. Many more Scots had been wounded or spent years in captivity.

Chapter Fifteen

1945–2004

Returning to normal took some time and defence became dominated by two apparently conflicting requirements. Uncertain political situations in the world, movements for independence in colonial territories and the advent of the Cold War all necessitated the maintenance of large conventional forces. Conscription had to be retained to man the substantial forces abroad until the end of 1962. There was also a need to have a small mobile army in support of the nuclear weapon, with which it was hoped to deter a potential enemy similarly armed. Later there came a realization that, if both sides had nuclear weapons, they cancelled each other out; substantial conventional forces would also be required for deterrence. The difficulty was in paying for both.

The inevitable result was that the British armed forces became over-stretched. The Royal Navy and Royal Air Force suffered severe cuts during the twenty-five years after the end of Hitler's war and, as a result, whole commitments had to be scrapped or reduced. The Army also suffered severe cuts but as is so often the case, many of its commitments could not be so easily given up. The inevitable outcome was a reduction in the number of soldiers detailed to do each job. This is a form of military deception in which the United Kingdom has often indulged. It is difficult and dangerous to operate, and hard on the soldiers concerned. It is only possible if the troops are high class in every way.

Luckily for Britain its troops were first class, and there was none better than the Jocks. Scottish regiments have given ample proof of their quality by their part in establishing or maintaining an uneasy peace around the world since 1945. In the peacekeeping tasks during the last days of the Indian Empire, in Palestine, the Caribbean, Cyprus and the African dependencies, they had to show tact and forbearance in addition to the normal soldierly qualities. The hunting down of Communist rebels in the jungles of Malaya, the vicious Mau Mau in Kenya and the conventional wars in Korea, Borneo and the Arabian Peninsula required sustained endurance and determination. All the campaigns (sixteen of which were recognized with a clasp to the General Service Medal) called for the same bravery and resilience shown by their predecessors through the centuries. In all of these operations the Scottish regiments served with distinction, contributing to the birth and survival of many nations. Their courage, sensitivity and humour sustained them through countless days and nights of jungle, desert and urban operations.

Private Peter Gilmour was the lead scout of his platoon in 1st Battalion The Gordon Highlanders during their operations against the communist rebels in Malaya in 1951. During the battalion's period of intense jungle operations he was involved in seven contacts with the enemy. In April he was on sentry when two bandits appeared down the track towards him. He stepped out onto the track, shot and killed one bandit who was about to throw a grenade and immediately gave chase to the other. Two months later he was one of a group that surprised five bandits. In the ensuing action four were killed and one wounded. Later that same day he was confronted by a further bandit; he opened fire and wounded him, and then gave chase. The other incidents were of a similar nature and reflected his consistent and calculated bravery and his determination to close with the enemy at every opportunity. For his actions he was awarded the Military Medal.

Two specific operations will long be remembered. In December 1962 1st Battalion Queen's Own Highlanders, then stationed in Singapore, was deployed to Brunei to re-capture the town of Seria after its vital oilfields had been seized by rebels. In a brilliantly planned and executed operation this was achieved without a single casualty to the battalion or to those taken hostage. Many of the rebels were killed or captured. The re-occupation of the Crater district of Aden by 1st Battalion The Argyll and Sutherland Highlanders on 3 July 1967 was another outstanding operation. Under their charismatic leader, Colonel Colin Mitchell from Argyllshire, the battalion overwhelmed the enemy by sheer determination and fighting spirit, and then, by their very presence, went on to dominate the district.

The Korean War is still the most intensive war in which the British Army has fought since the Second World War, certainly in terms of loss of life. 1st Battalion The Argyll and Sutherland Highlanders was deployed from Hong Kong to Korea on 29 August 1950 as part of the UK's contribution to the United Nations force countering the North Korean invasion of South Korea. Its most outstanding action was probably its first, the battle for Hill 282. This hill was taken, lost and then re-taken. At one stage the Argylls suffered the horrors of a napalm attack made in error by their supporting aircraft. During the battle Major Kenny Muir arrived on the hill with a stretcher party to collect the wounded as the position was being overrun by an enemy counterattack. He immediately took charge, retook the hill and evacuated the wounded. Although he was to be mortally wounded, others hung on. For his personal example and inspirational leadership Major Muir was awarded the Victoria Cross posthumously. The battalion went on to fight in the various battles to hold and then drive out the North Koreans, and in the early stages of the massive Chinese intervention. In a dawn attack on a hill near Songju two platoon commanders were both wounded. Red-haired Corporal Robert Sweeney from West Calder in Midlothian took immediate charge. He led the assault with bayonets fixed, surprising and routing fifty North Koreans near the crest. Thereafter he organized the defence and beat off dangerous enemy infiltration sometimes single-handed until he was eventually wounded. For his courage and leadership he was awarded the Military Medal. On 24 April 1951 the battalion handed over to 1st Battalion The King's Own Scottish Borderers, having gained the respect of allies and adversaries. Thirty-one men had been killed, 132 wounded and two were listed as missing during the nine months of operations.

The arrival of 1st Battalion The King's Own Scottish Borderers coincided with a major Chinese offensive. The battalion fought throughout the next eighteen months but one action stands out. It is best summarized in its Brigade Commander's Special Order of the Day:

> Sunday 4 November 1951 will be remembered and revered for all time in the annals of the King's Own Scottish Borderers. On this day you stood your ground from early dawn in the face of intense and accurate enemy bombardment and, as the afternoon wore on, you met and held a major Chinese attack and dealt the enemy a deadly blow. The actions fought by you all, both collectively and individually on this day, were beyond praise, and it is true to say that your gallantry and sacrifice saved the divisional front from being penetrated. Your adversary was clearly confident that his intense bombardment and human mass attack, in which he used one division (6,000 men), would overwhelm the defenders of the now famous Point 217 – Point 317 ridge line. He failed completely and utterly, however, to appreciate that he was opposed by men whose courage, tenacity and fighting skill was second to none – the 1st Battalion The King's Own Scottish Borderers.

Private Bill Speakman won the Victoria Cross for his inspirational leadership and heroism under fire at a critical time during this battle, in which 1,000 Chinese were killed. During its time in Korea the battalion lost sixty-six men killed and 229 wounded.

The 1st Battalion The Black Watch served in Korea in 1952–3 during which they fought in the 2nd Battle of The Hook on 18–19 November 1952. The Hook was a vital feature on a bend in the United Nations' line, commanding wide views over the junction of two main rivers. During the night, in temperatures of eight degrees below freezing, the Chinese mounted major sustained assaults and broke through the Black Watch defences. The battalion counter-attacked, bringing down artillery fire on their own positions, and eventually drove the enemy off. In scenes reminiscent of the First World War much of the fighting was hand-to-hand and often underground in the bunker and trench complexes. For this action the battalion received the Battle Honour 'The Hook 1952'. During the battle sixteen men of The Black Watch were killed, sixty-two wounded and a further twelve captured.

The story of Corporal Jim Laird from Glasgow is one of enduring courage. At the age of twenty-two, he was wounded in the back by shrapnel during the fighting on 7–8 May 1953 and paralysed from the shoulders down. Since then, his outstanding international sporting achievements and charity work have provided encouragement to many others facing similar challenges.

But perhaps the most difficult of all tasks soldiers have had to carry out since 1945 has been in Northern Ireland. This campaign started in 1969 and still continues, although a cease-fire has been in operation since 1996. The use of soldiers in support of the civil authority anywhere has always been fraught with political and military risk. When it takes place in your own country the strain is even greater. In this unenviable role the British soldier has excelled. The centuries' old affinities between the peoples of Scotland and Ireland often meant that Scottish soldiers understood the causes and nature of sectarian 'troubles' better than those from other parts of the United Kingdom. Every Scottish regiment, including the cavalry in an infantry role, has done numerous operational tours and they have received little thanks and no glory for doing their best to bring peace to this part of the United Kingdom. The names of 115 Scots are recorded on the National War Memorial as having lost their lives in Northern Ireland, of whom fifty-three were serving in Scottish regiments at the time. It has been a campaign of many small actions in which junior officers and NCOs have played a key part.

One such action involved eight men of 1st Battalion The King's Own Scottish Borderers. On 13 December 1989 an armoured lorry smashed into the compound in Derryard, County Fermanagh, followed by a van containing a large bomb. The IRA attack on the base had been well planned and involved at least twelve terrorists armed with rockets, flame throwers, rifles, machine guns and grenades. After ten minutes of close quarter fighting, the terrorists were beaten back. Two men of 1 KOSB were killed. Corporal Robert Duncan from Rutherglen and

Corporal Ian Harvey from Blantyre were both awarded the Distinguished Conduct Medal for their part in this action.

Much of the Army was committed to the campaign in Northern Ireland when, in 1982, Argentina invaded the Falkland Islands. A British Task Force was sent to recover the islands. 2nd Battalion Scots Guards, then stationed in London, was the only Scottish unit to participate in the operation. It received warning of the need for operational deployment on 15 April. With a speed reminiscent of preparations at the outbreak of the First World War, it found itself sailing for the South Atlantic just four weeks later. After a somewhat surreal journey to war on board the liner *QE 2*, it landed at San Carlos on East Falkland on 2 June. The battalion was then deployed to take part in the final battle for the mountains overlooking the capital, Port Stanley. Its objective was Mount Tumbledown held by the Argentinian Marines. The attack was carried out at night along the line of the ridge with companies passing through each other to take the peaks in succession. This was a soldiers' battle in every respect, fought in appalling weather, wet and cold with intermittent blizzards. By dawn on 14 June, Tumbledown was taken. Nine soldiers were killed and thirty-eight wounded, a tribute to the conduct of the battle and to the determination and courage of many individuals. One was nineteen year old Guardsman James Reynolds from Glasgow. During the attack his platoon came under fire from a group of enemy snipers, killing the Platoon Sergeant instantly. A confused situation developed and the section became separated. It was Guardsman Reynolds who immediately took command. Having located the snipers he silenced several of them himself. That done, and showing complete disregard for his safety, he moved forward to render first aid to a wounded comrade. He himself was shot in the hand but continued nonetheless to offer help to his colleague. While so doing, he was killed by enemy mortar fire. For this action he was awarded the Distinguished Conduct Medal.

In 1990 attention changed to the Middle East when Iraq invaded Kuwait. A British division was dispatched as part of a United States-led multinational force to liberate the country. Most of the Scottish regiments participated in this very rapid and successful operation. These included 1st Battalion The Royal

Scots which, by early 1991 was concentrated in the desert. Already highly trained, it had a further month to hone its skills, where preparation included inoculation against plague, a grim reminder of the type of potential threat they faced. On 25 February 1991 the battalion passed through the breach in the Border obstacle. Despite a last minute change to its initial objective, mines and unexploded ordnance, and the cold and wet, this and all the further objectives assigned to the battle group were taken. Many prisoners were captured. The overwhelming strength of the Allied air and ground forces was the major factor in this success which was achieved without any Royal Scots casualties, but this should not detract from the outstanding way the battalion prepared and fought the battle. Nor should the bravery of individuals be forgotten such as that of Private Thomas Gow from Glasgow who, on his own initiative destroyed a dug-in armoured vehicle and two bunkers, capturing seven prisoners. He was awarded the Military Medal. The citation records his initiative, aggression, determination and bravery.

The Royal Scots Dragoon Guards, equipped with Challenger tanks, was one of the armoured regiments that spearheaded the attack. Corporal Kenneth Anderson from Kilmarnock was one of its tank commanders. His tank broke down in the breach during the night advance. As soon as it had been repaired he pushed on, with the armoured personnel carrier (APC) that carried the REME repair team, to rejoin his squadron, unaware that his route led through enemy held territory. When he saw enemy infantry in front, he opened fire over their heads to force their surrender. They promptly dived into their trenches. Despite the poor night visibility he continued to close with the enemy, all the time shielding the vulnerable REME APC behind him. With enemy infantry all around him, Corporal Anderson stopped, switched on his headlights, dismounted and walked towards one group, all the time silhouetted, and persuaded them to surrender. They did so and a brigade objective was taken without a fight. For his personal courage and determination, Corporal Anderson was awarded the Military Medal.

Iraq continued to pose a threat and in March 2003 Britain invaded the country, again as part of an United States-led multinational force. The Royal Scots Dragoon Guards was again one of several Scottish regiments that took part in the operation. 1st Battalion The Black Watch had participated in this operation but it is its part in the subsequent peace enforcement operations between 27 October and 2 December 2004 that deserves special mention.

Initially the battalion had a reserve role in southern Iraq. However, the United States forces in central Iraq were determined to mount an operation to defeat the enemy in Fallujah. To do this they required an additional mechanized battalion to provide outer protection for the operation. Over three days the 1st Battalion The Black Watch moved 459 vehicles 673 kilometres into its designated area of operations. On arrival it found itself with no established base, no infrastructure and no intelligence. During the five-week operation, the battalion faced 120 serious incidents including suicide bombs, improvised explosive devices, mortars and rockets. Five soldiers were killed and seventeen wounded. In the most serious incident on 4 November, a car approached a 'D' Company checkpoint. Its driver was seen to smile before detonating a huge bomb. Four men of 1st Battalion The Black Watch and the Iraqi interpreter died and a further eight soldiers were wounded. Among them was Corporal Peter Laing from Ballingry in Fife. Laing, who had been awarded the Military Cross in 2003, looked about him in the aftermath of the carnage and saw every man in his section either dead or wounded. He himself had received a head wound and damage to one eye. With mortar fire incoming, Laing set about administering first aid to the casualties and organizing their subsequent evacuation by helicopter. For his bravery that day he was awarded the Queen's Gallantry Medal. There can be no more fitting conclusion to these examples of Jocks at War.

Chapter Sixteen

Today's Heritage

Scotland's military history could be simply divided into three stages. In the early years, before Scotland was one nation, there was almost constant internal fighting between regions and clans. At the same time the coast was constantly threatened by invaders from the sea. The Roman invasion did bring unity, albeit temporarily. Then for nearly 600 years Scotland's military history was dominated by war against England. This did more than anything else to forge national unity but it took a long time; clan rivalry frequently led to divisions and outbreaks of internal fighting. It was during this period that Scotland's military capability was enhanced by service in Scottish units in European armies. In the last stage of over 300 years, and since unification with England, Scotland's sword has been wielded in the service of the British Crown. Its forces played a major part in the European wars of the eighteenth and nineteenth centuries and the development of the British Empire. In the two World Wars of the twentieth century Scotland's contribution and sacrifice was proportionally greater than any other country. Today that legacy continues with many Scots serving as individuals in the Royal Navy, Army and Royal Air Force in addition to those in the Scottish regiments.

In the years following the Second World War the ten Scottish infantry regiments were each reduced to a single battalion. Further reductions were to follow as overseas commitments ended and financial pressures increased.

In 1959 The Royal Scots Fusiliers and The Highland Light Infantry were amalgamated to form The Royal Highland Fusiliers. While this may have been a logical decision, the regiments were so different that the merger caused considerable acrimony, particularly amongst the ex-servicemen of the two regiments.

Two years later, in 1961, the Seaforth Highlanders and The Queen's Own Cameron Highlanders were amalgamated to form the Queen's Own Highlanders.

In 1968 the four Lowland regiments again had to lose a battalion. This time it was decided not to amalgamate but to disband the junior regiment – The Cameronians. Scotland had been reduced to seven infantry regiments.

Three years later, in 1971, The Royal Scots Greys were amalgamated with the 3rd Carabiniers to form The Royal Scots Dragoon Guards. Although the regiment's area now extended outside Scotland it retained its identity as Scotland's regiment of cavalry. That same year the 2nd Battalion Scots Guards and 1st Battalion The Argyll and Sutherland Highlanders were reduced to company strength, although the decision was reversed the following year. 2nd Battalion Scots Guards was reduced again in 1993 and continues at company strength.

During these years the Territorial Army was also greatly reduced from the two divisions (51st Highland and 52nd Lowland) to brigade size formations. Battalions were frequently reorganized and renamed, reflecting the changes of organization in the Regular Army.

In 1994 the four Highland regiments were required to reduce to three. Largely on the basis of population figures, the Queen's Own Highlanders was amalgamated with The Gordon Highlanders to form The Highlanders (Seaforth, Gordons and Camerons). The Queen's Own Highlanders had existed for thirty-three years but in that short time had gained a fine reputation on operational service. In a country where a regiment's roots run deep in their respective communities, reflecting as they do centuries of history, every reorganization is traumatic for all concerned. This one was more difficult than most.

A further and more radical change is now underway. The six infantry regiments are to become part of a larger Royal Regiment

REGIMENTAL AREAS

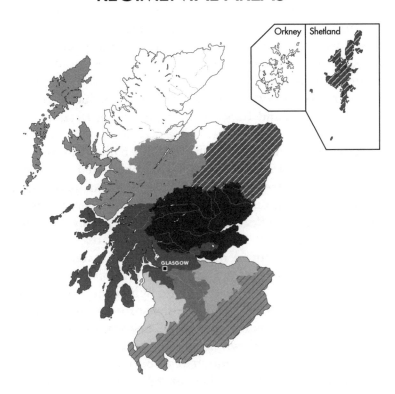

▨ The Royal Scots		■ The Black Watch	
▢ The Royal Scots Fusiliers		▢ Seaforth Highlanders	
■ The Highland Light Infantry		▨ The Queen's Own Cameron Highlanders	
▨ The Cameronians		▨ The Gordon Highlanders	
▨ The King's Own Scottish Borderers		■ The Argyll and Sutherland Highlanders	

Notes:

1. The Royal Scots Fusiliers and The Highland Light Infantry amalgamated in 1959 to form The Royal Highland Fusiliers (areas combined).

2. Seaforth Highlanders and The Queen's Own Cameron Highlanders amalgamated in 1961 to form Queen's Own Highlanders (areas combined).

3. The Cameronians disbanded in 1968.

4. Queen's Own Highlanders amalgamated with The Gordon Highlanders in 1994 to form The Highlanders (areas combined).

of Scotland. The justification for this change is the need to improve stability for soldiers and their families, to widen career opportunities, and to have more battalions available for the numerous operational commitments. The individual battalions will keep their regimental names and identities in an attempt to retain their heritage and their links with local communities. However, the six battalions have then to be reduced to five with The Royal Scots and King's Own Scottish Borderers 'battalions' being merged.

From earliest time Scottish forces have had a firm base in their home area. The frequent changes over the past fifty years have inevitably weakened that base but history has demonstrated that a new structure, given time, can build on the heritage it has inherited and be as effective in defeating an enemy as those that have gone before.

Soldiers' expectations have also changed over the past fifty years. Now well educated and very professional, they are probably better trained than ever before. When they are young they have the same sense of adventure that drove their forefathers to serve overseas. But as they get older they want stability for their families, to own their own homes and to have a good education for their children. Too much instability and separation discourages the best and most experienced. In all of this the Jocks are no exception.

But the Scot has also changed. Scotland's population has altered over the centuries with emigration, immigration and movement to the cities – particularly in central Scotland. This has broken down the traditional regional and tribal differences. The characteristics of the islander, highlander, lowlander and Borderer still exist in families that have been unaffected by the social changes but they are now comparatively few. There are now many more cosmopolitan Scots, a mixture of many ancestors and their individual characteristics.

These social changes have impacted on the identity of the Scottish soldier but in many ways the regiments, with their roots and heritage, have preserved all that is best. The character of the Scottish soldier, the Jock, has not changed. It is his fierce loyalty to his family and friends, and to his regiment, that takes him though the barriers of fear and thought of self to act with extraordinary courage, determination and self-sacrifice. It is his resilience that helps him overcome appalling adversity, to go where others might hesitate and to stand firm when others might falter. Loyalty, courage, resilience and pride define the Jock. In the Scottish regiments pride is a consequence of self-confidence, confidence in others, and an absolute confidence in the regiment.

These characteristics are part inherited from previous generations and part inherited through the regiments. It is they that make the Jock a formidable adversary in any organization. Others who join a Scottish regiment are instilled with these same qualities. Jocks are both born and made, to be firm friends and feared enemies. It has always been so.

The headquarters of The Royal Regiment of Scotland will be in Edinburgh Castle, alongside the regimental home headquarters of The Royal Scots Dragoon Guards, where the wealth of Scottish military tradition down the ages is concentrated. On the highest point of the Castle grounds stands the Scottish National War Memorial. A place of great beauty, the Memorial contains the separate shrines of each Scottish regiment, and memorials to the Scots who served in the Royal Navy and Royal Air Force. Here are recorded the deeds of Scots by land, sea and air in two world wars, and in all campaigns since. Its walls are hung with the Colours of the regiments decorated with the Battle Honours won in every corner of the world. It is surely a fitting tribute to the man whose hand has wielded the Sword of Scotland for 1,000 years – that incomparable soldier, the Jock.

Bibliography

Books

— *A Border Battalion, The History of the 7th/8th (Service) Battalion KOSB*, Private publication by The King's Own Scottish Borderers, Edinburgh, 1920

— *Transactions of Society of Antiquarians of Scotland*, Vol. II, Edinburgh, 1818

Alexander, Jack, *McRae's Battalion (The story of the 16th Royal Scots)*, Mainstream Publishing, Edinburgh and London, 2003

Anderson, A.O., *Early Sources of Scottish History,* Vol. II, Paul Watkins Publishing, Edinburgh, 1922

Anderson, P., *Culloden Moor*, Eneas Mackay, Stirling, 1921

Barbour, J., *The Bruce*, edited by Dr. John Jamieson, Maurice Ogle & Co., Glasgow, 1869 (See also translation by Archibald A.H. Douglas, William MacLellan, Glasgow, 1964)

Barclay, Brigadier C.H., *The London Scottish in the Second World War*, William Clowes and Sons, London, 1952

Bevan, David, *Drums of the Birkenhead*, Larson Publications, Aylesbury, 1972

Bewshire, Major F.W., *The History of the 51st (Highland) Division 1914–18*, William Blackwood and Sons, Edinburgh and London, 1921

Blake, G., *Mountain and Flood. The History of the 52nd Lowland Division 1939–46*, Jackson, Son & Company, Glasgow, 1950

Boece, H., *History of Scotland*, translated from the Latin by J. Bellenden, 1535 (original Paris, 1526)

Brownlie, Major W. Steel, *The Proud Trooper* (The History of the Ayrshire (Earl of Carrick's Own) Yeomanry from its raising in the Eighteenth Century till 1964), Collins, London 1964

Buchan, John, *The History of The Royal Scots Fusiliers 1678–1919*, Thomas Nelson and Sons, London, Edinburgh and New York, 1925

Bryant, Sir Arthur, *The Age of Chivalry*, Collins, London, 1963

Cameron Highlanders, *Historical Records of the Queen's Own Cameron Highlanders* Vol V, William Blackwood and Sons, Edinburgh and London, 1952

Carver, Lieutenant Colonel R.M.P., *Second to None, The Royal Scots Greys 1919–1945*, McCorquodale & Co., Glasgow, 1954

Chalmers, G., *Caledonia: or an Account, Historical and Topographic, of North Britain*, Vol. I, T. Cadell, London, 1807

Dickinson, W.C., *A New History of Scotland*, Vol. I, Thomas Nelson and Sons, Edinburgh, 1961

Doyle, Arthur Conan, *The British Campaign in France and Flanders 1915*, Hodder and Stoughton, London, 1917

Erskine, David, *The Scots Guards 1919 – 1955*, William Clowes and Sons, London, 1956

Ewing, Major John, *The Royal Scots 1914 – 1919*, Oliver and Boyd, Edinburgh and London, 1925

— *The History of The 9th (Scottish) Division 1914–1919*, John Murray, London, 1921

Fairrie, Lieutenant Colonel Angus, *Queen's Own Highlanders, Seaforth and Camerons – An Illustrated History*, Queen's Own Highlanders Amalgamation Trustees, Inverness, 1998

Ferguson, J., *William Wallace*, Alexander Maclehose & Co., London, 1938

Fordun, John of, *Scotichronicon*, edited by Walter Goodall, Edinburgh, 1759

Gunning, Captain Hugh, *Borderers in Battle*, Martin's Printing Works, Berwick-upon-Tweed, 1948

Gardyne, Lieutenant Colonel C. Greenhill, *The Life of a Regiment* (The History of The Gordon Highlanders Vols I and II 1794–1898), The Medici Society, London, 1901

Gardyne, Lieutenant Colonel A.D. Greenhill, *The Life of a Regiment* (The History of The Gordon Highlanders Vol III 1898–1914), The Medici Society, London, 1939

Gillon, Captain Stair, *The KOSB in the Great War*, Thomas Nelson & Sons, London, 1930

Grant, Peter, *A Highlander Goes to War*, Pentland Press, Edinburgh, 1995

Grierson, Lieutenant General Sir James, *Scottish Volunteer Force*, William Blackwood and Sons, Edinburgh, 1909

Hailes, Lord, *Annals of Scotland*, J. Murray, Edinburgh, 1776

Hennessy, William M., (ed.), *Annals of Ulster*, Alex Thompson and Company, Dublin, 1887–1901

Innes, T., *Critical Essay on the Ancient Inhabitants of Scotland*, William Innys, London, 1729

James, Harold and Denis Sheil-Small, *The Undeclared War*, New English Library, London, 1971

Johnstone, J., (ed. and tr.), *Norse Chronicles*, Edinburgh, 1884

Kemp, Colonel J.C., *History of The Royal Scots Fusiliers*, Glasgow University Press, Glasgow, 1963

Ker, W.P., *The Chronicles of Froissart*, Vol. III, translated by Lord Berners, 1525, D. Nutt, London, 1901–1903

Lindsay, Lieutenant Colonel J.H., *The London Scottish in the Great War*, Regimental Headquarters London Scottish, London, 1925

Mackie, Prof. J.D., *History of Scotland*, Penguin, London, 1964

Martin, Lieutenant General H.G., *Fifteenth Scottish Division 1939–1945*, William Blackwood and Sons, Edinburgh and London, 1948

Martin, Major D., *The Fifth Battalion The Cameronians (Scottish Rifles) 1914–1919*, Jackson, Son & Co, Glasgow, 1936

Maxwell, Sir Herbert, *The Lowland Scots Regiments*, James Maclehose and Sons, Glasgow, 1918

McGregor, John, *The Spirit of Angus*, Unwin Brothers, Woking, 1988

Mileham, Patrick, *The Yeomanry Regiments*, Spellmount, Staplehurst, 2003

Miles, Wilfrid, *Life of a Regiment* (The Gordon Highlanders) Vol 5, Aberdeen University Press, Aberdeen, 1961

Milner, Laurie, *Royal Scots in the Gulf*, Leo Cooper, London, 1994

Money-Barnes, Major R., *The Uniforms and History of The Scottish Regiments*, Seeley Service & Co, London and Plymouth, 1956

Muir, Augustus, *The First of Foot*, The Royal Scots History Committee, Edinburgh, 1961

Naylor, Murray, *Among Friends, The Scots Guards 1956–1993*, Leo Cooper, London, 1995

Oatts, Lieutenant Colonel L.B., *Proud Heritage, The Story of The Highland Light Infantry* Vols I to IV, Thomas Nelson & Sons, London, 1953

Paterson, Robert H., *Pontius Pilate's Bodyguard* (Regimental History of The Royal Scots), The Royal Scots History Committee, Edinburgh, 2001

Petre, F. Loraine, Wilfred Ewart and Major General Sir Cecil Lowther, *The Scots Guards in the Great War 1914–1918*, John Murray, London, 1925

Ray, Cyril, *Algiers to Austria, A History of 78 Division in the Second World War*, Eyre & Spottiswoode, London, 1952

Salmond, J.B., *The History of the 51st Highland Division 1939–1945*, William Blackwood and Sons, Edinburgh and London, 1953

Scobie, Major I.H. Mackay, *History of the Fencibles*, William Blackwood and Sons, Edinburgh, 1914

Shepperd, G.A., *The Italian Campaign 1943–1945*, Arthur Barker, London, 1968

Sigmond, Robert N., *Off at Last. An Illustrated History of 7th (Galloway) Battalion The King's Own Scottish Borderers 1939–1945*, RN Sigmond Publishing, 1997

Skene, W.F., (ed. and tr.), *Chronicles of the Picts and Scots*, HM General Register House, Edinburgh, 1867

Spooner, Keith, *The Battalion*, The London Scottish Regimental Trust, London, 1951

Stewart, Lieutenant Colonel J., *Fifteenth Scottish Division 1914–1919*, William Blackwood and Sons, Edinburgh and London, 1926

Strachan, Professor Hew, *Scotland's Military Identity*, Not yet published

Taylor, J., *Pictorial History of Scotland*, Virtue & Co, London, 1852

Thompson, Lieutenant Colonel R.R., *The Fifty-Second (Lowland Division) 1914–1918*, Maclehose, Jackson & Co, Glasgow, 1923

Thomson, Reverend P.D., *The Gordon Highlanders*, W. & W. Lindsay, Aberdeen, 1933

Stevenson, Joseph (ed.), *Wallace Papers. Documents Illustrative of Sir William Wallace, his life and times*, Edinburgh Printing Co., Edinburgh, 1841

Wauchope, A.G., *A History of The Black Watch in the Great War*, The Medici Society, London, 1926.

Wood, Stephen, *In the Finest Tradition* (The Royal Scots Dragoon Guards), Mainstream Publishing, Edinburgh, 1988

Woollcombe, Robert, *All the Blue Bonnets* (The History of The King's Own Scottish Borderers), Arms and Armour Press, London, 1980

Wyntoun, Andrew of, *The Orygynale Cronykil of Scotland*, edited by David Laing, Edmonston and Douglas, Edinburgh, 1872–9

Other sources

Black Watch Regimental Archives, Diary of Lieutenant Colonel J. Stewart DSO (0171), Account of Pte Williamson (0187), Letter of Captain Cameron (0186), Letter of Pte McFarlane (0953), Account of 5 BW (0275)

Highland Light Infantry Chronicle, MacLaren and Sons, Glasgow, 1893–1958

Red Hackle (The Chronicle of The Black Watch) No. 051, May 2005, Method Publishing, Inverness

Index

208

209